The Alienated Subject

The Alienated Subject

On the Capacity to Hurt

James A. Tyner

University of Minnesota Press
Minneapolis
London

Published by the University of Minnesota Press
111 Third Avenue South, Suite 290
Minneapolis, MN 55401-2520
http://www.upress.umn.edu

ISBN 978-1-5179-1134-8 (hc)
ISBN 978-1-5179-1135-5 (pb)

A Cataloging-in-Publication record for this book is available from the Library of Congress.

Printed in the United States of America on acid-free paper

UMP BmB 2022

To Meredith, Benilda, and Janet

Contents

Introduction

In late December 2019, a cluster of pneumonia cases, caused by a newly identified coronavirus later designated Covid-19, was documented in Wuhan, China. Patients exhibited a variety of symptoms, including fever, cough, fatigue, shortness of breath, and sore throat. The elderly and those with underlying medical conditions such as hypertension, pulmonary disease, diabetes, and cardiovascular disease appeared to be especially at risk.[1] Health experts realized that Covid-19 posed a serious risk to people. Preliminary studies indicated a case fatality risk of around 1 percent, making the disease several times more deadly than the typical seasonal influenza and comparable in severity to the 1918 influenza pandemic. With no vaccine available, virologists, epidemiologists, and other health experts recommended a combination of shelter-in-place policies, social distancing, and the wearing of protective masks to minimize the spread of the virus.[2]

The first case of Covid-19 was confirmed in the United States on January 21, 2020, and nine days later the World Health Organization (WHO) declared a "public health emergency of international concern," a designation reserved for extraordinary events that threaten to spread internationally.[3] However, as the virus inexorably swept across the globe, conservative politicians in the United States sat by idly. At first, President Trump downplayed the pandemic. Asked whether he was worried about a potential pandemic, Trump dismissed the question, replying "No. Not at all. And we have it totally under control. It's one person coming in from China. . . . It's going to be just fine."[4] Instead of marshalling resources in anticipation of critical shortages of medical supplies, ventilators, and personal protective equipment (PPE), he dismissed warnings issued by the Centers for Disease Control (CDC) and the WHO with false equivalences, suggesting that Covid-19 was comparable to the seasonal flu. Trump also politicized the pandemic, claiming that the disease was a "hoax" perpetrated by his "enemies."[5] Trump *knew* otherwise.

Trump in private described Covid-19 as a "killer" and called it "the plague."[6] However, 2020 was an election year, and he fervently sought a second presidential term. To that end, Trump continued to minimize the health risks. On February 26, he quipped, "You have 15 people," the president explained, "and the 15 within a couple of days is going to be down to close to zero."[7] Trump dithered, "You don't want to see panic, because there's no reason to be panicked about it. There's a chance it won't spread, too. And there's a chance it will."[8]

As the weeks turned into months, Trump's malicious unwillingness to adequately respond to the growing threat hardened and the number of infections and deaths mounted. Medical experts cautioned that immediate and drastic responses were necessary: mass production of medical supplies and the establishment of an efficient distribution system; the initiation of protocols for widespread testing and contact tracing; and the implementation of shelter-in-place orders to minimize community transmission. Trump, however, refused to initiate comprehensive plans at the federal level, preferring instead to delegate responsibility to the state level in a thinly veiled attempt to deflect any potential blame from his mishandling of the crisis. Indeed, on March 20 Jared Kushner—Trump's son-in-law and trusted advisor—met with several officials at the Federal Emergency Management Agency to determine how best to replenish the country's depleted reserves of PPE. In response to a comment that local businesses were eager to help and were looking for guidance from the federal government, Kushner reportedly brushed off the suggestion, stating that "Free markets will solve this. That is not the role of government."[9] Kushner's dismissive attitude—but really the entirety of the Trump administration—is indicative of a blind adherence to capitalist-led solutions to crises, but so too is it demonstrative of a pervasive indifference to the suffering of millions of people vulnerable to a pandemic.

When Trump did grudgingly respond publicly, he did so in a blatantly political fashion. As governors and other local officials across the country pleaded for critical medical equipment from a key national stockpile, the Trump administration favored Republican-led states over their Democratic-led counterparts. States including Oklahoma and Kentucky received more of some equipment they requested, while others, such as Illinois, Massachusetts, and Maine received considerably less.[10] Trump, for his part, touted his personal relationships with specific governors and declared, more broadly, that the federal government would not serve as a "shipping clerk" for local officials. "All I want them to do—very simple—I want them to be appreciative," Trump explained.[11]

In defiance of Trump, a growing number of state and local governments, notably in New York, Ohio, and Michigan, closed businesses and initiated shelter-in-place regulations. Only workers deemed essential—doctors, nurses, paramedics, transit workers—stayed on the job on-site. Not unexpectedly, unemployment rose precipitously. Within weeks, the number of people out of work surpassed levels not seen in the United States since the Great Depression of the 1930s, as the effects of the economic shutdown quickly rippled across the country, albeit uneven in scale and scope. By mid-April, more than 22 million people had filed for unemployment. Soon, millions of unemployed and underemployed workers faced mounting bills. And as the economic crisis deepened, Covid-19 laid bare the inequities of racial and wealth disparities present in the United States, with Black and Brown people most adversely affected.[12] By September 2020, as the death toll surpassed 200,000 people, grave differences with the U.S. population were evident. The mortality rate for African Americans stood at 97.9 deaths per 100,000, compared to a rate of 46.6 deaths per 100,000 for whites. Hispanics and Indigenous peoples were equally hard hit, with rates of 64.7 and 81.9 deaths per 100,000, respectively.[13]

Toward an Ontology of the Alienated Subject

It is easy—and necessary—to lay blame for the devastating death toll in the United States at the feet of President Trump, to decry his political and moral failings, his abrogation of responsibility, his racism and scapegoating of others, because, in the end, his inaction contributed to the premature deaths of hundreds of thousands of people. It is also easy to call out the irresponsibility and opportunism of federal, state, and local politicians. However, the unfolding tragedy reflected something deeper than the manipulations of an unqualified narcissist and his cabal of cronies that let victims of the coronavirus die needlessly. As Kevin Anderson explains, "too narrow a focus on Trump obscures how this abject failure illustrates the essential nature of capitalism, its 'normal' macabre workings, which are now revealed more openly."[14] Heather Brown concurs, noting that the overall response of the Trump administration "lays bare the crassness of contemporary capitalism. Trump is simply its most recent and clearest messenger."[15] For the Covid-19 pandemic uncovered a rot within the body politic of the United States, a rot long festering and long unchecked.

As Marx explains in the first volume of *Capital,* "Capital takes no account of the health and the length of life of the worker unless society forces it to do so. Its answer to the outcry about the physical and mental degradation, the premature death, the torture of over-work, is this: Should that pain trouble us, since it increases our pleasure (profit)?" As the *recorded* death toll in the United States inexorably rose throughout the spring and summer of 2020, politicians and protestors—mostly on the far right of the political spectrum—continued to demand businesses and most if not all sectors of the economy to open, thereby exposing workers (and consumers) to the lethal machinations of an indiscriminate virus. And yet, as we have seen, while Covid-19 does not discriminate in its targeting of hosts, one's exposure and risk to premature death are decidedly unequal. Structural inequalities, deeply entrenched in American society, produced a landscape of suffering disproportionately experienced by precarious workers, often persons of color. Indeed, the stark differences in mortality among Covid-19 victims highlights decades of racist, sexist, and other unjust policies and practices that separate not only the haves and have-nots but also those able to live and those left to die. Indeed, more wealthy members of U.S. society—who are disproportionately white—experienced the pandemic very differently. As Vicky Ward writes, many families viewed the pandemic as an extended vacation: One hedge fund billionaire stayed at his ranch in Texas, another isolated on a compound in Martha's Vineyard, and another couple relaxed at a villa in the Bahamas.[16] But it isn't just the country's wealthiest who are able to shelter-in-place in relative safety. Unlike the so-called essential workers, these people are able, more often than not, to work from home; they are able also to purchase groceries and other items online and have these delivered—by the essential workers. In the end, the privilege to place profits over potential premature death is a classed privilege, but it is also a white privilege, a gendered privilege, an ageist privilege, and an ableist privilege.

In a previous book, *Dead Labor: Toward a Political Economy of Premature Death,* I considered a set of interrelated questions: who lives, who dies, and who decides. However, these questions were mediated by a more insidious question, namely, who profits from the premature death of others? There, I premised that one's exposure to (premature) death is conditioned by one's position in capitalism; that is, the relationship between people laboring within the capitalist mode of production and the market logics of capitalism necessarily and materially mediate the relations between life and death. Inequalities manifest along the familiar axes of exploitation and oppression (such as ethnicity, gender, sexuality, citizenship, and physical and mental abilities) and materialize as inequalities in the vulnerability to premature death. To that end, I argued that we are witness to a new political economy of premature death, an emergent mode of existence identified as *necrocapitalism,* a neoliberal attitude on steroids in which the valuation and vulnerability of life itself is centered on two overlapping criteria: productivity and responsibility.[17] Capital values those bodies deemed both productive, that is, in a position to generate wealth, and responsible, conceived of as the ability to participate fully as producers and consumers in the capitalist system while simultaneously not incurring a net loss to the system. Those individuals who are deemed nonproductive or redundant, based on an economic bio-arithmetic, are disproportionately vulnerable and increasingly disallowed life to the point of premature death. They are, effectively, left to die so that others may enjoy the fruits of (dead) laborers. As such, necrocapitalism is marked by a distorted moral philosophy in which mortality constitutes individual risk and failure or a necessary cost of doing business. It is a supercharged utilitarian ethics whereby the lives of essential workers are sacrificed for politics, profit, or pleasure.

The capacity to hurt to the point of letting die, in other words, is inherent to capitalism at a structural level. Left unfettered, capitalism must continuously expand because, virus-like, it kills its host—that is, living labor—and thus requires newer, fresher hosts to infect. The failure to provide adequate safety measures and procedures, the life-saving masks and ventilators and testing kits, is not solely the consequence of immoral and/or incompetent leaders. The failure of not saving lives is not a tragic failure of capitalism but a critical feature of capitalism that expends lives in its perpetual expansion. Harm, as a systemic capacity to hurt, is intrinsic to capitalism; and this is why Marx focused on the structural relations inherent to capital as opposed to individuals. It is not that all capitalists (or the politicians who support them) are morally deficient; rather, the market logics of competition and continued accumulation impel owners to exploit workers. In doing so, capitalism itself infects the body politics and leaves behind an alienated society addicted to mindless consumption, indifferent to the suffering and premature death of others, and intolerant of demands to affect change.

The Covid-19 pandemic made visible legions of alienated subjects who, zombie-like, gleefully assembled in armed protests and made demands for greater sacrifices—not of themselves but of those workers—the grocery clerks and retail workers, transit employees and sanitation workers, farm laborers and farm processors—most vulnerable to premature death. In April, for example, several "Astro-Turf" social movements erupted, mostly in key swing states or states with Democratic governors, demanding an end to shelter-in-place rules and a return to "normal." Protesters, mostly white, frequently armed, and often waving Confederate flags, decried what they felt was an abrogation of their personal freedoms.[18] Trump, for his part, joined the chorus of white protestors, simultaneously downplaying the seriousness of the pandemic and elevating fears of vanishing liberties.[19] Outside the state capital in Olympia, Washington, for example, thousands of protestors gathered to call for the end of stay-at-home orders issued by Governor Inslee. Protestors carried American flags and Trump flags, gun rights advocates brought their firearms, and several held posters that read "Give Me Liberty or Give Me Covid 19." Republican Representative Robert Sutherland stoked the crowd with demands to "take back the state."[20]

In *The Alienated Subject,* I deepen my argument to consider the possibility of having a *meaningful life* within capitalism. This is a book about alienation and our need to overcome alienation. It is thus a story about our inability to live meaningful lives under capitalism, and of the necessity to chart a new path forward, a path of emancipation that foregrounds empathy over enmity. It is written against the backdrop of the Covid-19 global pandemic, but this crisis should not overdetermine the purchase of my argument.

Capitalism, as Marx argues, cares little about the life of laborers unless society compels it to do so. Moreover, capitalism values only those lives deemed productive, that is, those lives capable of producing objects not to sustain life but to accumulate profit and, by extension, sustain capitalism itself. Within the capitalist mode of production, valuable lives are lives valuable to capital; and the only lives that mean anything—the only lives that matter for capital—are productive lives. Thus, when health experts warned that a premature relaxation of precautionary measures would result in the premature death of thousands of people, conservative politicians and pundits displayed little empathy. Lt. Governor Dan Patrick (R-TX), for example, rationalized that there are more important things than living, and that it was incumbent that "we've got to take some risks and get back in the game and get this country back up and running."[21] The message was clear: the sacrifice of the elderly, of the precarious but essential workers, outweighed demands to patronize bars and bowling alleys, barber shops and beauty parlors. As the argument went, those who succumb to the disease (notably the elderly or those with comorbid conditions) would die anyway.

To this end, my concern with "meaning in life" strikes at the heart of a fundamental and steadfast theme of Marx, expressed most clearly in his so-called early writings but also apparent in his later works, this being the capability of human beings to enjoy a flourishing life. I do so, however, through a focus on our awareness of death. As Zygmunt Bauman writes, "The fact of human mortality and the necessity to live with the constant awareness of that fact, go a long way toward accounting for many a crucial aspect of social and cultural organization of all known societies."[22] The capability to experience a flourishing life is mediated by our awareness of death, of our finite, mortal existence. This is not the same as one's *fear* of death; this condition is too limiting. Instead, the primary factor is one's conscious awareness that death for all living organisms is a certainty. A person may fear death; alternatively, a person may even welcome death. These attitudes, moreover, are generally conditioned by one's belief about the existence (and possible experience) of an afterlife. Regardless of one's attitude toward death, however, the point remains that humans are *aware* of death and that this conditions how we live our lives and—importantly—interact with other, mortal beings. Indeed, an awareness of our shared mortality informs and mediates how we treat other living beings, human and nonhuman alike.

Catastrophes, such as the Covid-19 pandemic, push our awareness of, and response to, the specter of premature death to the forefront of daily life. For many people, the fear of exposure to the virus meant that everyday activities—banal on one level, but socially meaningful on another—could no longer be taken for granted. For those individuals who abided by shelter-in-place orders, life became severely circumscribed: the ability to visit friends and families, to eat at a restaurant or watch a film at the local theater, or to hug and console others in times of grief became all but impossible. Myriad activities that once provided meaning in life seemed to heighten one's vulnerability to a premature death. From weddings to birthday parties, vacations, and playdates, all of these activities that otherwise help nurture meaningful lives suddenly forced people to stare into the abyss of their own mortality and the mortality of those individuals who give meaning to their lives.

Governmental and public responses in the United States (and elsewhere) to the pandemic reveal particular attitudes—both subtle and direct—toward the vulnerability of different persons to premature death. Most clearly expressed in policies geared to the meatpacking industry, the Trump administration and (mostly) Republican governors laid bare a callousness in their calculus of human life. Workers—especially migrant laborers and persons of color—were confronted with a Hobson's choice of two equally and potentially fatal options: go to work in unsafe conditions and risk exposure to a deadly virus, or stay home and get fired, thereby losing both income and insurance. And those people (mostly Trump supporters) who protested the imposition and continuance of shelter-in-place orders and other measures designed to minimize the deadly effects of the virus demonstrated an arrogance and insensitivity in their behaviors, expressing minimal regard for the well-being of others as they promoted their own self-interests. Indifferent at best, these people were largely intolerant to the point of letting die a sizable portion of the public.

The Covid-19 pandemic highlights also that the market logics of competition and capital accumulation are structured not to promote or sustain life—meaningful or otherwise—but to transform the living into the dead. In turn, alienated subjects may see salvation not in the collective care of others but through the coveting of commodified articles of consumption. As such, we witness not only the ravages of a pandemic and economic crisis; we witness also the gradual unfolding of a crisis of indifference, in which the plight of the poor and the vulnerable are neglected and ignored, as an alienated society demands the right to visit a barbershop or to buy lawn fertilizers. In short, the pandemic swept aside the curtains of capitalist confusion and exposed the idolization of false profits rather than the promotion of an ethics of meaningful empathy.

The Covid-19 pandemic offers an opportunity—and I use this term cautiously—to think about who and what we value in society, with value determined not on conditions set by capital but instead based on our capacity to achieve meaning in life. In doing so, I critically interrogate the ontology of the *alienated subject* as a counterbalance to the more conventional "liberal subject." As Frank Michelman explains, "To speak of the liberal subject is to call to mind the sort of being theorists have in view when they undertake to justify a liberal constitutional conception by showing some benign relation between the favored conception and the values of human lives."[23] To this end, long enshrined in the canons of Western political philosophy, the liberal subject is heralded as the embodiment of rational thought, self-reflection, and self-interest.[24] However, the liberal subject is also invariably an economically privileged, heterosexual, white male.[25]

How—and why—the liberal subject became a disguised substitute for heterosexual white men is a story of slavery, colonialism, and genocide. As Lisa Lowe writes, notions of "liberal freedom did not contradict slavery but, rather, served precisely as a means to rationalize and implement slavery and its aftermath."[26] Lowe explains that "many of the liberal concepts that were used to justify slavery were also employed differently at other times to justify settler occupation, theft of land, imperial war, and overseas empire."[27] To this end, the attributes of the liberal subject, including rational thought, self-determination, and free will, gain their purchase precisely because these are not universal but instead monopolized through acts of physical and symbolic violence. Lowe concludes:

> As modern liberalism defined the human and universalized its attributes to European man, it simultaneously differentiated peoples in the colonies as less than human. Even as it proposes inclusivity, liberal universalism effects principles of inclusion and exclusion; in the very claim to define humanity, as a species or as a condition, its gestures of definition divide the human and the nonhuman, classify the normative, and pathologize deviance. Universalizing concepts of reason, civilization, and freedom divide humanity according to a coloniality of power, affirming freedom for modern man while subordinating the colonized, enslaved, and dispossessed whose material labors and resources were the conditions of possibility for that liberty.[28]

On this point, as Eduardo Bonilla-Silva explains, the presumption of a universal subject, who by definition is color-blind and genderless, sidesteps that people of color are not part of white people's moral universe, which limits white people's capacity to empathize with "sufferers" of color.[29] In other words, the fact that our subjectivities are deeply racialized, for example, is discordant with the forwarding of legal, political, and social ideologies premised on the uncritical presumption of the liberal subject. At the very least, such presumptions work against taking seriously the racist foundation of the political economy of the United States; at worst, it reaffirms and codifies the implicit superiority of whiteness. Thus, and in contradistinction to the liberal subject, I introduce the litmus figure of the alienated subject to accompany us on our path forward.

In ordinary speech, alienation "is often taken to describe vague feelings of malaise or meaningless, particularly with respect to work."[30] Conceived as such, there is a tendency to position the alienated subject as the subaltern, that is, a figure beaten down by exploitative relations inherent to capitalism. This in fact informs many accounts of Trump's popularity, in which members of the so-called *white* working class express their "class anxiety" through their support of Trump.[31] For example, many journalists, academics, and commentators intimate that the sentiments of anger, intolerance, and outright hatred evinced by especially white men, coupled with a pervasive indifference, result from deep-seated feelings of alienation and thus demand a modicum of empathy to their plight. Bonny Wells, to this end, details that in the months leading up to and following the election of Trump, many of these narratives attempted to understand the mentality of the so-called working class—invariably presented as rural, low-income white people in areas that are economically depressed and have been neglected by politicians and institutions. She notes that framings often attribute Trump's success to several factors, but that in many cases racism and economic depression are prominent. Notably, however, these accounts *also* use "economic anxiety" arguments, that is, alienation, to refute or complicate the notion that white voters were motivated by Trump's racist, xenophobic, and misogynistic platform. In doing so, these accounts—whether sympathetic or vindictive to the white working class—pointed to the failure of existing structural problems and institutions unable or unwilling to remedy the economic ills of the *white* working class.[32] Indeed, a common thread running through many of these narratives is the so-called Left Behind thesis, that is, poor working-class whites—the stereotypical alienated subject—supported Trump because, economically speaking, they did not benefit in the wealth-generating promise of capitalism. Representative examples include Katherine Cramer's (2016) *The Politics of Resentment: Rural Consciousness in Wisconsin and the Rise of Scott Walker*; Justin Gest's (2016) *The New Minority: White Working Class Politics in an Age of Immigration and Inequality*; Arlie Hochschild's (2016) *Strangers in Their Own Land: Anger and Mourning on the American Right*; and James Vance's (2016) *Hillbilly Elegy: A Memoir of a Family and Culture in Crisis.*[33]

This explanation was (and remains) popular both among conservatives and liberals.[34] And yet, it is patently false. In fact, many of these accounts are actually premised on the experiences of middle-income whites and not the dogged blue-collar workers struggling in the face of economic precarity. Exit polls throughout the 2016 Republican primaries and the subsequent presidential campaign routinely indicated that the "average" Trump supporter was economically better-off than those voters who did not support him. According to one survey, for example, the median household income of a Trump voter was $72,000, compared to a national median income of $56,000.[35] And yet, for many political prognosticators, the mythology of the working-class support of Trump proved intoxicating and, accordingly, the alienated subject continued to play a central role in the spectacle of Trumpism.

In actuality, what is being described is a relative loss of privilege among the better-off *white* segment of society rather than any real account of serious and systemic economic decline that is uniquely affecting white citizens in the United States.[36] Indeed, the "ordinary" white Trump supporter was not among those "left behind" but instead one who fears a perceived loss of what gives them meaning in life—white racial superiority.[37] Concurrently, those who *have been* left behind economically, notably people of color and nonwhite immigrants, are "scapegoated for inequalities of material conditions that are increasingly . . . shared by both black and white workers, as well as others."[38] Effectively, the concept of alienation has been whitewashed, both unintentionally and intentionally.[39] On the one hand, the normative whiteness of much Marxist analysis leaves white bodies racially unmarked. On the other hand, reference to the working class serves as a dog whistle for racist conservatives and liberals alike.

Alienation is an important mediator of our present moment, but not for reasons usually forwarded by pundits and politicians. This is difficult to see, though, because alienation is too often couched in the color-blind and race-neutral rhetoric of the liberal subject, that is, a rational being who becomes aware of its alienated condition and organizes in solidarity with other class-conscious people. If we acknowledge, alternatively, that capitalism in the United States is a form of settler colonialism and racial capitalism, it follows that alienation must be similarly understood. And yet, with a few notable exceptions, most discussions of alienation remain woefully inadequate in their account of racism and other forms of structural oppression. Thus, to uncritically attribute the rise of Trumpism to the "class anxieties" of the (white) working class is to fundamentally misunderstand the locus of alienation within a system of white supremacy. As Eduardo Bonilla-Silva explains, "Although it is true that white workers have lost ground and that progressives should show empathy to them," too often pundits and scholars "give this segment of the white group a pass on their racialized, gendered, and xenophobic consciousness. More problematic, they ask for empathy for their white brethren, but show little understanding and empathy for the plight of poor Black and Brown folks."[40]

From the *Communist Manifesto* onward, as Peter Goodwin writes, the self-emancipation of the working class was central to Marx's thought.[41] Subsequently, the question of the revolutionary potential of the working class has been central in the development of Marxist-inspired scholarship and practice for generations.[42] From Engels to Kautsky, Lenin to Luxemburg, and Trotsky to Gramsci, countless Marxists wrestled with the ideas developed by Marx in anticipation of a socialist revolution that seemed always on the horizon. And whether implicit or explicit, the condition of alienation remained crucial, for foundational to Marx's notion of emancipation was the premise that the alienated proletariat embodies the revolutionary potential necessary to transform capitalism and to construct a society free of exploitation and oppression.

It is necessary, therefore, to work through Marx's premise that the working class holds the key toward *universal* emancipation from the exploitative and alienating conditions of a *racial* and *gendered* capitalism. And to do so, we proceed cautiously. Particularly in his early writings, Marx cherished a rather romantic image of the proletariat, for as David Lovell explains, the proletariat for Marx gained moral stature because it endured its suffering without losing its human qualities.[43] However, to romanticize the proletariat, as Georg Lukács warns, is to risk losing sight of the fundamental condition of the alienated subject, that is, a subject estranged from society.[44] While Marx's theory of alienation upholds the revolutionary and emancipatory potential of the working class, in other words, the class of men and women most often identified with Trump and conservative politics, we find the anger and hatred of many of the so-called alienated working class directed not toward structures of oppression and exploitation but instead toward other marginalized people. Such reductive accounts that position the working class as predominantly composed of white cis men too often ignore the alienation of women, immigrants, and persons of color.

Consequently, an *intersectional* approach to alienation is required, for the alienated subject inhabits multiple and intersecting geographies and, as such, may simultaneously oppress and be oppressed.[45] This follows from the particular social and material relationships that intersect within the alienated subjects' everyday life. Concretely, we see this in the intolerance and antipathy directed toward impoverished persons of color by members of the so-called (white) working class; and we see this in the support of patriarchal programs by (often, white) women. But the alienated subject is also Black, Asian, Latinx, or Native American; the alienated subject labors as an assembly worker in an automotive factory but also works as a domestic worker; and the alienated subject is racist but also antiracist. For in the end, there is no single, essentialist alienated subject if by *subjectivity* we understand the subject's form of life as necessarily conditioned by its social, political, and economic position.[46]

Effectively, the alienated subject *was never a liberal subject* for it always embodied multiple and contradictory subject positions. The alienated subject is capable of extending care to some, while revealing a harmful indifference or intolerance to others. In some cases, a person or a group of persons might sometimes benefit from systemic exploitation while at other times be the ones who are being exploited.[47] For example, when white workers benefit from white privilege, they benefit from the hyperexploitation of persons of color while still being exploited themselves. However, the deleterious effects of exploitative relations are lessened—or, perhaps, rendered more palatable—by the privileges accorded to them through the "psychological wages of whiteness."[48] Likewise, when men benefit from patriarchy, they benefit from the hyperexploitation of women. Ultimately, the alienated subject embodies an ethical ambiguity, and indifference, manifested materially in the intolerance toward difference and the attendant capacity to hurt.

From an ontological standpoint, there is no universal or transhistorical *condition* of alienation; nor, for that matter, is there any universal or transhistorical *meaning* in life. Rather, both alienation and meaningful life are mediated by one's material conditions. This is not to say that meaning, for example, is dictated or determined by one's wealth or lack thereof. Rather, it is to call attention to the constellation of social relations that comprise one's quotidian existence, and how these social relations are organized such as to make life itself possible. As John Fischer writes, "a meaningful life is not just a matter of pleasant internal states—pleasures or other experiences. It is in part a matter of how we are connected to the external world."[49] In other words, a meaningful life should also be a meaningful social life, and this suggests we must consider how life is experienced not as isolated individuals but as members of something beyond our immediate self-interests. Ultimately, I argue that the transformation of the *alienated subject* to an *emancipated subject* is conditioned by one's ability to overcome indifference, intolerance, and the capacity to hurt through a moral philosophy founded upon an ethics of care and empathy. This requires an effort to cultivate, at a minimum, a meaning in life through our actions and inactions that promote and do not inhibit the life and well-being of others. This extends an understanding of our shared mortality to include an awareness of our uneven vulnerability to premature death, and in the process to actively work toward the constitution of meaningful life as a social good.

What then does this hold for the revolutionary potential of the so-called working class? For many scholars, as Erik Olin Wright explains, the working class (both in a material and a discursive sense) has become increasingly fragmented, internally unequal, and heterogenous in all sorts of ways, impeding the broad class solidarity needed for sustained collective action against capitalism.[50] Indeed, Wright clarifies that part of the problem is the variegated landscape of labor and the lack of a "historical subject" comparable to Marx's vision of the proletariat required for cohesive forms of solidarity needed for an emancipatory overthrow of capitalism.[51] The *alienated subject*, for example, has become thoroughly politicized, so much so that within systems of racial capitalism the *white* alienated subject accrues psychological comfort—that is, meaningfulness in life—through the mere fact of being identified as white. To a certain extent, therefore, the emotional satisfaction of white privilege offsets or counterbalances the stultifying conditions of being exploited. The "psychological wages of whiteness" continue to undermine class solidarity and pervert many whites into believing that they must defend their racial position in society through an "any means necessary" approach that includes violence, voter fraud, and the inscription of inequality into the legal framework of the nation.[52] So too patriarchal ideologies, misogynist practices, homophobia, and ableist narratives obviate against class solidarity in any meaningful sense.

The Path Ahead

The Covid-19 pandemic, Heather Brown writes, lays bare capitalism's quest for limitless value creation and of the deference to profits over lives.[53] This of course is a point underscored repeatedly by Marx. Writing in *Capital,* for example, Marx observes that "within the capitalist system all methods for raising the social productiveness of labor are brought into effect at the cost of the individual laborer."[54] In other words, capital survives—indeed, flourishes—at the expense of those who make its perpetuation possible, namely, the exploited and alienated workers forced to sell their labor in the absence of other life-sustaining activities. As Anderson grimly remarks, how true Marx's comments ring at a time when U.S. workers, but especially Black and other minority workers, are being forced back to labor in workplaces rife with Covid-19.[55]

Throughout *The Alienated Subject* I provide neither a history of alienation nor a reconstruction of Marx's theory of alienation; nor do I provide an exhaustive account of alienation in the United States, although my primary examples are drawn from Trump's America. Instead, I offer a critique of the alienated subject in an effort to understand better the manifest indifference toward, intolerance of, and capacity to hurt others within the capitalist mode of production. More broadly, the task I set to accomplish in the following chapters is twofold: On the one hand, to reflect on the *becoming* of the alienated subject and, on the other hand, to explore the possibility of the *overcoming* of alienation, that is, the transformation of the alienated subject into an emancipated subject. Throughout, I premise that the alienated subject is indifferent to, or intolerant of, the suffering of others and, as a corollary, incapable of seeing the meaningfulness of other lives. These attitudes of indifference and intolerance are expressed as racism, misogyny, homophobia, transphobia, and xenophobia. This is not to say these attitudes are unique to capitalism; indeed, these forms of prejudices pre-date the advent of capital. However, indifference, intolerance, and the capacity to hurt others acquire a particular, concrete form under capitalism in that they relate to, and are mediated by, specific social relations that underpin the material necessities required to sustain a meaningful life.

For someone to *be alienated* is also to say that someone may *not be alienated.* What is the condition of not being alienated? Any satisfactory answer requires an engagement with the human condition; of what it means to be human and, specifically, to be a human in a nonalienated existence.

Throughout his writings, Marx focuses on creative, productive activity. Building on this premise, in chapter 1 I forward the argument that a meaningful life is conditioned by one's awareness of death. As Martin Hägglund explains, "Only in light of the apprehension that we will die . . . can we ask ourselves what we ought to do with our lives and put ourselves at stake in our activities."[56] I disagree, however, with the presumption that *shared mortality* provides the basis for an emancipatory politics. Indeed, the concept of shared mortality, while biologically accurate—*all* living organisms *will* ultimately die—reifies a liberal conception of subjectivity that deflects attention from structural inequalities that conditions one's vulnerability to premature death. In the end, by repositioning the alienated subject as a mortal being aware that a meaningful life is mediated by one's vulnerability to premature death, we circle back to the historical-materialist approach of Marx, notably, the first premise of satisfying those materials necessary for the production and reproduction of life itself. As Marx writes, "Man can only live if he produces means of subsistence, but he can only produce these means if he holds the means of production, the material conditions for labor. It is easy to understand that, if the worker is deprived of the means of production, he is also deprived of the means of subsistence."[57]

Having sketched the contours of a flourishing but mortal life, in chapter 2 I provide an overview of capitalism. Capitalism is a distinct mode of production in which all participants—producers and consumers—depend on the market for their basic needs.[58] As a form of economic organization, made possible by the exaltation of private property, capital's foundation is the social (class) separation of direct producers from the means of production. It is because of this social relation that workers—although formally free—are forced by material circumstances to sell their labor-power to capitalists, who own the means of production.[59] Within capitalist social relations, work tends to be an alienating rather than self-affirming activity.[60] Understanding why this is so provides a first step toward the transcendence of the alienated subject by the emancipated subject. Thus, I continue chapter 2 with an engagement of Marx's conceptualization of alienation. Marx presents his account of alienation most fully in the posthumously published *Economic and Philosophic Manuscripts of 1844*. Here, he conceives of alienation as comprising four broad relations that cover the totality of human existence: workers' relationships to (1) their productive activity, (2) their products, (3) other people, and (4) the species-being, i.e., humanity.[61] First, alienation is experienced when laboring activities become external to the worker. Those workers assigned to assembly lines, for example, exist as mere appendages to the factory; they do not control their own productive activities but instead function at the beck and call of those who own the means of production. Second, under such conditions workers become alienated from the object of their labor: the commodities produced are owned not by the worker but rather by those who own the means of production. Workers derive no satisfaction for their labor activities. Third, workers become alienated from other people; all become mere cogs in the machinery. Lastly, workers become alienated from humanity itself. This final form, "species alienation," we will see is of a qualitatively different type that should be understood not as alienation from an ideal human nature but as alienation from historically created human possibilities, and especially from the human capacity for creativity.[62]

Alienation is not universal but is manifest in particular ways in specific modes of production. To this end, I conclude chapter 2 with an extension of Marx's conceptualization of alienation to consider the multiple subject positions of the alienated subject. Accordingly, I begin the task of repositioning the alienated subject *as abstract figure* within the specific contours of actually existing capitalism. In the United States, for example, capitalism does not exist in a vacuum but instead intersects with other structures and social relations, notably racism and patriarchy. As such, the alienated subject assumes a particular form, redolent of struggles beyond that of class and, in so doing, mediates one's vulnerability to premature death.

In chapter 3 I continue my discussion of how alienation is systemic to the productive processes inherent to the capitalist form of social organization, that is, to the concrete structural and social relations that give rise to the alienated subject. However, I expand my discussion to argue for an intersectional epistemology for the study of alienation. Simply put, any account of the alienated subject that remains faithful to the myopia of the liberal subject will always and necessarily be insufficient, that is to say, to position the alienated subject as unmarked by race, gender, sexuality, and so on is to circumscribe the concrete realities of class struggle through a neglect of intersectional forms of oppression. Thus, we must remain vigilant to the operative question, who comprises the working class? When Marxists posit racial or gender relations, for example, as epiphenomena to class struggle, they conveniently discount the crucial, and divisive, role played by racism and sexism in society.[63] We must, in other words, decenter whiteness from the study of alienation; we must decenter the male subject from the study of alienation; we must decenter heteronormative sexuality from the study of alienation; we must decenter citizenship from the study of alienation.

Building on the theoretical scaffolding developed in chapters 2 and 3, in chapter 4 I excavate the *white* alienated subject within the historical geographies of white supremacy in the United States and its relation to the Black Lives Matter movement and the counterclaim that "All Lives Matter." My purpose in this chapter is not to provide an exhaustive account of the Black Lives Matter movement—see, for example the work of Barbara Ransby and Keeanga-Yamahtta Taylor.[64] Instead, I offer a critical interrogation of the *white* alienated subject, detailing how this subject figure is necessarily defined in relation to its Other. That is, the iconic white worker—and especially the alienated white worker—derives and connotes meaning by what it is not, whether that Other appears in the form of an immigrant of color or a Black criminal. Stated differently, the abstract white alienated worker is produced and reproduced primarily but not exclusively through anti-Black violence.[65]

Black matters, Katherine McKittrick reminds us, are spatial matters.[66] To that end, McKittrick continues, "social practices create landscapes and contribute to how we organize, build, and imagine our surroundings. Black subjects are not indifferent to these practices and landscapes; rather, they are connected to them due to crude racial-sexual hierarchies and due to their (often unacknowledged) status as geographic beings who have a stake in the production of space."[67] In opposition therefore to the anti-Black violence that largely defines whiteness, the Black Lives Matter movement disrupts "a seemingly stable white, heterosexual, class" geography.[68] My underlying focus, therefore, remains on the hope provided by the Black Lives Matter movement, for the simple yet powerful affirmation that "Black Lives Matter" speaks forcefully to the everyday spatial struggle of survivability within capitalism. This hope, however, remains conditional upon the peculiar manifestation of alienation as mediated by settler colonialism and racial capitalism. For under conditions of settler colonialism and racial capitalism, white workers, although exploited and alienated, have little incentive to overstep—let alone overthrow—a system in which they overwhelmingly benefit to the detriment, collectively, of women, persons of color, and members of the LGBTQ community.

In chapter 5, by way of conclusion, I consider the possible and potential transformation of the alienated subject into an emancipated subject.

In doing so, I draw heavily on Eric Fromm's political philosophy of sadomasochism and the art of loving.[69] My take is somewhat unconventional; indeed, such an approach seems discordant with much of the Marxist-inspired literature on alienation and revolutionary emancipation. The term itself is, as Lynn Chancer concedes, a "loaded and quite controversial term" fraught with misunderstandings.[70] Chancer explains, for instance, that "Sadomasochism frequently is taken to connote sexual and/or violent exchanges between two individuals—the sadist and masochist—who play out relationships of domination and subordination in a language of explicit physicality." However, as a political philosophy, sadomasochism directs attention toward concrete social relations as embedded in hegemonic structures of production, distribution, and consumption, that is, in particular modes of social organization, and, as such, offers a particularly salient vantage point from which to interpret alienation. In other words, sadomasochism, conceptually, underscores the fluid asymmetries of power within myriad social relations in which the alienated subject interacts in its everyday life. Chancer elaborates, noting that sadomasochism accords with the highly stratified and inequitable structures of social experience in modern life—patriarchy, white supremacy, heteronormativity, and capitalism—to which we have become habituated.[71]

From his reading of Marx, Fromm premised that alienation is a social and structural relation systemic to the capitalist mode of production. In addition, Fromm surmised that *alienated* social life in contemporary society is debilitating, stressful, and dehumanizing but, crucially, modes of behavior that are deemed normal or adaptive under these conditions are neither healthy nor fulfilling, but rather undermine the ability of people to lead meaningful, flourishing lives.[72] These maladaptive behaviors, notably the (masochistic) submission to authoritative figures *and* the (sadistic) yearning to dominate others, appear normal—a condition Fromm describes as "the pathology of normalcy."[73] In other words, alienation is so pervasive that subjects do not readily recognize their estrangement; nor do they comprehend that indifference, intolerance, and the capacity to hurt are similarly reactions to structural and social relations of capitalism. Subjects are thus both unaware of their own alienation and therefore complicit in their alienation, insofar as they perpetuate illusions about their own "free" conditions.[74] As Fromm postulates, "Man lives with illusions because these illusions make the misery of real life bearable."[75]

I conclude that Fromm's insights, in particular his social psychological reading of Marxist alienation, offer a framework toward the promotion of a radical ethics of giving.[76] Drawing inspiration from a much broader corpus of feminist writings that call for a radical ethics of care and, specifically, the affirmation of love as a revolutionary concept, I premise that love, understood as a productive act of giving, offers the potential, and the promise, to transcend alienation. In doing so, love offers a path forward to transform a society subsumed to the dictates of capital into an emancipated society conditioned by socially just relations of production, distribution, and consumption. Ultimately, to overcome the deadening qualities of capitalism requires efforts that liberate humanity from the structural and social relations of exploitation and alienation that negate the possibility for living a meaningful, flourishing life. Only in this way is it possible to achieve a society centered upon beloved relations and productive love.

1

A Flourishing, but Mortal Life

According to Marx, under capitalism, men and women—but humanity as a whole—are precluded from developing an unalienated, unestranged consciousness. As Bertell Ollman writes, "The human species is deprived of its reality, of what it requires to manifest itself as the human species."[1] Indeed, the exploitative practices of a society built upon a system of production for exchange reduces humanity "to performing undifferentiated work on humanly indistinguishable objects among people deprived of their human variety and compassion."[2] It was for this reason that Marx believed a socialist revolution, as a collective, nonindividuated form of production—was necessary to overcome the alienated life that typified capitalism. Such a revolution, accordingly, was premised not solely to affect political and economic change; it would occasion a *moral* transformation. With the abolition of those social and spatial relations that bring about alienation, work would be experienced as a free and meaningful expression of a flourishing life.[3]

As Martin Hägglund explains, at the time when Marx lived, there was a growing secular recognition that *we are what we do* and that we can do things differently. In other words, we do not have to subject ourselves to the dictates and doctrines of religion *or* capitalism; that we can transform our historical situation through collective action and create institutions that work toward the betterment of all humankind.[4] This sense of optimism is developed most explicitly in Marx's so-called early works, notably the posthumously published *Economic and Philosophic Manuscripts* of 1844. Here, Marx makes a bold statement: "The capitalist can live longer without the worker than can the worker without the capitalist."[5] In this single sentence, Marx effectively captures the mortal consequences and moral wrongness of capitalism, namely, the profound structural and social inequalities that mediate one's vulnerability to premature death. On this point, Marx never turns away from his concern with the human condition and, by extension, how capitalism prevents some people the opportunity to lead a meaningful, flourishing life.[6] Indeed, Marx was well aware of the misery and suffering associated with the advent of capitalism, of lives cut short. For this reason, alienation remained a critical construct in Marx's political philosophy; it is not something he left behind as he moved toward his more extensive economic analyses of capitalism.[7] As Marx explains, "The intimate connection between the pangs of hunger suffered by the most industrious layers of the working class, and the extravagant consumption, coarse or refined, of the rich, for which capitalist accumulation is the basis, is only uncovered when the economic laws are known."[8]

As such, when Marx calls attention to the disparities between the life of the worker and that of the capitalist, he challenges the liberal conception of universal, shared mortality. In other words, Marx underscores the notion that death—or, more precisely, one's awareness of death—is pivotal toward the understanding and practice of living a flourishing, meaningful life. Marx acknowledges the truism that all living beings are mortal. However, Marx understands also that the sustenance of life is *conditional,* that is, dependent upon the structural and social relations that constitute society. Hägglund explains: "A living being cannot simply exist but must do something to stay alive."[9] This *something* is productive labor, that is, the conscious and deliberate production of the basic necessities that make life possible. For Marx, the notion of alienation points to the fact that production under capitalism negates free, cooperative activity.[10] For this reason, the alienated subject must become an emancipated subject.

Marx is no nihilist, for there is hope. Indeed, insofar as alienation is constituted, it can also be changed, transformed, and overcome.[11] To this end, from the 1840s onward, the "working class" became a central part of Marx's thinking, for it was the alienated condition of the proletariat, in particular, that impelled Marx in his interrogation of capitalism.[12] Why Marx places such faith in the proletariat is addressed in chapter 2. First, however, it is necessary to explore more fully Marx's conception of human nature and of how humanity's awareness of its own mortality conditions the ability to lead a flourishing, meaningful life.

A Materialist Conception of Human Nature

Our moral foundations are premised upon particular understandings of human nature, that is, different conceptions of human nature lead to different views about what we ought to do and how we can do it.[13] Within the Western philosophical canon, Socrates and Plato began a tradition of rational inquiry into how we should live predicated, in part, by our distinctive human nature.[14] Plato, for example, premised that human beings are social beings. Humans are not self-sufficient and have needs that cannot be met in isolation, and, consequently, a well-ordered, "just" society is one in which each class of person plays its distinctive role, in harmony with each other.[15] Aristotle, likewise, understood human beings as ineradicably social beings and believed that our human nature reaches its full development only when we live as members of an organized society.[16] Marx aligns with this tradition, drawing especially on the writings of Aristotle.[17] Indeed, Marx's very conception of being human—what philosophers often call "human nature" and what Marx calls "species-being"—supervenes upon Aristotle's theory of the good life.[18]

When Marx writes about species-being, he raises a question similar to that asked by Aristotle in the context of human *ergon*.[19] The term *ergon* is problematic, and classicists continue to debate its precise meaning used throughout the writings of Aristotle.[20] Variously defined as "work," "activity," or "deed," *ergon* implies a functionality inherent both to organic and inorganic objects; thus we may speak of the *ergon* of plants, of animals, and of human beings, as well as shovels or oxcarts.

So what is the human *ergon*? As Thomas Nagel writes, "Humans do a great many things, but since some are done equally well, or better, by plants, fish, and animals, they are not among the things to do which is to be human."[21] We can begin by answering, following Aristotle, what *ergon* is not. Life—as we have seen—is an activity shared by all living organisms, including plants, and therefore is not distinctive of human beings. Perception, likewise, is shared both by human beings and nonhuman beings, and also must be ruled out. For Aristotle, there is only one other general function in the animate world, and humanity's *ergon* consists in this: action with *logos*.[22] In other words, the human *ergon* is a particular form of life, or activity, in accordance with reason.[23]

Marx, following Aristotle, conceives also the human species-being as conditioned by productive activity.[24] Writing in *The German Ideology*, Marx (with Engels), presupposes that humans begin to distinguish themselves from nonhuman animals "as soon as they begin to *produce* their means of subsistence, a step which is conditioned by their physical [corporeal] organization."[25] It is not life of a general nature nor the mere use of tools that is characteristic of universal human nature. Rather, it is "free conscious activity [that] constitutes the species-character of man" and that "In creating an objective world by his practical activity, in *working-up* inorganic nature, man proves himself a conscious species being."[26] The central point that Marx makes is that it is through productive activity *with a conscious plan* that human beings actualize, that is, self-realize, themselves as human beings.[27]

For Marx and Engels, "The first premise of all human history is . . . the existence of living human individuals. Thus, the first fact to be established is the physical [corporeal] organization of these individuals and their consequent relation to the rest of nature."[28] This imparts a particular spatiality to the human condition. As Ian Shaw and Marv Waterstone write: "Our sense of self is bound to the spaces that we inhabit. Space is the canvas of our being: we impress in the world our individuality, passing from the obscurity of inexistence to the security of coexistence."[29] We inhabit a material world, and we imbue this world with meaning. Through our daily activities we interact with other people and other places; our thoughts and actions are affected by these encounters. At the same time, our presence, our connections, reflect back upon those spaces. Just as we are transformed through our everyday pursuits, so too are the spaces that we inhabit transformed. Our being-in-the world, however, is conditioned by social and structural relations that are antecedent to our existence. This is not to condemn humanity to a nihilistic existence, or to resign ourselves that our fate is predetermined because of where we live or who we are. Instead, our awareness of the conditionality of life underscores that other worlds are always possible.

Marx identifies a basic, universal condition of all living things, that is, the necessity to survive and reproduce. Indeed, scattered throughout Marx's writings is the concept *Anlage,* a term imbued with biological connotations, including both the capacities and limiting factors required to sustain and reproduce life. On the one hand, living organisms have physiological needs and bodily limits and constraints and, on the other hand, certain attributes to deal with those needs and limitations. Taken together, the satisfaction of bodily constraints is the absolute precondition of a living existence and provides the impetus and telos of production. Corporeal limitations and bodily capacities are universal for living organisms; the need to acquire by whatever means possible the basic necessities of life itself are held in common by all living creatures and thus are elements of a *general nature.* These dispositions—the need to acquire food and water, and to seek shelter, cannot therefore be considered distinctly human.

On this point, Marx's use of "labor" as being the distinctive capacity of the human species is striking.[30] Marx acknowledges that certain species of nonhuman animals also produce. However, Marx writes: "An animal only produces what it immediately needs for itself or its young. It produces one-sidedly, while man produces universally." He elaborates that nonhuman animals "produce only under the dominion of immediate physical need, while man produces even when he is free from physical need and only truly produces in freedom therefrom."[31] Echoing Aristotle, Marx maintains that nonhuman animals produce *instinctively* in a set pattern, whereas human production is flexible and can be based on specific judgments about how to treat the materials that are to be transformed.[32] To this end, for Marx, "An animal forms things in accordance with the standard and the need of the species to which it belongs, while man knows how to produce in accordance with the standard of every species, and knows how to apply everywhere the inherent standard to the object. Man therefore also forms things in accordance with the laws of beauty."[33] Thus, in a well-known passage of *Capital,* Marx writes:

> A spider conducts operations which resemble those of the weaver, and a bee would put many a human architect to shame by the construction of its honeycomb cells. But what distinguishes the worst architect from the best of bees is that the architect builds the cell in his mind before he constructs it in wax. At the end of every labor process, a result emerges which had already been conceived by the worker at the beginning, hence already existed ideally. Man not only effects a change of form in the materials of nature, he also realizes his own purpose in those materials.[34]

Both cooperation and conscious thought (*logos*) are foundational to Marx's abstract conception of human nature. As Marx and Engels write, "The production of life, both of one's own in labor and of fresh life in procreations, now appears as a twofold relation: on the one hand as a natural, on the other as a social relation—social in the sense that it denotes the co-operation of several individuals, no matter under what conditions, in what manner and to what end. It follows from this that a certain mode of production . . . is always combined with a certain mode of co-operation."[35] In addition, as Morgan explains, "As a species, humans are creatures who are necessarily self-conscious, active, planning, creative and cooperative (sometimes competitive but in ways that can require mutuality, dependencies, reliance and perhaps trust). They are also able to change their own lived circumstances and the broader material environment precisely because of the nature of their being, which includes sociality."[36] Human beings are thus *knowing* beings. Equipped with a consciousness and an ability to reflect upon themselves, human beings can willfully create and produce for a manifold of purposes, both as individuals and as a collective.[37] This is a point that bears repeating. As Aristotle premised—and Marx followed—a person should seek to transcend not only his or her individual practical concerns, but also those of society or humanity as a whole.[38] Consequently, this enables Marx "to argue that there is no a priori restriction based upon a theory of human nature, that would prohibit the formation of a society governed by an overall identification of people with one another as fellow beings."[39]

For Marx, therefore, productive activity with *logos* both is unique to human beings and provides a way forward for the betterment of being human. This is not to say that Marx *privileges* humanity over other nonhuman animals or nature itself. Nor does Marx advocate an instrumentalist valuing of nonhuman nature.[40] Instead, Marx advances a dialectic understanding of human/nature, a framing influenced by both his knowledge of Greek philosophy and contemporary scientific thought. On the one hand, Marx drew inspiration from the Greek philosopher Epicurus (341–270 BC), namely, the relationship between life and death—a topic I visit later in this chapter. Here, we begin with Epicurus's argument that death has no meaning for humans or, for that matter, any living, sentient creature. In other words, death from the standpoint of the living may be feared, but from the standpoint of the dead, there is nothing to fear.[41] Consequently, when Marx writes that "nature fixed in isolation from man—*is nothing for man*" he is not reducing all of nonhuman nature to some form of instrumentality but instead finds connection with Epicurus's proposition that "Death is nothing to us."[42] Marx underscores the idea that human beings are objective, corporeal, sensual beings, and that when removed (alienated) from the sensual connections to earth and other living beings, nature (in Epicurean terms) is "nothing for man."[43] Hence, instead of positing a dualist conception of human and nonhuman nature, Marx advances a human/

nature dialectic whereby "Nature is man's inorganic body—nature, that is, insofar as it is not itself the human body. Man lives on nature—means that nature is his body, with which he must remain in continuous intercourse if he is not to die. That man's physical and spiritual life is linked to nature means simply that nature is linked to itself, for man is a part of nature."[44] As Foster and Clark conclude, divorced from nature, human beings, like nonhuman animals, would have no existence. Rather than representing a separation of humans from other animals or a moral justification for the utilitarian use of the latter, Marx acknowledges our shared *universal* existence as corporeal spatial beings.[45]

On the other hand, Marx studied the scientific advances of his day and, specifically, incorporated the concept of metabolism, in a much broader fashion, into all his major political economic works from the 1850s onward.[46] Indeed, for Marx the concept of metabolism provides the necessary fulcrum with which to interpret the dialectic between human and nonhuman nature.[47] As Foster explains, Marx's conceptual use of metabolism was not simply (or even mainly) an attempt to solve a philosophical problem but rather an endeavor to ground his critique of political economy materially in an understanding of concrete human-nature relations emanating from the natural sciences of his day. Accordingly, the concept of metabolism became central to his analysis of both the production of use-values and the labor process.[48] To this end, social metabolism for Marx encompasses human labor and production in relation—both socially and spatially—to the larger biophysical world and, effectually, captures the complex interchange of matter and energy between human beings and nature.[49]

Marx understood that natural systems, such as the nutrient cycle, had their own metabolism, which operated independently of and in relation to human society, allowing for their regeneration and/or continuance. However, with the onset of capitalism, a new social metabolic order came to dominate the material interchange between society and nature. Marx recognized that the tendency of capital—because capital "freely" *robs* from nature—is to violate the natural conditions that ensure nature's vitality, undermining the base on which ecological and human sustainability depends.[50] On that point, as Foster and Clark explain, "capitalism has both an inner force that propels it and objective conditions outside itself that set its boundaries, the relations to which are forever changing. The inner dynamic of the system is governed by the process of exploitation of labor power, under the guise of equal exchange, while its primary relation to its external environment is one of expropriation."[51] Notably Marx employs the concept of metabolic rift to capture the material and spatial estrangement, or alienation, of human beings in capitalist society from the natural conditions of their existence.[52] Marx explains, "Instead of a conscious and rational treatment of the land as permanent communal property, as the inalienable condition for the existence and reproduction of the chain of human generations, we have the exploitation and the squandering of the powers of the earth."[53] Under capitalism, therefore, an alienated form of labor mediates the human-social relation to nature.[54] This is a point demanding additional clarification. The social and spatial separation implicit in Marx's conception of the metabolic rift does not reestablish a dualism between "humans" and "nature"; rather, it underscores a maladaptive *relationship* in that under capitalism, labor is abstracted to only maximize the accumulation of wealth. Labor no longer functions to fulfill human needs and, as such, no longer provides meaning in life.

Returning to the matter of productive activity, our discussion thus far has focused on human nature *in the abstract,* that is, of the presupposition of a universal human nature. Marx and Engels readily understood that abstractions, including those of human nature, "divorced from real history, have no value whatsoever. They can only serve to facilitate the arrangement of historical material. . . . But they by no means afford a recipe or schema . . . for neatly trimming the epochs of history."[55] To this end, Marx and Engels conclude that "Empirical observation must in each separate instance bring out empirically, and without any mystification and speculation, the connection of the social and political structure with production." As such, alongside an abstract, transhistorical conception of human nature, Marx forwards an historical conception, whereby "The essence of man is no abstraction inherent in each single individual. In its reality it is the ensemble of the social relations."[56] Stated differently, the concrete manifestation of being human arises from the fact that human beings participate in, and live through, particular social relations over time and across space.

In his *Contribution to a Critique of Political Economy,* Marx expands upon this idea. He writes: "In the social production of their existence, men inevitably enter into definite relations, which are independent of their will, namely, relations of production appropriate to a given stage in the development of their material forces of production."[57] In this passage, Marx does not promote a determinist position but instead acknowledges the historical and geographical continuity (and adaptability) of human activity. Recall that Marx and Engels presuppose that human beings distinguished themselves from animals as soon as they began to produce their means of subsistence.[58] This "first historical act" thus marked the production of the means to satisfy the reproduction of life itself, but to do so required the development of tools by which nature was transformed and specific objects were created that satisfied these needs.[59] In turn, the satisfaction of initial biological needs creates new needs (and new tools); these needs, in turn, require new products and, in an ongoing process, subsequent needs and products are produced. Therefore, as Marx and Engels conclude, any given "mode of production must not be considered simply as being the reproduction of the physical existence of the individuals. Rather it is a definite form of activity of these individuals, a definite form of expressing their life, a definite mode of life on their part. As individuals express their life, so they are. What they are, therefore, coincides with their production, both with what they produce and with how they produce. Hence what individuals are depends on the material conditions of their production."[60] Consequently, "The production of ideas, of conceptions, of consciousness, is at first directly interwoven with the material activity and the material intercourse of men—the language of real life. . . . The same applies to mental production as expressed in the language of the politics, laws, morality, religion, metaphysics, etc., of a people. Men are the producers of their conceptions, ideas, etc., that is, real, active men, as they are conditioned by a definite development of their productive forces and of the intercourse corresponding to these, up to its furthest forms."[61]

The process by which we transform the material world therefore is simultaneously a process by which we continually create within ourselves new needs and, thus, can be said to change our nature.[62] As Marx explains in *The Eighteenth Brumaire of Louis Bonaparte,* "Men make their own history, but they do not make it just as they please; they do not make it under circumstances chosen by themselves, but under circumstances directly encountered, given, and transmitted from the past."[63] In other words, Marx recognizes that people are *born into* particular societies; and that this fact alone shapes subsequent human activity, both from an individual and collective standpoint.

To recap our discussion thus far: Marx's *historical* (that is, particular) conception of human nature is grounded in a robust *transhistorical* (that is, universal) conception of human nature.[64] Marx, as such, promotes a dialectic interpretation of human nature that operates both at an abstract and concrete level, whereby the latter refers to the specific forms of human social organization organized around particular modes of production while the former refers to the general form that human social activity takes place.[65] At this point, it is necessary to consider more closely the individual human, that is, the embodied subject, within Marx's historical-materialist framework.

On the one hand, there is a "natural" body, the living organism subject to death in the absence of food, water, and shelter. This is a universal conception, for as Sébastien Rioux explains, the importance of the natural body lies precisely in its foundational, transhistorical character, for it is the natural body that must inevitably die.[66] On the other hand, there is the "laboring" body—that entity "engaged in the social production of material life by metabolizing nature through labor in order to meet human needs and survive."[67] Thus, the natural body and the laboring body are not separate entities but exist *in totality* and operate at different levels, similar to the transhistorical and historical forms of human nature.

The separation of abstract and concrete conceptions both of human nature and of embodied subjects is crucial insofar as alienation, for Marx, is *not* a universal condition of humanity in general but instead denotes a particular social relation specific to the capitalist mode of production. A detailed assessment of capitalism as generative of alienation must wait until chapter 2. First, however, I turn my attention to a concept intimately associated with that of human nature, this being *meaningful life.*

Marx and Meaningful Life

It is not uncommon for people to complain that their lives lack meaning, that they yearn for *something* to give them purpose. However, as John Fischer explains, "When people ask about the meaning of life, they are not typically wondering about the purpose of human life in general. Rather, they are asking about meaning (or meaningfulness) in human life."[68] To this end, questions about *meaning in life* direct attention toward attendant concepts such as nihilism, suffering, misery, morality, and death itself.[69]

Ontological questions surrounding one's meaning in life do not figure prominently in most accounts of Marx, and yet the potential of living a flourishing—that is, meaningful—life is a central concern of Marx. Indeed, "Marx's epic critique of capitalism may be understood as an analysis of the way that capitalism systematically denies the majority of people the requirements of a 'good life.'"[70] The capacity to live a meaningful life, as forwarded by Marx, is heavily indebted to Aristotle's concept of *eudemonia.*[71] Itself a contested term, *eudemonia* is variously translated as "happiness," "wellness," "goodness," or "flourishing."[72] For Aristotle, *eudemonia* describes the realization of a "good" or ethical life and thus refers to a way of living, a way of carrying out the trajectory of one's life.[73] In short, for Aristotle, *eudemonia* relates directly to the natural purpose of being human, that is, it is teleologically determined by human nature.[74]

Aristotle's view was that every living being has a *telos,* some good that it naturally strives to actualize.[75] Consequently, his teleological conceptualization of *eudemonia* was premised on a categorical distinction between human and nonhuman nature.[76] Both human and nonhuman beings, Aristotle acknowledges, require material resources in order to survive. However, human beings have an innate ability to consciously shape and control their environment. Such capabilities require intelligence and, in turn, require a capacity for reason and the freedom to shape one's own life through deliberation and choice.[77] *Eudemonia,* accordingly, is conceptually related to *ergon.* As Richard Kim explains, "the argument is that for anything that has a characteristic function or activity (*ergon*), that thing's good resides in its functioning well. And since, Aristotle claims, the characteristic activity of a human being is to engage in rational activities, it is the engagement of rational activities in accordance with the virtues or excellences, over a lifetime, that constitutes [eudemonia]."[78]

Given Aristotle's understanding that the ability to live in accord with reason is unique to humans, it follows that he proposed that the most complete way to live according to reason was to live virtuously. For Aristotle, the virtues specific to human beings included living in a reflective way that embraced our best values and engaged our highest talents and civic concerns, including friendship, justice, and truthfulness.[79] Notably, Aristotle held that "the pinnacle of human excellences was the philosophical or contemplative life."[80] Aristotle, in short, provides a way of determining what constitutes a meaningful life by appealing to human nature and the characteristic activities of human beings.[81] For Aristotle, "a person could be more or less characterized as a person who lives (or has lived) a good life, insofar as that individual pursued or lived in accordance with the specific human virtues. By engaging in these personal and civic virtues and excellences, and when conditions allow, actualizing them, Aristotle expected persons to be most fulfilled."[82] Marx builds on this foundation, but does so with a scaffolding predicated on an historically contingent conception of being human. Briefly stated, for Marx, meaning in life is related to productive activity. As Marx and Engels write in *The German Ideology*:

> The phantoms formed in the brains of men are also, necessarily, sublimates of their material life-process, which is empirically verifiable and bound to material premises. Morality, religion, metaphysics, and all the rest of ideology as well as the forms of consciousness corresponding to these, thus no longer retain the semblance of independence. They have no history, no development; but men, developing their material production and their material intercourse, alter, along with this their actual world, also their thinking and the products of their thinking. It is not consciousness that determines life, but life that determines consciousness.[83]

In other words, the capacity to achieve meaning in life is inseparable from one's productive activity. And yet, so conditioned are we to the alienating tendencies of capitalism that such an assertion rings discordant to contemporary ears. Indeed, it is strange to conceive of work, that is, laboring activities, to hold the potential for meaningful life. For many people, working under the conditions of capitalism becomes something they have to do, instead of something they want to do. However, as Sven-Eric Liedman explains, Marx lived in a time when the word *labor* itself contained an expanded meaning, one that encompassed intellectual and artistic activities.[84]

For Marx, all forms of labor—whether materially productive or socially reproductive—entail human self-realization; the essence of labor, therefore, lies not in its exchange value (as premised under capitalism) but in its capacity to fulfill the needs of the human species.[85] To this end, we understand *eudemonia* not as an emotion or a feeling, but instead as a guide toward living itself. As Todd May explains, "The telos of a human life is not an end result, where one becomes something and then spends the rest of one's life in that condition that one becomes."[86] Instead, meaning in life is actively cultivated and requires a degree of autonomy and self-determination, that is, free will. This is only possible, however, within an ensemble of social relations, for human beings are necessarily communal beings.

For Marx, existing material conditions, and therefore concrete potentials, are important parts of his definitions of humanity, and this privileging of potentiality is the key conceptual lever that generates Marx's critical development.[87] As Wallimann explains, in Marx's investigation of the nature of social organization, he found that throughout most of history individuals have not been able to live according to their capabilities.[88] Paradoxically, human beings by nature are capable of subjecting production and the product of their labor to their conscious control and yet, in actuality, they are often prevented from doing so.[89] For Marx, capitalism is especially noteworthy in this regard. Indeed, for Marx, capitalism is anti-*eudemonic* precisely because it impairs the realization of human capabilities, restricts the exercise of intelligence or creativity, restricts the exercise of deliberation and freedom in productive activities, narrows life's compass to the sale of labor-power as a means to obtain life's necessities, and reduces social relations among people to that of objects.[90] In short, a good life is not that of the rich and famous; a flourishing life is one that promotes well-being in others as opposed to being well off.

Capitalism, with its systemic promotion of endless material accumulation, is anathema to a flourishing life. Indeed, we can take this assertion one step further and argue that capitalism is not only *not* conducive to living a meaningful life, it is anathema to life itself. As Sandro Mezzadra writes, "We are confronted with an intensification of exploitation that goes hand in hand with its extension—to the point that, to mention just a couple of instances, the poorest of the poor are exploited through the financialization of their life, the boundaries between production and reproduction are blurred by the penetration of finance into households, [and] mobility and migration connect and recombine geographic scales of exploitation and resistance."[91] For these reasons, I expand upon Marx's concern with a flourishing life. I do so in a way that resonates strongly with his materialist conception of history, namely, humankind's awareness of its own mortality.

Toward a Marxist Thanatology

An essential feature of human life—indeed, a constituent component of human nature—is that we are aware, either explicitly or implicitly, of its finitude.[92] That is, human beings are conscious of our mortality and, in fact, the mortality of all living organisms. "It may be," May suggests, "that humans are the only animals with an ongoing sense of their own death."[93] Nonhuman animals, to be sure, fear danger; but, as May elaborates, "to seek to remain alive when one's life is threatened . . . is not the same as having an ongoing awareness of one's death."[94] To this end, human species-beings' *knowledge of the certainty of death* and the constant awareness of that fact conditions the social and cultural organization of all known societies.[95] Truly, as Olivia Stevenson and colleagues observe, "Death and bereavement are inevitably central to everyday life across culture, although associated social and cultural practices vary by time and place, ranging from sequestered social taboo to an integral part of ongoing social life."[96]

For Zygmunt Bauman, "Once learned, knowledge that death may not be escaped cannot be forgotten—it can only not be thought about for a while, with attention shifting to other concerns."[97] In other words, human life is an ongoing process of learning to live with death.[98] This is seen in our practices as they relate to the dying and the dead, for example, in the ways we grieve, mourn, and remember the dead.[99] In addition, our attempt to live with the inevitability of death informs our understanding of the possibility of living a meaningful life. For many people, death is "bad" in part because it deprives us of the ability to pursue projects that give our lives meaning. As Martha Nussbaum writes, "The intensity and dedication with which very many human activities are pursued cannot be explained without reference to the awareness that our opportunities are finite."[100]

An awareness of death leads naturally to a consideration of other, more metaphysical questions, such as the existence of God, spirituality, and the afterlife. Indeed, as human beings, many of our beliefs about living meaningful lives are conditioned by attendant beliefs about what happens after death occurs.[101] In various Christian accounts, for example, one's immortal soul ascends to heaven and thereupon dwells in eternal peace.[102] These interpretations, among others, speak to the deep human desire felt by many that our worldly existence should have some ultimate meaning or purpose or significance.[103] By way of contrast, existentialist philosophers such as Søren Kierkegaard, Jean-Paul Sartre, and Albert Camus denied the existence of an afterlife. Consequently, death itself lends no meaning to life.[104] More recently, scholars have considered how technological advances, especially in the fields of medicine and health care, have altered conceptions of death, to the extent that death is not only something undesirable but something to be mastered and overcome.[105] Regardless, though, of one's attitude toward death—be it fear or ambivalence, something to be welcomed or avoided, or of the existence of an afterlife in whatever form—the point remains that humans are *aware* of death. This awareness, I suggest, figures prominently in the conceptualization of alienation and one's potential to lead a meaningful life.

Marx does not present an explicit framework of death; rather, his conception of human mortality—and of an awareness of death—is scattered throughout his works, usually in reference to the harmful, material conditions of laboring within the capitalist mode of production. For example, when Marx and Engels presuppose the "first premise of all human existence" is that "men must be in a position to live in order to be able to 'make history,'" they point specifically to the physiological imperative of bodily survival and reproduction.[106] Indeed, they recognize that the first activity of being human relates to survival, that is, "pushing back the moment of death, extending the life-span, increasing life expectation and thus life's content-absorbing capacity, making death a matter of concern, a significant event."[107] As Marx, writing with Engels, elaborates:

> But life involves before everything else eating and drinking, housing, clothing and various other things. The first historical act is thus the production of the means to satisfy these needs, the production of material life itself. And indeed this is an historical act, a fundamental condition of all history, which today, as thousands of years ago, must daily and hourly be fulfilled merely in order to sustain human life.[108]

Here, Marx implies that the human body needs a certain number of calories to reproduce its cells, a certain amount of liquid to prevent dehydration, a certain amount of shelter to maintain its temperature within a fairly narrow range, and a certain amount of oxygen, rest, and sleep.[109] However, beyond the materiality of life itself, Marx demonstrates a keen awareness that one's mortal existence is mediated by definite social relations that are largely independent of one's will. As May explains, "We live in the shadow of the fact that we will die. What we do, how we do it, the attitude we take towards it, happens against the background knowledge that each of us is mortal."[110] This knowledge is nevertheless conditioned by the concrete social and structural relations in which one inhabits. Within the capitalist mode of production, for example, Marx writes, the worker "can live as a worker only insofar as he exchanges his labor capacity for that part of capital which forms the labor fund [wages]. This exchange is tied to conditions which are accidental for him, and indifferent to his organic presence."[111] In other words, capital is indifferent both to the organic presence, that is, the living existence, of the worker, and the worker, in turn, is able to live only through the "chance" of obtaining gainful employment. Under perilous and uncertain conditions, "the worker is maintained as a living being through the mercy of others."[112]

Marx's thanatology elides readily with his conception of productive and meaningful activity, in that one's awareness of death is the ultimate condition of cultural creativity as such.[113] As Bauman explains: "Death, when it comes, will brutally interrupt our work before our task is done, our mission accomplished. This is why we have every reason to be worried about death now, when we are still very much alive and when death remains but a remote and abstract prospect."[114] The imbrication of mortality and meaningful life, however, raises another conceptual problem, notably the philosophical basis of why death in and of itself is bad. For Marx, there is an implicit understanding that the shortening of workers' lives under capitalism is inherently wrong. In drawing out comparisons between capitalists and wage workers during economic hard times, Marx writes, "In those cases where worker and capitalist equally suffer, the worker suffers in his very existence, the capitalist in the profit on his dead mammon."[115] Effectively, economic downturns threaten the capitalist with diminished profits, and for the workers, a diminished, meaningful life to the point of an early death.

Stepping back for a moment, though, we note that there is no consensus among philosophers or theologians if death (in the abstract) is good or bad. For Epicureans, for example, you must exist in order to be harmed. Since death negates the existence of someone, no harms can come to the dead and thus we should not fear death. For others, however, the badness of death results from the opportunities lost. As Fischer explains, "As we live our lives, and even as we get older, we have preferences for pursuing projects that give our lives meaning. . . . Death now, rather than later, may thwart these preferences."[116] Not surprisingly, it is this attitude that often informs our response to learning of the death of an infant or child as opposed to a more elderly person. For some people, the *premature* death of a young person is more tragic than that of an older person, for the simple calculus that the former has had fewer years to pursue their dreams whereas the latter, supposedly, has already achieved theirs.[117] Such an attitude was on blatant display during the Covid-19 pandemic in the spring of 2020, for example, as conservative pundits in the United States downplayed the severity of the disease since the elderly were thought to be more susceptible to death as opposed to younger (and, presumably, more productive) members of society.

If death constitutes a bad thing for an individual insofar as it deprives them of what could have been on balance a meaningful continuation of life, premature death is infinitely worse.[118] However, premature death as a theoretical concept is notoriously difficult to define.[119] As Watson explains, "We often call the death of a young person tragic, a wasted potential and the feeling that they have suffered a great misfortune. But for an individual who affirms their life and does not wish it to end, at least prematurely, death at any point before then would seem a necessary harm."[120] On this point Watson asks, if death is a harm because of what it deprives us of, then are all deaths then premature?[121]

Given the slipperiness of premature death as a concept, it is helpful to consider the *modernist* origins of the term. According to Zohreh Bayatrizi, premature death emerged as crucial concern during the seventeenth century and subsequently was the main impetus behind the birth of population statistics and demography. She explains that major killers such as plague epidemics drove efforts to quantify and contain the causes of premature death, and this contributed to the development of new scientific techniques for measuring longevity and mortality rates and for identifying the most common causes of death.[122] Conceptually, therefore, premature death *is death in the abstract.* As Bayatrizi explains, death "came to be treated as a form of risk, that is, as an avoidable, indeterminate, and manageable contingency. The construction of death as a preventable risk entailed an overt "instrumentalization" of the knowledge of mortality, making death amenable to political management (as in public health projects) and even economic profit-making (as in life insurance calculations."[123] Understood as such, premature death refers *not* to the application of violence or death by harmful intent, but instead the abstract application of instrumental calculations. And this, in fact, is how premature death is most often understood in the medical community. Epidemiologists, for example, frequently utilize a measure known as "years of potential life lost" that is calculated by subtracting the various ages at which individuals in a population die from the average life expectancy or an arbitrarily chosen number such as age sixty-five.[124]

Consider, for example, two scenarios. In the first, we have a young woman in the United States—perhaps in her early thirties—who is diagnosed with cancer. She is admitted to the hospital and receives exceptional care. Still, the disease spreads rapidly, and, in spite of the efforts of her doctors, she dies. In this example, we may describe her death as premature, in that she died well before the average life expectancy for women in the United States. We may even question the meaning of her death and wonder why she died at such an early age. However, we would probably not describe her death as the result of deliberate harm. In our second example, we again have a young woman in the United States, also in her thirties, who is diagnosed with cancer. In this scenario, however, she is denied access to medical treatment because of her inability to afford health insurance. Without treatment, the woman succumbs to the disease.

In both cases the deaths of the women are premature; and yet, the term *premature* at this point sounds hollow. My sense is that when we talk of premature death we are referencing something *beyond* the calculation of years lost. Rather, there is an implicit understanding that premature deaths result from harm being done to someone, that death—regardless of age—stems from some form of violence, whether direct or structural. People who are denied medical treatment and people who are shot and killed are harmed; this is why their deaths are morally wrong. Ruth Wilson Gilmore captures this idea: "Fatalities—premature deaths—are not simply an objective function of any kind of power differential. . . . Rather, the application of violence—the cause of premature deaths—produces political power in a vicious cycle."[125] In other words, when we consider the "reality" of violence, of premature death, we must do so through an understanding of how power and difference are sedimented into society.[126] To this end, in a previous work, I forwarded the concept of "truncated life."[127] Premature death *as truncated life* is that life which ends abruptly. Fundamentally, truncated life directs attention to social and structural relations that mediate harmful practices that result in death. It includes obvious situations, such as homicide by firearms, but it includes also the harm brought about by intransigent governments that refuse to enact gun control measures. It includes the premature deaths that result from a lack of affordable health care, and it includes those deaths resultant from lax occupational safety regulations. In short, as Emma Laurie and Ian Shaw conclude, "truncated life names the injustice of premature death."[128]

We need to take seriously *truncated life* as foundational to the conditions of precariousness and precarity. Judith Butler explains that "Lives are by definition precarious: they can be expunged at will or by accident; their persistence is in no sense guaranteed."[129] For Butler, *precarious* is a condition of all life—including both human and nonhuman animals—in that all living organisms will die, that is, life in the collective marks a condition of *shared mortality.* However, as Christopher Harker explains, the concept of precariousness does not explain why certain subjects and populations experience a greater risk of death and injury than others.[130] There is, in other words, a mediation to precarity itself, for while all living things will at some point die, that point is highly conditional. As Sean Hill writes, deployment of the term *precarity* often fails to address broader systems and institutions responsible for precarity, notably racism, sexism, and ableism, and how differently marginalized people experience a precarious existence.[131] Building on this premise, premature death as truncated life is mediated by concrete structures and social relations, including but not limited to racism, sexism, and ableism.[132] In chapter 3 I develop this argument further; here, I call attention to the salience of intersectionality as an epistemology toward a reworking of the notion of shared mortality. For example, Kimberlé Crenshaw details that the location of women of color at the intersection of race and gender makes their actual experience of domestic violence and rape qualitatively different than that of white women.[133] Crucially, the concept of intersectionality "refuses a liberal and additive theorization of power and justice" and, in doing so, highlights how structural oppressions mediate the inequalities and injustices surrounding one's vulnerability to a truncated life.[134] Indeed, the concept of shared mortality falters precisely because it is predicated on a classical sense of universal human nature. As Martha Fineman explains, throughout much of the world today, "dominant political and legal theories are built around a universal subject defined in the liberal tradition."[135]

From the standpoint of the so-called liberal subject, Fineman continues, equality "is the expression of the idea that all human beings are by nature free and endowed with the same inalienable rights."[136] Accordingly, the promotion of the liberal subject is based on the idea of a "sameness of treatment," whereby various classifications, such as ethnicity, gender, sexuality, religion, and national origin, define individual legal identities and form the main axes around which claims for equal protection are made.[137] To this end, differential life expectancies are to be corrected through the equal application of law: all persons, regardless of "identity," are to have equal access to employment, housing, and so on. In practice, however, institutions are structured so as to preclude equal treatment under the law. Indeed, this forms the basis of distinguishing between equality, equity, and justice.

Certainly, all human beings are mortal and thus experience a shared mortality. However, because we are positioned differently within a web of economic, political, and institutional relationships, our vulnerabilities to a truncated life through premature death are conditioned and experienced in particular ways.[138] Those conditions that are productive of truncated life are decidedly *not* universal but instead manifest differently at different times and in different places. For example, as Kathryn Gillespie and Patricia Lopez write, "racialized social relations in the United States, characterized by uneven social and economic hierarchies of support and privilege, make black bodies (and black male bodies, in particular) killable and disproportionately exposed to bodily violence, incarceration, and premature death."[139]

Conclusions

Under the conceptual guise of human species-being, Marx presents a theory about the nature of being human. Marx articulates a framework whereby it is the potential capability of human beings to freely shape the material world in accordance with a consciously adopted and nonexploitative plan that provides the essential conditions for human fulfillment.[140] In so doing, Marx calls to question the deleterious effects of capitalism on one's capacity to live a flourishing, meaningful life. In other words, Marx underscores the structural and social inequalities inherent to capitalism and how these mediate both one's ability to live a meaningful life and, subsequently, one's vulnerability to premature death. Marx writes, "It is true that labor produces for the rich wonderful things—but for the worker it produces privation. It produces palaces—but for the worker, hovels. It produces beauty—but for the worker, deformity."[141] Notably, Marx's repeated references to the concept of species-being "is a reminder that there is a human who can flourish or be harmed and the systemic weirdness of capitalism fundamentally means that human well-being is not an explicit concern of capitalism in general."[142] For Marx, the primary consideration is always "the real individuals, their activity and the material conditions of their life."[143]

Under the capitalist mode of production, Marx details, the "human species-being is not allowed to realize human freedom, but functions merely to keep the worker alive. Whereas the satisfaction of our animal needs for food, clothing, and shelter ought to function as the means toward a realization of our specifically human natures, under the capitalist form of social organization, this relationship is reversed—inverted."[144] Aware of their own mortality—and that of their family and those dear to them—workers come to the realization that they utilize all their capabilities for labor simply in order to sustain life itself.[145] In doing so, workers become alienated in their productive activities. Labor no longer holds any meaning or provides a purpose in life beyond mere survival. Alienation is thus "something produced or constituted through society, at the core of which . . . is the way work is organized, since this is central to the whole of society."[146]

Capitalism, but more precisely the social relations of productive activities oriented around private property and commodity exchange, sunders people from their potential to lead meaningful lives. On this point, alienation is not a transhistorical, immutable feature of humanity but instead a mutable, historically contingent production of being human. Effectively, capitalism inhibits one's capacity to live a meaningful life, and this limitation constitutes an alienated existence: thus, the production of the alienated subject.

2

The Alienated Subject

For Zygmunt Bauman, the United States is a "society of consumers" whereby meaning is found not in the satisfaction of creative, productive activities conducted individually and collectively but rather in the incessant drive and consumption of *stuff.*[1] In other words, the insatiable desire to consume *for consumption's sake* becomes desirable in and of itself and, in the act, appears natural and normal.[2] Consumption, effectively, *appears* to provide meaning in life. As Nolen Gertz explains: "If a life of acquisition and consumption is the only life we know, then we would not see a life of meaningless labor for meaningless money for meaningless goods and services for meaningless fulfillment as a *meaningless life,* instead we would see it as *the real world.*"[3] Consequently, as John Holloway elaborates, "It is the very fact that wealth appears as a collection of commodities to us who live in capitalist society that makes us take this appearance for granted. We are used to seeing wealth in that way."[4]

Marx sees things differently or, rather, hopes to make things different. Marx wants us to reconsider our understanding of wealth and, in doing so, to reevaluate what we find meaningful, as social beings, in our lives. As Chris Byron observes, Marx's comments on human nature, from his early writings through the *Grundrisse, Capital,* and *Theories of Surplus Value* are not divergent. Rather, when his views on labor, species-being, human nature, and alienation are analyzed together, some very consistent themes are identified, notably that humans, individually and collectively, produce both with purpose and creativity and that their free and conscious production serves to generate meaning in life.[5] Thus, in the *Grundrisse,* Marx writes: "In bourgeois economics—and in the epoch of production to which it corresponds—this complete working-out of the human content appears as a complete emptying-out, this universal objectification as total alienation, and the tearing-down of all limited, one-sided aims as sacrifice of the human end-in-itself to an entirely external end."[6] However, Marx counters, "when the limited bourgeois form is stripped away, what is wealth other than the universality of individual needs, capacities, pleasures, productive forces etc., created through universal exchange?"[7] That is, for Marx, meaning in life *outside of capitalism* "is collective, it is social, the product of human interaction—the richness of what is often referred to as 'the common.'"[8] Marx effectively stakes out a "world of tension," a contrast between a society of meaningless production and consumption and a society of meaningful, communal interaction among people.[9] As Holloway concludes, this communal richness is "the richness of a street filled with different traditions and ways of living, the richness of the turn of the seasons in the countryside, the richness of a voice raised in song, be it human or bird."[10]

A society of wealth premised upon a deeper, more meaningful sense of freedom, we will see, is denied the alienated subject. This assertion, however, requires clarification, for the term *freedom* carries myriad connotations, many of which are routinely used toward particular political ends. As Bauman writes, "The oft-repeated assurance 'this is a free country' means: it is up to you what sort of life you wish to live, how you decide to live it, and what kinds of choices you make in order to see your project through."[11] However, within a capitalist, consumer-oriented society, especially as currently configured in the United States, people believe they are free because they can choose among a near infinite variety of breakfast cereals or potato chips, where freedom *appears* in the form of cheese-filled sausages or raspberry-infused beer. The confusion of concrete choices with constraints in the abstract masks the degree to which the alienating tendencies of capitalism have distorted one's subjectivity and, by extension, one's ability to live a meaningful, unalienated life.

The basis of alienation for Marx is not at its foundation religious or philosophical doctrine but rather economic life.[12] That said, neither is alienation an intrinsic or transhistorical feature of production—and thus an essential trait of humanity. Instead, the tendency toward alienation is mediated by particular forms of social organization.[13] That is to say, alienation is conditioned historically, geographically, and morally.[14] On this point, alienation is a social condition mediated by the capitalist mode of social organization in two fundamental ways: through a fragmentation of the human person and through a prohibition, or limitation, on the exercise of human productivity.[15] The operative question, though, becomes how alienation is manifest in the structural and social relations of capitalist organization.[16] For as Sandra Lee Bartky discerns, alienation is not a condition into which someone might stumble by accident; rather, it is the manifestation of myriad structural and social relations that comprise capitalism.[17] My aim in this chapter, to this end, is not to reconstruct an orthodox account of Marx's conception of alienation—a topic covered extensively elsewhere—but instead to theorize the place of the alienated subject under capitalism, for as Ian Shaw and Marv Waterstone explain, alienation presents as a profound loss, that is, a loss of one's *place in the world*.[18]

We begin with Marx, not because Marx is the ultimate arbiter of alienation but rather because Marx provides a robust account of capitalism both as a mode of production and a way of life. Together, Marx calls to question the structural and social relations inherent to capitalism as obstacles to the simple fact of being human, in short, how the capitalist mode of production negates our capacity to live meaningful lives. Simply put, capitalism precludes a meaningful life for many because exploitation and the ever-present specter of a truncated life through premature death are built into the organization of society. That said, Marx's project is incomplete.

Marx readily understands that the history of capitalism "is written in the annals of mankind in letters of blood and fire."[19] He recognizes that "the discovery of gold and silver in America, the extirpation, enslavement and entombment in mines of the indigenous population of that continent, the beginnings of the conquest and plunder of India, and the conversion of Africa into a preserve for the commercial hunting of blackskins, are all things which characterize the dawn of the era of capitalist production."[20] Here, Marx—unlike many of his predecessors—locates colonialism, slavery, and genocide as pivotal to social and structural relations of capitalism. However, Marx does not elaborate on the salience of racism, for example, in his conceptualization of alienation or for the transcendence of alienation. It will become necessary, therefore, to rearticulate Marx's account of alienation in concert with the formation of myriad subject positions within capitalism. Following Epifanio San Juan Jr., we need to remain sensitive to the fact that "the capitalist labor process and its conditions overdetermine the location of groups whose ethnic, racial, gender, and other characteristics acquire value within that context."[21] Neither whiteness nor patriarchy, for example, are autonomous factors operating apart from the totality of social relations systemic to the capitalist mode of production, for as San Juan Jr. concludes, a critique of ideologies of racism and sexism operating in the arena of class antagonism becomes crucial in the effort to dismantle their efficacy.[22] This discussion appears in chapter 3. First, however, my objective is to sketch the contours of the capitalist mode of production. As Mészáros writes, the basis of Marx's assertion was not simply recognition of the unbearable dehumanizing effects of alienation but, rather, the profound understanding of the objective ontological foundation of the processes that remained veiled from his predecessors.[23] That is to ask, what makes capitalism so degrading and destructive that precludes one from living a flourishing, meaningful life?

Producing the Laboring Subject

For Marx, the phrase "mode of production" refers to a set of social and structural relationships. His clearest exposition appears in his *Contribution to the Critique of Political Economy,* whereby Marx explains that people "inevitably enter into definite relations, which are independent of their will, namely relations of production appropriate to a given stage in the development of their material forces of production."[24] Stated differently, a mode of production entails two components: the forces of production and the relations of production. Here, the "forces of production" consist of the means of production, such as land and labor, and the existent tools and technologies. The "relations of production" refers to the social organization of production, distribution, and consumption, that is, the ways in which the means of production are effectively controlled, and by whom.[25]

In presenting his concept of the mode of production, Marx uses the architectural metaphor of "base" and "superstructure." Marx writes that the "totality of these relations of production constitutes the economic structure of society, the real foundation, on which arises a legal and political superstructure and to which correspond definite forms of social consciousness."[26] The foundation, or base, is the unity of the forces of production, which include the technological, geographical, and physical means of production together with human labor power, and the relations of production, which are the social and property relations; the superstructure, in turn, comprises ideologies and institutions, such as the state, religion, and criminal justice systems.[27] Marx's metaphor, unfortunately, has been widely misunderstood and misappropriated, both by supporters and detractors. Indeed, Marxism has been accused repeatedly of being teleological, reductionist, dogmatic, and mechanistic.[28] In his brief and incomplete discussions of noncapitalist modes of production, for example, Marx's heuristic has been reduced to an overly simplistic caricature of economic forms: "primitive communist," "slave," "ancient," and "feudal." Marx, of course, never devoted much attention to theorizing these alternative modes of production as thoroughly as he did capitalism; this lacuna has contributed to much confusion in the applicability of Marx's method.[29]

Marx does not present history as unfolding in a preordained, linear fashion; nor is this his intent. Rather, Marx's purpose in elaborating the concept of the mode of production and applying it to the development of different types of society was, according to John Haldon, to employ it as a heuristic, as a means of asking questions about the basic structure of society that informed the ways a given socioeconomic system worked.[30] The mode of production, in other words, is an abstraction, derived from historical examples but in the end representing no specific society, but rather one set of possible social relations of production.[31] To this end, Marx's framing "of historical reality in terms of base and superstructure within modes of production is an attempt to compel us to think about the relationship between material production and all the political, cultural, legal, ideological and social manifestations of each human society."[32]

In addition, Marx provides a means by which to explore and evaluate the structural transformations that give rise to different modes of production. In his *Contribution,* Marx explains that "at a certain stage of development, the material productive forces of society come into conflict with the existing relations of production."[33] For Marx, this begins an "era of social revolution" whereupon the "changes in the economic foundation lead sooner or later to the transformation of the whole immense superstructure."[34] In short, through class struggle a new mode of production begins to undermine and replace the previous mode of production, a process that involves not only a reorganization of the relations of production but also the social, political, and ideological superstructure.[35] Accordingly, Marx presents an *inclusive* conceptual framework rather than a reductionist account of staid economic forms. Marx is concerned with the totality of human societies, of the ways in which all social apparatuses, including but not limited to law and politics, are internally related to the dominant mode of production at any given time or place. Consequently, any particular mode of production "must not be considered simply as being the reproduction of the physical existence of individuals. Rather it is a definite form of activity of these individuals, a definite form of expressing their life, a definite *mode of life* on their part. As individuals express their life, so they are. What they are, therefore, coincides with their production, both with *what* they produce and with *how* they produce. Hence what individuals are depends on the material conditions of their production."[36] To this end, within capitalist mode of production, the alienated subject arises from the material conditions of commodity production.

A commodity, Marx writes, is an external object, that is, "a thing which through its qualities satisfies human needs of whatever kind."[37] That need, moreover, may derive from our mortal existence, such as the need to eat and drink; conversely, the need may arise from productive and creative activities, such as the need for a basket or shovel. Consequently, commodities, as needed objects, are inseparable from the human species-being. Within capitalism, however, there is more to the commodity than meets the eye. As Marx explains, "a commodity appears at first sight an extremely obvious, trivial thing. But its analysis brings out that it is a very strange thing."[38] This strangeness arises from the argument that "ordinary, sensuous" things under capitalism are transformed into "extrasensory" things.[39] As Marx explains, "The mysterious character of the commodity-form consists . . . simply in the fact that the commodity reflects the social characteristics of men's own labor as objective characteristics of the products of labor themselves."[40] In other words, commodities are not merely needed objects in and of themselves but instead signify particular social relations that emanate from concrete human activities inherent to the production process.

Within the capitalist mode of production, commodities exhibit a dual character, being composed of use-value, that is, something needed for a particular task, but also of exchange-value. This latter element appears as a quantitative relation, the proportion in which use-values of one kind exchange for use-values of another kind.[41] In a well-known illustration, for example, Marx considers the relation between the values of two commodities: 20 yards of linen = 1 coat. Here, Marx explains that the value of linen is expressed in relation to that of a coat. It is not possible, he notes, to express the value of linen in linen, for a "definite quantity of linen [can only be] considered as an object of utility."[42] The value of linen must be expressed, quantitatively, in terms of another commodity. The first commodity, linen, is expressed as the *relative value* whereas the second commodity, coat, constitutes the *equivalent form of value.* The obverse also holds true. It is possible to state that one coat is equivalent to 20 yards of linen. This indicates that "value cannot be grasped within an individual use value."[43] Here,

Marx wonders if there is something underlying exchange-value governing the relationship between commodities.[44]

Marx argues that commodities are not exchanged according to their usefulness; instead, there is a quantitative relation that appears in all commodities that facilitates their exchange. This common denominator, Marx concluded, was labor-power, that is, labor in the abstract. This proposition is important in that it establishes a foundation by which "labor" is evaluated within capitalism. As Joseph Choonara explains, commodities have value—which is different from their price—because they are products of abstract labor; exchange-value, consequently, is merely the form through which this value is expressed.[45]

Historically, most production was directed toward consumption—that is, the immediate or near-immediate use of products. Capitalism, conversely, is a system of generalized commodity production *for exchange.*[46] For Marx, therefore, the circulation (exchange) of commodities is the starting point of capital, for the distinction between money as money and money as capital is nothing more than a difference in their form of circulation.[47] Here, Marx identifies two general forms of circulation. The direct form entails the conversion of a commodity (C) into money (M), and the reconversion of the money into a commodity (C); this is represented as C-M-C.[48] The first transformation, C-M, represents the conversion of a commodity into money, for example, the act of selling a bushel of corn, while the second transformation, M-C represents the conversion of money into a commodity, for example, the act of buying a bottle of wine. Hence, this single process is two-sided: from one pole, that of the commodity owner, it is a sale, and from the other pole, that of the money owner, it is a purchase, that is, an individual sells a bushel of corn in order to obtain money in which to buy a bottle of wine.[49] Broadly conceived, this circuit represents the circulation through which every commodity passes to become a use-value for its owner; here, money simply serves as a medium of exchange.[50]

Alongside this form of circulation is a second form of circulation: M-C-M, the transformation of money into commodities, and the reconversion of commodities into money.[51] Here, during the first phase, M-C (the purchase), money is changed into a commodity while, during the second phase, C-M (the sale), the commodity is changed back again into money.[52] Whereas the first circulation resulted in the exchange of commodities (albeit mediated through money), under the second circulation there is an exchange of money for money via commodities. This latter form of circulation appears, on the surface, to be meaningless. As Elena Lange explains, while the first commodity in C-M-C denotes a *qualitatively different* commodity than the second one, the exchange for money (M-C-M) seems tautological: there is no qualitative difference if one spends money to purchase a commodity and then sells the commodity *at the same price.*[53] Here, Marx finds the unique feature of capitalism in that "the circulatory process of M-C-M would be absurd and empty if the intention were, by using this roundabout route, to exchange two equal sums of money."[54] Marx explains that "in the simple circulation of commodities [C-M-C] the two extremes have the same economic form. They are both commodities, and commodities of equal value. But they are also qualitatively different use-values, as for example corn and clothes."[55] However, within the second circulation, "both extremes have the same economic form. They are both money, and therefore are not qualitatively different use values, for money is precisely the converted form of commodities."[56] Consequently, the "process M-C-M does not . . . owe its content to any qualitative difference between its extremes, for they are both money, but solely to quantitative changes."[57] As Harvey writes, "M-C-M only makes sense if it results in an increment of value," this being surplus-value and is thus rewritten as M-C-M'.[58]

The production of *surplus* value, that is, the conversion of money (M) into *more* money (M') functions as the general formula for capital, namely, profit for profit's sake. Indeed, Marx cautions that use-values must never be treated as the immediate or even final aim of the capitalist.[59] This is a point well worth underscoring, for as a form of social organization, a general system of production for exchange necessarily imparts a particular ideology that permeates all social relations. What is decisive for Marx is that the movement of capital does not aim at the satisfaction of *particular human needs*; rather, the movement of capital aims at self-valorization and its quantitative transformation into a larger sum of money.[60] Effectively, under capitalism, the fundamental rationale for production is neither need nor use, but simply profit.

Marx's account highlights the importance of *productive* labor, that is, value-generating labor, under the capitalist mode of production. Marx writes that "since the immediate purpose and the authentic product of capitalist production is surplus value, labor is only productive, and an exponent of labor-power is only a productive worker, if it or he creates surplus value directly, i.e. the only productive labor is that which is directly consumed in the course of production for the valorization of capital."[61] Considerable misunderstanding exists vis-à-vis Marx's separation of productive and unproductive labor, and it is necessary to clarify these terms before proceeding. Marx, for example, does not minimize the role of activities that take place outside the formal production process. He does not make the argument that *housework,* for example, and those tasks necessary for the reproduction of daily and generational life are less important to the functioning of capital. Rather, Marx insists that *capitalism* values only those activities that are productive *for capital,* namely, labor that not only produces commodities (marketed use-values), but also is employed by capital and creates *surplus value.*[62] Thus, within the capitalism mode of production, unpaid household work constitutes a "free gift" to capitalists while paid domestic workers are generative of value, that is, profit. The former represents a form of oppression and the latter a form of exploitation. Regardless of the form, capital benefits, but it does so in particular ways that greatly mediate the intersectionality of other forms of oppression.

If we consider production *from the viewpoint of the capitalist,* as does Marx, we see that only certain types of labor are productive, in other words, capable of generating exchange-value. This, to clarify, is not Marx's position but rather his critique of bourgeois political economists who diminish the contributions of activities outside the formal circuits of capital. Indeed, Marx stresses that "it is only bourgeois obtuseness that encourages the view that capitalist production is production in its absolute form."[63] In key respects, Marx's observation is supported by the Republican response to the Covid-19 pandemic, for these politicians demanded that *productive* workers—mostly immigrants and persons of color—return to work despite the known risks they faced.

Marx's discussion of productive and nonproductive labor is, in the main, an explication of the commodification of society. As Murray Smith explains, this entails two crucial postulates: that living labor is the sole source of all new value at the level of the capitalist economy as a whole, and that value exists as a definite quantitative magnitude precisely because it is a social substance that has a real existence in the relations comprising the social division of labor.[64] Together, these claims have a direct bearing on the "laws" of motion of capitalism, namely, the "self-expanding" value of capital. Here, the value-expansion process upon which capital feeds is precisely the process of producing and expropriating surplus value, that is, the valorization process.[65] The valorization process signifies capitalism's "imperative need to expand in terms of total production" and thus sets capitalism on a path toward the "commodification of everything."[66]

The valorization of capital, that is, the accumulation of profit, begins with the mobilization of labor-power and assumes two basic forms, distinguished by whether they originate outside or within the realm of capitalist rule.[67] The *formal* subsumption of labor under capital is characterized by labor practices that preexist the imposition of capitalism but are subsequently brought under the rule of capital, such as traditional farming practices or craftwork.[68] For Marx, this form of subsumption is formal, in the sense that the substance of the labor process remains unchanged; the workers continue to perform the same operations, but do so within a new context.[69] Conversely, the *real* subsumption of labor to capital occurs when new (or modified) production techniques and management strategies are introduced. These labor practices are generated within capital and are fundamentally different than the pre- or noncapitalist practices that were incorporated in the formal subsumption processes.[70] The introduction of the assembly line, for example, marks one technique introduced under the capitalist mode of production that radically transformed productive activities. Marx's materialist outlook holds that by nature humans produce cooperatively in their community. However, when this cooperative productivity happens in a way that is imposed upon people, then this becomes an unnatural situation and, as we will see, an alienating condition.[71]

Marx's distinction between formal and real subsumption is important not only because it calls attention to the particular ways in which societies (and attendant labor processes) are brought under the purview of capitalism. For Marx, the processes of formal and real subsumption correspond to two fundamentally different ways in which capital is valorized, these being *absolute surplus value* and *relative surplus value.* First, under the formal subsumption of labor, the capitalist "buys" the commodity labor-power from the worker for a given period of time and, in return, the worker receives in wages in order to purchase the material necessities (e.g., food, water, shelter) necessary for the worker to reproduce him- or herself as a worker.[72] However, it is a peculiar feature of the capitalist-laborer relation that the period of work time established by the contract will always be longer than this necessary labor time. Otherwise, "there would be no gain for the capitalist and thus no reason to bother with the whole affair."[73] Workers, for example, may produce enough value in six hours to offset their reproduction. And yet capitalists purchase labor-power for a longer period of time, say, ten hours. The remaining four hours, Marx argues, appear as *absolute* surplus labor time. Marx explains: "The fact that half a day's labor is necessary to keep the worker alive during 24 hours does not in any way prevent him from working a whole day. Therefore the value of labor-power, and the value which that labor-power valorizes . . . in the labor process, are two entirely different magnitudes; and this difference was what the capitalist had in mind when he was purchasing the labor-power."[74] In other words, workers produce enough value to cover the costs of their wages in just a part of the working day; the labor performed for the remainder of the day, therefore, does not have to be paid for—it is "surplus labor" that produces "absolute surplus value."[75] As Mandel explains, when the producer is performing necessary labor, he or she is producing a necessary product; when the laborer is performing surplus labor, he or she is producing a social surplus product.[76] The social surplus product is thus that part of social production which is produced by the laboring class but appropriated—without compensation—by the ruling class, regardless of the form the surplus product may assume.[77] Simply put, under the capitalist mode of production, the product of labor belongs not to the person who produced it, but rather, the person who hired the laborer.

Capitalism is oriented toward neither the sustainability nor continuance of life but instead toward the accumulation of capital. Capitalism, in this way, is inherently detrimental to the production and reproduction of the human species-being, for the simple fact that not only do workers not produce for their immediate need but also because production is not even directed toward future need. As such, living laborers "live only so long as they find work, and [they] find work only so long as their labor increases capital."[78] In this manner, the formal subsumption of labor-power to capital establishes the initial—and alienating—context of the human species-beings' vulnerability to premature death from a truncated life. As Marx identifies, there are physical limits on the extent to which capitalism can depend on the production of absolute surplus value. The working day, for example, can only be extended so long. This, of course, is a peculiarity of capital's adaptability to the diurnal rhythms of the Sun-Earth relationship; in principle, employers are not necessarily bound to measuring labor productivity in twenty-four-hour blocks. More problematic, for capital, is the physical stamina of the human species-being. Marx elaborates:

> In its blind and measureless drive, its insatiable appetite for surplus labor, capital oversteps not only the moral but even the merely physical limits of the working day. . . . It is not the normal maintenance of labor-power which determines the limits of the working day . . . but rather the greatest possible expenditure of labor-power, no matter how diseased, compulsory and painful it may be. . . . By extending the working day, therefore, capitalist production . . . not only produces a deterioration of human labor-power by robbing it of its normal moral and physical conditions of development and activity, but also produces the premature exhaustion and death of this labor-power itself.[79]

Given the very likely prospect of workers succumbing to premature death, capital (as embodied by capitalists) seeks ways around the physical limitations of the human body. It is not necessarily that the capitalist evinces concern over the plight of any given worker; rather, if "the unnatural extension of the working day, which capital necessarily strives for in its unmeasured drive for self-valorization, shortens the life of the individual worker, and therefore the duration of his labor-power, the forces used up have to be replaced more rapidly, and it will be more expensive to reproduce labor-power."[80] Consequently, other means of increasing profit must be sought. Here, "one of Marx's most profound insights into the functioning of capitalism," Prahhat Patnaik explains, "was that the system could not do without a reserve army of labor."[81] Michael McIntyre concurs, noting that for Marx the creation of an industrial reserve army was not an aberration; it was an ordinary product of capitalist accumulation.[82] As Marx writes, "What experience generally shows to the capitalist is a constant excess of population, i.e., an excess in relation to capital's need for valorization at a given moment, although this throng of people is made up of generations of stunted, short-lived and rapidly replaced human beings, plucked, so to speak, before they were ripe."[83]

Surplus populations do not constitute a monolithic or homogenous group but instead may be differentiated by their position within the capitalist mode of production.[84] To that end, Marx subdivides surplus populations into three categories: *floating, latent,* and *stagnant.* The floating population consists of those workers who cycle in and out of the labor force, that is, those workers who are "sensitive to fluctuations in the production process, outsourcing, and long-term economic trends."[85] Capitalism does not proceed uniformly but instead is reflective of recurrent periods of expansion and contraction. This follows from the inherent contradictions within the capitalist mode of production. Thus, in times of economic growth, surplus workers enter the ranks of the formal waged-labor sector. Unemployment levels decrease—but this is only temporary. Subsequent economic slowdowns result in massive lay-offs, hence a replenishing of the surplus population. Also included are those individuals made redundant as a result of technological innovations.[86] The latent population includes those with insecure employment. Notable in this regard are those in agriculture and artisanal industries who are made redundant under processes of real and formal subsumption. The dispossession and displacement of subsistence farmers, for example, constitutes a principle means by which latent surplus populations are produced. As Marx writes, "as soon as capitalist production takes possession of agriculture . . . the demand for a rural working population falls absolutely, while the accumulation of the capital employed in agriculture advances."[87] Third, the stagnant population is composed of those workers who are only rarely employed. It is the stagnant population, in particular, that forms the massive ranks of the "inexhaustible reservoir of disposable labor-power."[88] This population includes those workers engaged in part-time, casual, or "informal" labor, with the largest part to be found in "domestic industries," which consists of "outwork" carried out through the agency of subcontractors on behalf of manufacture, and dominated by so-called cheap labor, primarily women and children.[89] To these three categories of surplus populations Marx adds a fourth: the *lumpenproletariat.*[90] Distinguished *morally* from the working-class proletariat, this "lowest sediment" of society includes vagabonds, criminals, and prostitutes; those able to work but who do not (e.g., paupers); and those unable to work because of particular incapacities.[91] This latter subset was composed of "people who have lived beyond the worker's average life-span; and the victims of industry, whose number increases with the growth of dangerous machinery, or mines, chemical works, etc., the mutilated, the sickly, the widows, etc."[92]

For Marx the production of surplus populations is systemic to capitalism. Marx identifies a tendency within capitalism to "overproduce" workers—a paradoxical condition that exists alongside but apart from biology.[93] Marx writes: "Independently of the limits of the actual increase of population, [capitalism] creates a mass of human material always ready for exploitation by capital in the interests of capital's own changing valorization requirements."[94]

The ability to exploit the labor-power of surplus populations also is neither infinite nor always practical. Accordingly, other techniques are required by capitalists to expropriate surplus-value beyond the extension of the working day or the possibility of tapping into the so-called reserve army of labor. To this end, Marx introduces the concept of *relative surplus value.* Unlike absolute surplus value, this value is generated not through the prolongation of the working day but instead through the intensification of the labor process itself, that is, through the real subsumption of labor to capital. Here, Marx introduces the concept of "socially necessary labor time," that is, the quantity of labor necessary under the average conditions of labor productivity existing in a given country at a given time.[95]

As an abstract concept, socially necessary labor time transfers the level of argument from any individual capitalist to society as a whole.[96] An increase in average production, for example, increases the average number of commodities produced per unit of time; it thereby decreases the amount of socially necessary labor time required for the production of a single commodity and, hence, the value of each commodity.[97] Greater efficiencies of scale lesson the costs of production, thereby facilitating greater profits. With an increase in the productivity of labor—through refinements in the division of labor or through the introduction of machinery—the value of labor-power falls and the portion of the working day necessary for the reproduction of that value will be shortened. For example, if a technical improvement in the conditions of production cheapens the consumer goods that workers buy with their wages, then the value of labor-power has fallen; less time is required to reproduce labor-power, and the portion of the working day devoted to necessary labor will fall, with the remaining hours of the working day appearing as surplus.[98] Consequently, "with the production of relative surplus-value the form of production is altered and a specifically capitalist form of production comes into being."[99]

How much socially necessary labor time is required to reproduce labor-power?[100] For Marx, the concrete determination contains both a historical and moral element, the amount mediated by struggles between capitalists and workers.[101] In the abstract, however, the amount is sufficient to return the worker to such a condition that they can once more sell their labor-power to a capitalist; this value may also include the cost of raising subsequent generations of workers and perhaps also the cost of supporting a nonworking partner.[102] Marx explains: "The owner of labor-power is mortal. If then his appearance in the [labor] market is to be continuous . . . the seller of labor-power must perpetuate himself."[103] Moreover, given that "the labor-power withdrawn from the market by wear and tear, and by death, must be continually replaced by, at the very least, an equal amount of fresh labor-power," it follows that "the sum of means of subsistence necessary for the production of labor-power must include the means necessary for the worker's replacements, i.e., his children."[104] In short, capitalists seek to provide the *minimum* wage possible to ensure the daily and generational reproduction of its workforce, for as Marx writes, "The wages of labor have thus exactly the same significance as the maintenance and servicing of any other productive instrument, or as the consumption of a capital, required for its reproduction with interest; or as the oil which is applied to wheels to keep them turning.[105] Beyond this, "the lowest and the only necessary wage-rate is that providing for the subsistence of the worker for the duration of his work and as much more as is necessary for him to support a family and for the race of laborers not to die out."[106] Capital, in other words, "has an immanent drive, and a constant tendency, towards increasing the productivity of labor, in order to cheapen commodities and, by cheapening commodities, to cheapen the worker himself."[107]

Notably, the relations established under the formal subsumption of labor do not disappear; indeed, the direct subordination of the labor process to capital remains. However, on this foundation "there now arises a technologically and otherwise specific mode of production—capitalist production—which transforms the nature of the labor process and its actual conditions. Only when that happens do we witness the real subsumption of labor under capital."[108] Marx continues: the "real subsumption of labor under capital is developed in all the forms evolved by relative, as opposed to absolute surplus-value. With the real subsumption of labor under capital a complete . . . revolution takes place in the mode of production, in the productivity of the workers and in the relations between workers and capitalists."[109]

The problem with capitalism, Marx identifies, is that the productive activity of laboring appears to humans as simply the means of satisfying their need to maintain their own physical existence.[110] To this end, systematic exploitation occurs when a form of social organization (capitalism) develops an economic, political, or legal framework that locks alienation in place and allows one class routinely and "legitimately" to exploit another, all behind the mask of appearing to act in the general interest of the population.[111] In the process, the alienated subject also comes into being. For as Lynn Chancer explains, "A sense of powerlessness and dependency results for the worker forced to accept conditions of work set by the more authoritative capitalist."[112] In other words, the exploitative and alienating conditions of capitalism are effectively sadomasochistic in orientation.

The Alienated Subject

On April 28, 2020, President Trump issued an executive order that declared meatpacking plants to be "critical infrastructure" under the Defense Production Act of 1950. Democratic politicians had for weeks pressured Trump to invoke this act in an attempt to jump-start the production of much-needed life-saving medical equipment to combat the coronavirus. When Trump did react, however, his concern was not centered on the production of ventilators and respirators but instead sausages and sandwich meats. To this end, the executive order prohibited the closure of meatpacking plants and provided their parent companies legal immunity from liability claims filed by workers or their families.[113] Notably, there was little concern expressed by politicians—or even the media—over the plight of these working-class folk, most of whom were Black or Latinx. Unlike the iconic *white* coal miner or the *white* steel worker, these people who were forced to work during a pandemic elicited little sympathy, especially by Trump, the so-called president of the working class.

Trump's response, in part, reflected his political narcissism, for the meatpacking industry had long been a supporter of the Republican Party. More broadly, however, the executive order confirmed for many the callousness of *racial* capitalism. Throughout the early months of the Covid-19 pandemic, meatpacking plants across the country emerged as hotspots for the transmission and infection of the virus. From Wilkesboro, North Carolina, to Tama, Iowa, hundreds of workers—mostly low-income people of color—tested positive for the coronavirus, with many subsequently dying. Indeed, by September 2020 a nonprofit investigative news organization discovered that over 42,000 meatpacking workers tested positive in nearly 500 plants; at least 203 died. Representatives of the Occupational Safety and Health Administration acknowledged that many of these plants failed to provide a workplace "free from recognized hazards that were causing or likely to cause death or serious physical harm to employees in that employees were working in close proximity to each other and were exposed to" the coronavirus.[114] Compounding the vulnerabilities of meatpacking workers were mandatory work orders that compelled them to remain on the job—despite the known risks. Iowa governor Kim Reynolds, for example, announced that slaughterhouse employees who refused to show up for work would be ineligible for unemployment benefits. The choice was clear: stay on the job and risk possible death or stay home and risk possible eviction, destitution, loss of health care, and death.[115]

Writing in the *Communist Manifesto,* Marx and Engels assert that the majority of people under capitalism "live only so long as they find work, and [they] find work only so long as their labor increases capital."[116] Their words echo in the meatpacking plants and provide a grim epithet for those men and women compelled to work so that the nation's supply of bacon or chicken tenders not be disrupted. As Crystal Rodriquez, a single mother of four who worked in a meatpacking plant in Greeley, Colorado, explained, "I'm kind of angry because I don't understand why everybody's lives are being put at risk just to make the product." By the time of her interview, six workers had already succumbed to the coronavirus, with 200 other workers infected. Rodriquez herself would later test positive and spend nearly a month in the intensive care unit.[117]

The plight of meatpacking workers and of the myriad other "essential workers" compelled to work illustrates the devastating effect of capitalist production on human beings, on their physical and mental states, and on the social and spatial processes of which they are a part.[118] Their plight also depicts the mediation of living a meaningful life conditioned by one's awareness of premature death. To this end, we readily understand the life-or-death tradeoffs forced upon workers dispossessed of the means of production, where the only recourse is seemingly to accede to the demands of capital. Accordingly, the separation of human beings from meaningful work forms the basis upon which alienation *in its capitalist form* materializes.

Humans depend on functioning ecosystems to sustain themselves.[119] That is to say, there is a *metabolic interaction* between humans and nature, "a process by which man, through his own actions, mediates, regulates and controls the metabolism between himself and nature."[120] This is not to say that humans *dominate* nature but rather to acknowledge that each mode of production generates a particular social metabolic order that influences the society-nature relationship, regulating the ongoing reproduction of society and the demands placed on ecosystems.[121] To fully appreciate this dialectic, however, it is necessary to clearly differentiate between *appropriation* and *expropriation.* For example, writing in the *Grundrisse,* Marx explains that "all production is appropriation of nature on the part of an individual within and through a specific form of society."[122] This is the material basis of labor and production, for there can be no human existence without the appropriation of those resources necessary for biological continuance and reproduction. Appropriation, in other words, is an inherent feature of human life and is present in all societies; appropriation constitutes the fundamental basis by which life is made possible.[123] Notably, there is an implicit recognition that appropriation is sustainable. Humans require food, water, and materials necessary for clothing and shelter; these can be understood as the "conditions of reproduction." As Paul Burkett clarifies, "Free appropriation need not imply wasteful, destructive or unsustainable appropriation. The degree to which nature's gifts are cherished and cared for depends on the particular social organization governing their use."[124]

Appropriation differs from the practice of expropriation. Expropriation, in this sense, refers to appropriation "without exchange" or "without reciprocity." In other words, production for exchange value imparts a rift in the metabolic interaction between humans and society. As Marx writes, "A presupposition of wage labor, and one of the historic preconditions for capital, is free labor and the exchange of this free labor for money, in order to reproduce and realize money, to consume the use-value of labor not for individual consumption, but as use value for money."[125] There, it follows that "it is not the unity of living and active humanity with the natural, inorganic conditions of their metabolic exchange with nature, and hence their appropriation of nature, which requires explanation or is the result of a historic process, but rather the separation between these inorganic conditions of human existence and this active existence, a separation which is completely posited only in the relation of wage labor and capital."[126] In short, for Marx the separation of humanity's productive activity and its ensuing subsumption to the dictates of capital marks a radical break, one in which an emergent alienated subject comes into being, a subject "reduced to performing undifferentiated work on humanly indistinguishable objects among people deprived of their human variety and compassion."[127]

Expressed most clearly in his unpublished 1844 *Economic and Philo-*

sophic Manuscripts, Marx presents alienation as comprising four broad relations that, taken in their totality, cover the whole of human existence, namely, alienation from a person's productive activity, their product, other people, and, ultimately, humanity itself.[128] As Ian Shaw and Marv Waterstone write, "Alienation is a disorienting sense of existential exclusion: to be separated from the material conditions that enable humans to flourish."[129]

To begin, for Marx the human species-being is a productive agent. It is through self-conscious, cooperative labor that humans find meaning in life. Human beings exist as conscious, knowing beings, equipped with the ability to reflect upon themselves and their environment. Species-being, recall, is the human capacity to consciously and freely transform the world, through our work, to meet our creative needs.[130] And to that end, human beings are able to deliberately create and produce for myriad reasons, both as individuals and as members of society.[131] Capitalism, however, is antithetical to life in the collective. Productive activity under capitalism is an inherently alienating activity.[132] As Shaw and Waterstone explain, "To be alienated is to be denied this liberty of meaningful work: we cannot take hold of the world, our place in it, and insist, I matter. The alienated are denied an ability to reshape their simple being-in-the-world."[133]

An alienated existence arises because of the peculiar social and spatial relations that comprise capitalism as a whole, namely, that capitalism is based on the separation of workers from the means of production. For this unusual relation to arise, however, two conditions are necessary. First, "labor-power can appear on the market as a commodity only if, and in so far as, its possessor, the individual whose labor-power it is, offers it for sale or sells it as a commodity."[134] In other words, capitalism requires workers to obtain waged employment. Second, "the possessor of labor-power, instead of being able to sell commodities in which his labor has been objectified, must rather be compelled to offer for sale as a commodity that very labor-power which exists only in his living body."[135] This holds tremendous importance for Marx, who elaborates:

> [The] fact that labor is *external* to the worker, i.e., it does not belong to his essential being; that in his work, therefore, he does not affirm himself but denies himself, does not feel content but unhappy, does not develop freely his physical and mental energy but mortifies his body and ruins his mind. . . . His labor is therefore

> not voluntary, but coerced; it is *forced* labor. It is therefore not the satisfaction of a need; it is merely a *means* to satisfy needs external to it.[136]

In claiming that productive activity under capitalism does not belong to humanity's species-being, Marx presupposes that human beings deny rather than affirm their existence.[137] Accordingly, as production is more fully subsumed to the dictates of capital, workers become mere appendages to the production process. "Modern industry," Marx and Engels describe, "has converted the little workshop of the patriarchal master into the great factory of the industrial capitalist. Masses of laborers, crowded into the factory, are organized like soldiers. . . . Not only are they slaves of the bourgeois class, and of the bourgeois state; they are daily and hourly enslaved by the machine, by the overseer, and, above all, by the individual bourgeois manufacturer himself."[138] Marx elaborates this in *Capital,* detailing the transformations wrought by the advent of modern capitalism on once-creative, productive people who produced *useful objects* instead of *commodities*:

> In handicraft and manufacture, the worker makes use of a tool; in the factory, the machine makes use of him. There the movements of the instrument of labor proceed from him, here it is the movements of the machine that he must follow. In manufacture the works are the parts of a living mechanism. In the factory we have a lifeless mechanism which is independent of the workers, who are incorporated into it as its living appendages. "The wearisome routine of endless drudgery in which the same mechanical process is ever repeated, is like the torture of Sisyphus; the burden of toil, like the rock, is ever falling back upon the worn-out drudge."[139]

For Marx, it is insufficient to render the deleterious aspects of alienation in abstract terms; instead, he underscores the sensory-mental condition it generates.[140] Marx writes:

> Factory work exhausts the nervous system to the uttermost; at the same time, it does away with the many-sided play of the muscles, and confiscates every atom of freedom, both in bodily and in intellectual activity. Even the lightening of the labor becomes an

> instrument of torture, since the machine does not free the worker from the work, but rather deprives the work itself of all content. Every kind of capitalist production, in so far as it is not only a labor process but also capital's process of valorization, has this in common, but it is not the worker who employs the conditions of his work, but rather the reverse, the conditions of work employ the worker. . . . Owing to its conversion into an automaton, the instrument of labor confronts the worker during the labor process in the shape of capital, dead labor, which dominates and soaks up living labor-power.[141]

Ben Hamper provides a particular apt description of the drudgery of alienation under the capitalist mode of production. Working on the assembly line at the General Motors plant in Flint, Michigan, Hamper describes how the time-clock dominated living labor: "But the clock was a whole different mammal altogether. It sucked on you as you waited the next job. It ridiculed you each time you'd take a peek. The more irritated you became, the slower it moved. The slower it moved, the more you thought. Thinking was a very slow death at times."[142] Hamper's reference to the slow death of workers as a feature of monotonous factory life is especially revealing, for capitalism is indifferent to living laborers beyond their usefulness in the valorization of capital. As Lisa Marie Cacho puts it, "The value of life is subjected to an economic analysis and assessed accordingly: How has this person contributed to society? What will he or she accomplish in the future?"[143]

As Highmore explains, "What makes the assembly line such a telling exemplification of everyday modernity is not the specificity of the factory environment, but the generalized condition that it points to: 'plodding,' 'monotony'—the emptiness of time."[144] And these are not unique to the factory or to the assembly line. In its quest for efficiency, that is, to facilitate and increase productive output, tasks become tedious and, when viewed in isolation, pointless. There is no purpose in work other than to garner a wage in order to buy the material necessities needed to live day to day.

For Marx, the nature of the human species-being is to form "things in accordance with the laws of beauty."[145] In other words, the essence of being human, that which provides meaning in life, is derived from the life-activities of producing both consciously and freely. Under capitalism, however, the human being is denied this. Objects are produced primarily for exchange-value and, as such, the relationship between producer and produce is irrevocably altered. Specifically, the productive activities associated with the capitalist mode of production establish a "hostile" and "alien" relationship between the producer, that is, the worker, and the object produced. As Marx explains: "The worker puts his life into the object; but now his life no longer belongs to him but to the object. . . . The alienation of the worker in his product means not only that his labor becomes an object, an external existence, but that it exists outside him, independently, as something alien to him, and that it becomes a power on its own confronting him; it means that the life which he has conferred on the object confronts him as something hostile and alien."[146] Consequently, the object "does not belong to his essential being" and so through his work "he does not affirm himself but denies himself."[147] If, however, the product of labor is alien to the one who produced it, if it confronts the direct producer as something alien and external, to whom does it belong?[148]

The short answer is, the capitalist. Marx elaborates:

> If the product of labor does not belong to the worker, if it confronts him as an alien power, this can only be because it belongs to some other man than the worker. If the worker's activity is a torment to him, to another it must be delight and his life's joy. . . . Thus, if the product of his labor, his labor objectified, is for him an alien, hostile, powerful object independent of him, then his position towards it is such that someone else is master of this object, someone who is alien, hostile, powerful, and independent of him. If his own activity is to him an unfree activity, then he is treating it as activity performed in the service, under the dominion, the coercion and the yoke of another man.[149]

In *Capital,* Marx underscores that people sell their labor only after they have been robbed of their own means of production, that is, only when people are prevented by law or by force from living outside the parameters of capitalism. Indeed, as Chancer explains, "The capitalist's ability to impose his or her will is solidified and made all the more intimidating in being reinforced and supported by the coercive powers of the capitalist state. And so the worker confronts labor from a position of alienation, estranged from a process of which he or she had once been able to exert participatory and independent self-control; under capitalism, the labor process is experienced as though it were the sole prerogative, right, and belonging of others."[150] To this end, the lack of ownership of the means of production is directly related to wage labor and is the reason why, under capitalism, the worker is coerced into entering a subordinate relationship to an alien will.[151] Consequently, the rendering of free activity to the dictates of capital degrades humanity and alienates workers from their humanity. As Martin Hägglund writes, "Insofar as we spend our time working a job that is not fulfilling but merely serves as a means for our survival, our labor time is unfree, since we cannot affirm that what we do is an expression of who we are. Instead of being free to engage the questions of what makes our life worth living—the question of what we *ought* to do with our time—our lives are mortgaged to a form of labor that is required for our survival."[152] In the process, the alienated subject becomes oblivious to the source of its discontent and so must seek solace in pursuits and interests beyond productive activity. This is a point worth underscoring. Unable to engage in creative, productive tasks, the alienated subject seeks salvation elsewhere and, in the process, alienation becomes a source of further capitalist accumulation.[153] To this end, capitalism transforms the alienated subject into an "addict of commodity consumption."[154] Meaning in life, for the alienated subject, is achieved in part through the insatiable desire for senseless consumer objects.

Thus far, our focus has centered on the alienated proletariat. This is not to suggest that capitalists are not also alienated.[155] Marx was sensitive to the fact that capitalism, in its totality, engulfed all people, including those who owned the means of production. Under such a system, employers and employees alike were subject to the market logics of production for exchange and, in the process, alienated. That said, capitalists experience alienation in profoundly different ways than do workers. Marx expands this idea in *The Holy Family*: "The propertied class and the class of the proletariat present the same human self-alienation. But the former class finds in this self-alienation its confirmation and its good, its own power; it has in it a semblance of human existence. The class of the proletariat feels annihilated in its self-alienation; it sees in it its own powerlessness and the reality of an inhuman existence."[156] We should not read into this, however, that the proletariat is *more* alienated than the capitalist, but instead that the experience of alienation varies according to one's subject position.

Remarkably, the alienated subject, whether in the form of employer or employee, is not necessarily aware of its alienated existence or that of other alienated subjects. As Sandra Lee Bartky describes, alienation "serves to make the work of domination easier by breaking the spirit of the dominated and by rendering them incapable of understanding the nature of those agencies responsible for their subjugation."[157] To this end, capitalism thrives off the illusion of freedom and choice; indeed, it is this illusory component that helps maintain order and stability.[158] Because alienated workers, for example, *want* to believe that markets operate on their own, and thus are realms of equality and freedom, they too often fail to properly scrutinize how the workings of the market actually concentrate wealth in the hands of a few.[159] They fail to see that they occupy a decidedly unequal position in the social relation of exchange, or that the wages paid are not equal to the value created. Moreover, alienated workers often fail to see in their employer the source of their alienation. Instead, alienated subjects look for scapegoats—often in the form of ethnic or gendered minorities—to apportion blame for whatever failings are experienced. In this fashion, the fetishized social relations of capitalism contribute to a toxic environment of intolerance and hostility, with hatred directed not toward the source of exploitation and alienation but rather toward other human beings.

The prevalence of attitudinal indifference shapes social relations both within and beyond the workplace. Within a commodified society, the waged labor market becomes the model on which social relations are structured. A competitive, atomistic worldview is promoted, and it is a worldview predicated on assumptions of scarce and finite resources to be fought over in an unending struggle for personal survival. Indeed, the alienated subject's awareness of the finitude of life mediates its attitudes toward the plight of others. Eschewing a solidarity formed around notions of shared mortality, the alienated subject sees in a life a zero-sum game, where its own life chances are necessarily threatened by those of other subject-beings. Conservative ideologies—and moralities—have only deepened discriminatory and prejudiced attitudes of alienation. In many contemporary capitalist societies, notably the United States, the myth of the "self-made man" is pervasive—and underscores feelings of indifference and intolerance toward the destitute and downtrodden. A commonly held belief, for example, is that the ability to succeed—as defined by accumulated wealth—is rooted in one's hard work and perseverance, and that external structures, such as white privilege and patriarchy, play a minimal role in one's ability to succeed. Conversely, those who are seen as failures in society, that is, members of the so-called underclass, are presumed to have failed because of their individual—and moral—deficiencies. Here, the term *underclass*—unlike the positive connotations associated with the working class—implies a society that is anything but constructive. As Bauman explains, the "underclass" evokes an image of an aggregate of people who have been declared off-limits in relation to all classes and the class hierarchy itself, with little chance and no need of readmission: people without a role, making no useful contribution to the lives of the rest, and in principle beyond redemption.[160] In societies marked by racial capitalism, the distinction between members of the underclass and the working class pivots on racism.

On this point, journalistic and scholarly accounts routinely describe members of the (white) working class as alienated, and thus somehow justified in their anger directed toward immigrants and other minorities for "stealing" their jobs or driving down wages. Members of the so-called underclass are rarely portrayed as alienated, but instead as indolent or irresponsible. And because their failings are seen as the result of their own negligence and carelessness, they are deemed unworthy of any assistance—beyond, perhaps, charitable contributions. Too often, the subjugated are viewed with indifference; more frequently, they are shunned and scorned, vulnerable to acts of hostility. The irony, of course, is that members of both the so-called working class and underclass are alienated; they both are exploited within a productive system indifferent to their mortal existence and both are made vulnerable to premature death by a system that privileges profit over vital needs.

Alienated Subjectivities

Thus far, we have theorized the production of the alienated subject through a critical interrogation of the capitalist labor process. To leave our discussion at this point, however, would ultimately fail to capture fully the variegated experiences of alienation. Indeed, a too-narrow, class-based understanding of Marx will necessarily struggle to provide any meaningful account of how patriarchy, racism, nationalism, and other structures of oppression condition the day-to-day existence of the alienated subject.

The alienated subject is an abstract subject. As such, the alienated subject stands in opposition to the more prevalent figure of the "liberal subject." As Martha Fineman explains, the "liberal subject informs our economic, legal, and political principles" and it does so from the standpoint "of autonomy, self-sufficiency, and personal responsibility, through which society is conceived as constituted by self-interested individuals with the capacity to manipulate their independently acquired and overlapping resources."[161] In contradistinction to the liberal subject, I postulate the alienated subject as one who embodies the violence of indifference that is endemic to capitalism, itself understood as an ensemble of social relations mediated by one's access to the means of production. The alienated subject, accordingly, embodies the pursuit of material wealth not as a means of cultivating a flourishing life for all but instead for an egotistic need to accumulate for the sake of accumulation. The alienated subject exhibits—in Zygmunt Bauman's phrase—a particular "moral blindness" and thus remains "insensitive to human suffering" beyond its own self-defined and limited community.[162] Indeed, it is this moral blindness that enables the alienated subject to remain indifferent to the suffering of others or to engage in harmful activities directed toward those it is intolerant of.

As an abstraction, the alienated subject is conditioned by its relation to capital. Capitalism, though, is itself conditioned by myriad social and structural relations beyond that of one's access to the means of production. Indeed, Michael Hardt and Toni Negri extend Marx's conception of the real subsumption of *labor* under capital to the real subsumption of *society* under capital.[163] For Hardt and Negri, this extension is necessary, for it provides a means to evaluate the penetration of the capitalist mode of production beyond the factory floor, that is, to theorize "the extraordinarily wide and deep extension of capitalist relations of production throughout the social fabric."[164] In doing so, they argue, it is important to recognize that analyses of contemporary capitalist society in terms of a real subsumption do not indicate a process of social homogenization.[165] Capitalism, in other words, does not give rise to a society populated by "one-dimensional men" as argued by Herbert Marcuse but, following Hardt and Negri, a composition of multiplicities.[166]

The recognition that all social relations, not just labor, are subsumed under the capitalist mode of production refocuses attention toward the complex interplay of dominant and subordinate subjectivities conditioned along racial, gender, sexual, and other axes of oppression apart from but alongside class divisions. This has a tremendous bearing for our understanding (detailed in chapter 5) of the varied subject positions of the alienated subject as sadomasochist. As alluded to in the preface, the so-called working class is commonly rendered, implicitly if not explicitly, white and male. David Harvey, for example, correctly identifies that "workers alienate their labor-power when they enter the factory to do whatever the capitalist commands" but that "alienation has a broader meaning that entails the loss of trust, fairness or reciprocity."[167] For Harvey, the exchange of labor for wages is legal but has the feel of something fraudulent and, consequently, for the laborers "the response is a sense of loss and unfairness, of powerlessness and loss of dignity, which is prone to provoke resentment, anger, and frustration."[168] The workers' ire and animosity, however, are not necessarily directed toward the employer but, instead, toward others. Harvey continues: "They want to tear down and destroy the existing order of things. They want scapegoats to blame. The capitalist class feeds them racial minorities, women, and immigrants as easy targets for blame."[169] Harvey concludes: "In this kind of world, we should not be surprised that right-wing populism and bigoted nationalist and racist movements thrive. With mass alienation, somebody like Trump could come along and blast his way into power. . . . For alienated, disempowered, frustrated and angry people . . . Trump is the President of alienation."[170]

Harvey's account is attractive, in that is purports to explain the indifference, intolerance, and capacity to hurt expressed by *white* members of the *working class.* Harvey downplays, however, that the "racial minorities, women, and immigrants" targeted as scapegoats for the working-class white men are also alienated members of the working class. For Harvey, the alienated subject—as a white, working man—is premised to behave in response to perceived slights attributed to his subject position. But what of the Black alienated subject, for example? What of the vulnerable people of color forced to work in slaughterhouses during a pandemic?

If we premise that alienation is not transhistorical but instead manifest in particular ways under particular circumstances, we need to extend Marx's argument *in accordance with* Marx's own method. We need, in other words, to pick up where Marx left off and to consider how intersecting systems of oppression prohibit the transcendence of alienation. The alienated subject, in short, may be racist or the target of racist attacks; the alienated subject may be a misogynist or the victim of sexual abuse; the alienated subject may be a religious bigot or the object of religious persecution. Ultimately, the alienated subject exhibits a capacity to hurt, but also a capacity to be hurt, to dominate but also to submit. Required, therefore, is recognition that the subject formation of the alienated subject always takes place within contours of sadomasochism. Indeed, as Chancer explains, "That capitalism as a social system operates on sadomasochistic principles seems less than far-fetched when some of capitalism's fundamental premises are unearthed, even superficially." She elaborates: "For wage earners, the vast majority of those under its aegis, capitalism has inextricably tied work to survival; one has no choice but to labor in order to meet basic subsistence needs. Yet, although a job is a requisite to the substance of life, its provision is not taken to be a simple human right. Under capitalism, the likelihood of ongoing work is continent on a variety of factors over which most individuals have little and often no control."[171] Not surprisingly, many of these factors appear as racism, misogyny, homophobia, and xenophobia.

To this end, scholars of racial capitalism and patriarchal capitalism effectively extend the analyses of formal and real subsumption and, in so doing, provide a necessary reconfiguration of the alienated subject.[172] Capitalism in the United States, for example, has since its inception been deeply racialized.[173] To this end, Cedric Robinson coined the term "racial capitalism" in an effort to articulate the centrality of race in the historical development of capitalism.[174] Building on the writings of W. E. B. Du Bois, C. L. R. James, and other Black radical scholars, racial capitalism forwards the idea that capitalist accumulation requires human difference and, in the process of exploiting it, reifies sociospatial differentiation.[175] As Laura Pulido writes, "A focus on racial capitalism requires greater attention to the essential processes that shaped the modern world, such as colonization, primitive accumulation, slavery, and imperialism."[176] In so doing, Pulido explains, "By insisting that we are still living with the legacy of these processes, racial capitalism requires that we place contemporary forms of racial inequality in a materialist, ideological and historical framework."[177]

The historical development of world capitalism, Robinson argues, was influenced in a most fundamental way by the particular forces of racism and nationalism.[178] In other words, the geographic expansion of the capitalist mode of production "enlisted and deployed—formally subsumed—racial markers and racial hierarchies within its own structures of rule."[179] As Robin D. G. Kelley explains, "capitalism emerged within the feudal order and flowered in the cultural soil of a Western civilization already thoroughly infused with racialism. Capitalism and racism, in other words, did not break from the old order but rather evolved from it to produce a modern world system of 'racial capitalism' dependent on slavery, violence, imperialism, and genocide. Capitalism was 'racial' not because of some conspiracy to divide workers or justify slavery and dispossession, but because racialism had already permeated Western feudal society."[180] To this end, as Hardt and Negri emphasize, "the fact that race and racial hierarchies pre-existed capital (and were subsequently incorporated and redeployed in capitalist society) provides one means to recognize that race is not an accidental or incidental feature of the capitalist system. Race is constitutive of the capitalist mode of production and essential to the continuing rule of capital."[181] We should note also though that capital is constitutive of racism, to the extent that the racism is subsumed to the logic of capital. To this end, if we premise that racism and capitalism are co-constitutive, it follows that alienation is always and already racialized. The alienated subject is not *naturally* white.

Racial capital is of course mediated by myriad other structures of oppression, including but not limited to gender, sexuality, and ableism. Feminist scholars, for example, document that patriarchy and misogyny, similar to racism, preceded the advent of capitalism but were subsequently incorporated into the capitalist mode of production.[182] As such, it is imperative to understand, on the one hand, that "racism and patriarchy are not incidental features of the capitalist system and not subordinate to its rule, as if they were merely secondary enemies in the primary struggle against capital. They are relatively autonomous structures that have been subsumed formally within it. On the other hand, racial and gender hierarchies are not historically mutable but instead have been thoroughly transformed, reinvented, and redeployed—that is, really subsumed—within 'properly capitalist' society."[183] Thus, to the degree that "the ideas of the *ruling class* are in every epoch the ruling ideas," it holds that a society founded upon the dominance of white men of the propertied class will reflect these conditions.[184] For example, in British North America—what would become the United States—settler colonists created and developed a logic of race that placed white European men at the pinnacle of the social hierarchy and all others in various positions of subordination.[185] Subsequently, an ideology of white supremacy permeated the evolving political, economic, and legal structures that in their totality "valorized whiteness and sanctioned the violence of white domination, enslavement, and genocide while bolstering Eurocentric understandings of land use, private property, and wealth accumulation."[186] Indeed, Marx and Engels conclude: "The class which has the means of material production at its disposal, consequently also controls the means of mental production, so that the ideas of those who lack the means of mental production are on the whole subject to it. The ruling ideas are nothing more than the ideal expression of the dominant material relations, the dominant material relations grasped as ideas."[187]

Conclusions

As we move forward into the twenty-first century, many progressives question the long-term salience of Marx, notably his apparent privileging of the proletariat for its emancipatory potential. For as Erik Olin Wright observes, "We now live in a world very different from the one in which Marx formulated his theoretical ideas, and it is difficult to sustain the exuberant optimism of Marx's theory of the future beyond capitalism."[188]

Marx discerned the potential *political* power of the working class, that is, the revolutionary and emancipatory promise of the alienated subject.[189] Marx believed fervently that members of the working class would eventually overcome alienation through collective realization and regain control over their productive activity, whereby people would live free from exploitation and of an alienated egoism of unfulfilled dreams of material possessions.[190] In doing so, the emancipation of the proletariat would encompass the emancipation of all people. Marx's exploration of alienation is, therefore, a hopeful foray into humanity's existence, for if alienation was an essential trait of being human, there would be no possible way of overcoming alienation. However, our consciousness of alienation generates an awareness that a nonalienated existence is possible, just as our awareness of death mediates our experience of life. And yet, a Marxian proletariat has yet to emerge. For this reason, as David Lovell writes, Marxism after Marx has been a series of attempts to come to terms, theoretically and practically, with the actual working class.[191] The issue, quite simply, is this: Is the failure of a revolutionary proletariat to appear inherent in Marx's conception of the alienated subject?[192]

Marx was correct when he premised that "the capitalist can live longer without the worker than can the worker without the capitalist."[193] The stark mortality rates between the wealthy and the working class in the midst of a global pandemic provide grim confirmation of this relation. As Michael Yates writes, "Whether in health care, farm fields and labor camps, food delivery, grocery stores, food banks, Fed Ex and UPS trucks, post offices and postal delivery vehicles, buses, subways, trains, airplanes, boats, warehouses, or construction sites, those who labor risk their lives to work, with many becoming sick and dying."[194] Furthermore, as indicated earlier, disparities in the exposure to premature death are decidedly shaped by social and structural relations of racial, gendered, and sexual oppression. Through September 2020, the age-adjusted mortality rates of Black, Hispanic, and Indigenous peoples were three times that of whites.[195]

However, it is equally clear that *capitalism* is unable to reproduce itself without the labor of the working class. Indeed, the working class holds a unique position in that if workers stopped working, the system shuts down. Historically, this accounts for the violent repression of the ruling class to unions, mass strikes, work stoppages, slowdowns, and any other technique that places the ongoing accumulation of profit in jeopardy. Tellingly, as Heather Brown notes, Covid-19 "has the potential for a mass disruption of the workforce, the blocking of the production process, the profits of capital, and above all the reproduction of capitalist production relations."[196] And members of the working class readily grasped this reality. Throughout the United States, workers rose up in defiance of orders to continue to labor under unsafe conditions. In New Orleans, Louisiana, for example, sanitation workers went on strike in May 2020, demanding hazard pay, adequate personal protective equipment, and a $15 living wage.[197] Other sectors, including food service, meat processing, retail, manufacturing, transportation, health care, and education also experienced wildcat strikes, walkouts, and protests as "essential workers" likewise demanded better pay and safer working conditions.[198]

That said, the Covid-19 pandemic makes clear also the diverse composition of the working class. As Roland Simon explains, "exploitation doesn't produce a homogenous social entity of the working class." There is no singular proletariat "able to be conscious of itself as a social subject, in the sense habitually given to this, that is to say able to have a consciousness of itself as a relation to itself, facing capital."[199] In other words, the proletariat *in the abstract* still assumes a fundamental role toward the abolition of capital; but its role is mediated by myriad other social and material relations that comprise the totality of the capitalist mode of production. To this end, as Simon clarifies, "having lost its centrality as a principle organizing the totality of the labor process, the big factory which gathered a large number of workers together has not disappeared, but it is not the principle organizing the labor process and the valorization process anymore. . . . In the contradiction between proletariat and capital, there isn't anything sociologically given *a priori* (as was the 'mass-worker' of the big factory) anymore."[200]

The *concrete* working class, that is, those who labor under conditions of "actually existing capitalism," comprise a diffuse, divided, and disintegrated subject body. Class struggle remains important; but the struggle is mediated by competing and often contradictory subject positions that each, in their own particular way, provide meaning to one's life. White members of the working class, for example, may forgo class solidarity to take advantage of white privilege; the *racist* alienated white worker disdains class solidarity with other exploited but nonwhite workers. Indeed, this alienated subject may increasingly become intolerant of government interventions, such as affirmative action programs, perceived as unfairly benefiting nonwhites. Working-class men, similarly, may refuse class solidarity in favor of patriarchal superiority. In other words, the alienated subject may attempt to find meaning in life outside of the workplace, that is, in *other places* and, in doing so, the alienated subject embodies an ethical ambiguity that may foster an indifference to and intolerance of others. Ultimately, we find the alienated subject exhibits a social and spatial liminality whereby it is both capable of hurting and being hurt in the process of *being-in-the-world.* Consequently, we need to acknowledge, both in theory and in practice, the intersectionality of alienation, for the emancipation of the alienated subject is only possible through the concurrent fostering of a society free from all forms of oppression. As Hardt and Negri maintain, "if racism, patriarchy, and capital [among other forms of oppression] are mutually constitutive, then feminist, anti-racist and anti-capitalist struggles must intersect on equal terms."[201]

3

The Intersectionality of Alienation

After four years of incessant rallies and campaign events, Trump's stump speeches by 2020 displayed a discomforting familiarity of dog whistles and gaslighting: racism, sexism, ableism, and xenophobia matched with not-so-subtle support for physical violence. To this end, a notable mainstay was his paean to the "American worker." Indeed, during his many reelection rallies held during the 2020 presidential campaign, Trump repeatedly appealed to America's downtrodden and neglected "working class." In Dayton, Ohio, for example, Trump accused Joe Biden, the Democratic nominee, of selling out American workers. Billing himself as the "blue-collar president," Trump ranted, "For 47 years, Joe Biden shook the hands of American workers and then stabbed them in the back." Trump continued: "The Democrats literally waged war on the American workers for half a century. Look what they've done." At a separate rally held in Toledo, Ohio, Trump bellowed, "Proud citizens like you helped build this country, and together we are taking back our country. We are returning power to you, the American people."[1]

That Trump's blatant and obsequious cajolery to the working class was coded language for *white* workers should come as no surprise.[2] What is remarkable, however, is the *power* of Trump's rhetoric, for he effectively tapped into a cherished myth of the United States. Ideologies of "rugged individualism" and of "pulling one's self up by the bootstraps" have long shaped the ethos of a supposed American exceptionalism, and politicians across the spectrum have capitalized on these platitudes. Likewise, these ideologies harken to the liminal position of the working class in the United States, namely, the government's relationship to the working class, for not all poor people are held as worthy of admiration. As Mechele Dickerson explains, many Americans subscribe to the idea that the government has a duty to assist the "deserving" poor enough to help them pull themselves up by their bootstraps, but balk at the idea of providing assistance to the unemployed but able-bodied, which is seen as morally corrupting and fostering an attitude of economic dependency.[3] To this end, Trump is no exception.

It is noteworthy, though, how Trump's style conveys more than simply the specter of material loss. Drawing on his slogan, "Make America Great Again," Trump assured his audiences that *together* they would "take back *our* country" and in doing so restore the luster to a sullied country. Certainly, Trump's phrasing is a not-so-veiled racist diatribe against his predecessor, Barack Obama, the first Black president of the United States. Relatedly, though, Trump's verbiage warns of the loss of something intangible yet equally important, an emotional loss bordering on spirituality, a loss of the psychological "wages of whiteness."

In *Black Reconstruction in America,* W. E. B. Du Bois argues that while white workers historically have received low wages, they also have been "compensated in part by a sort of public and psychological wage."[4] Du Bois elaborates: "They were given public deference and titles of courtesy because they were white. They were admitted freely with all classes of white people to public functions, public parks, and the best schools."[5] In short, white workers were offered the opportunity to cash in on their "privilege" of simply being white in a society founded upon racial prejudice, discrimination, and violence. Trump's campaign rhetoric effectively ties into the fear that the privileges afforded to whiteness among the working class are under duress, threatened by undeserving minorities favored by traitorous liberal politicians prepared to stab American workers in the back. To this end, Trump imagines an alternate reality whereupon both the materiality and meaningfulness of being white is discarded in favor of misguided policies and programs geared to promote equity and inclusiveness. For Trump, the *white* alienated subject becomes the flag-bearer of a restored America, rebuilt through the labors of the working class. Gilded with irony no doubt lost on Trump and his supporters, Trump echoes the suppositions of Marx, precisely that the working class, in the abstract, occupies center-stage in historical revolutions.

In this chapter I expand upon my discussion of the structural and social relations that give rise to the alienated subject. Precisely, I argue for an intersectional epistemology for the study of alienation. On this point, I establish that any account of the alienated subject that remains faithful to the myopia of the liberal subject will always and necessarily be insufficient, for the alienated subject does not remain unmarked by race, gender, sexuality, and other forms of positionality. Thus, I build upon Marx's conception of class struggle to consider Sartre's spatially inspired postulates of group formation. This is a necessary step, for it provides a concrete path toward an intersectional repositioning of the alienated subject.

Class Struggle and the Working Class

In his 1859 *Contribution to the Critique of Political Economy,* Marx outlined the broad historical preconditions for revolution: "At a certain stage of development, the material productive forces of society come into conflict with the existing relations of production or—this merely expresses the same thing in legal terms—with the property relations within the framework of which they have operated hitherto. From forms of development of the productive forces, these relations turn into their fetters. Then begins an era of social revolution."[6] In other words, revolutionary change is internal to society, based on the contradictions existing within each mode of production.[7] On the one hand, every mode of production in its own way advances the material development of society but, on the other hand, does so only within the limits of existing social relations of production. When social relations hinder the development of material forces, class conflict and struggle results.

The key concept of Marx's political economy is that of contradictions.[8] Contradictions give rise to problems, and thus to a set of possibilities and the need to find a solution, and therefore to the need to make a choice.[9] There are, for example, contradictory processes and possibilities, and there are contradictory viewpoints or ideologies held by oppositional groups. Modes of production, such as feudalism or capitalism, are conditioned by contradictions. The capitalist mode of production, for example, consists of several contradictions, such as that between use-value and exchange-value, production and reproduction, and monopolies and competition.[10] For Marx, the principal contradiction of capitalism is the contradiction personified by the social relations inherent to the labor process. This is no surprise, really, in that Marx assumes that creative, productive activity is the raison d'être of the human species-being. In capitalism, the entire product belongs to the owner (the capitalist), who does not labor but who owns the productive process. This capitalist stands in opposition to the worker who does labor, that is, who produces commodities but owns neither the means of production nor the object produced. However, there is an additional contradiction embodied by the workers, in that they are both producers and consumers. As waged workers, laborers produce commodities; as consumers, they are required to purchase these commodities on the market. Now, in an effort to garner greater profits, the capitalist may introduce "labor-saving" devices or attempt to hire workers at lower wages. This poses a contradictory crisis, however, in that workers-as-consumers have less money to purchase commodities. Simply put, it matters little how many products are made if they remain unsold; capitalism only continues to the extent that commodities are purchased.

The Covid-19 pandemic illustrates these contradictions systemic to capitalism. Under quarantine guidelines encouraging people to shelter at home, workers are neither producing nor consuming commodities. Capitalism slows down, with predictable ripple effects moving through the economy. From this vantage point, the pandemic posed a potential economic crisis, but also a crisis of *meaning.* For underlying the pandemic was a struggle not only to sustain the valorization of capital but also over the valorization of life itself.

Crises are moments of transformation in which capital typically reinvents itself and morphs into something else.[11] To continue the preceding example: in response to workers not having enough money collectively to buy things, capitalists (instead of raising wages) extend credit to workers. However, as David Harvey explains, the resolution of one contradiction may be better or worse for the people even as it stabilizes the reproduction of capital.[12] Here, the extension of credit allows workers-as-consumers to continue to buy products, thus facilitating the reproduction of capital. Unfortunately, readily available credit leads also to widespread debt. Consequently, workers become even more dependent upon their access to waged work in order to pay bills and buy food and pay rent. The resolution of one crisis thus potentially contributes to the further immiseration and hardship of the working class. As Marx concludes, "Capitalist production therefore reproduces in the course of its own process the separation between labor-power and the conditions of labor. It thereby reproduces and perpetuates the conditions under which the worker is exploited. It incessantly forces him to sell his labor-power in order to live, and enables the capitalist to purchase labor-power in order that he may enrich himself."[13] The Republican-led response to Covid-19, again, demonstrates this tendency, in that both federal and state officials threatened meatpackers and other "essential" workers to remain on the job despite a lack of adequate safety measures and equipment.

For Marx, the objective of socialist revolution is the social and economic emancipation of the working class.[14] Under capitalism, the industrialization and automation of the labor process initiated unprecedented levels of productive power. Paradoxically, these transformations brought about a fundamental societal contradiction. Marx observed in England, France, and a handful of other European countries that capitalism had increased to the point that all basic material needs could be satisfied, and yet throngs of men, women, and children continued to live in conditions of extreme poverty. Production under capitalism should have provided the means to humanize labor, reduce the working day, and lead to greater freedoms.[15] Yet, under capitalism, societal inequalities deepened. This contradiction, fundamentally, underscores the asymmetries of power within the capitalist mode of organization. Simply put, as Chancer identifies, "The class division between proletariat and bourgeoisie central to Marx's conceptualization of capitalism is simultaneously an interpersonal relationship steeped in experiences of extreme domination and subordination."[16] Accordingly, when we observe the gross inequalities of capitalism, of the coexistence of obscene wealth and abject poverty, we can only conclude that capitalism isn't broken; instead, it's operating according to design.

The overcoming of capitalism, Marx premised, was necessary to transcend the stultifying and sadomasochistic conditions of exploitation and alienation; in turn, the socialist transformation would provide the necessary freedom for the development of human creativity and personal fulfillment. When Marx drafted the rules for the International Workingmen's Association (IWA) in 1864, he openly declared the primacy of the working class as revolutionary agent—but only insofar as the proletariat struggled for universal emancipation. "The emancipation of the working classes must be conquered by the working classes themselves," Marx writes, but quickly adds, "the struggle for the emancipation of the working classes means not a struggle for class privileges and monopolies, but for equal rights and duties, and the abolition of all class rule."[17] Here, Marx postulates the overcoming of alienation as all-encompassing, that is, a revolutionary transformation not simply for one class or even one species, but as a necessary condition for the flourishing of nature itself. As Marx concludes, "all living things must also become free."[18]

Why does Marx place such a great responsibility on the working class? The answer rests in part on Marx's conceptualization of the alienated condition of the proletariat. As detailed in chapter 2, Marx insists that the economic subjugation of workers to those who control the means of labor lies at the bottom of servitude in all its forms, of all social misery, mental degradation, and political dependence.[19] However, social conditions of immiseration and suffering are insufficient to affect revolutionary change. As Marx acknowledges, many people—including those excluded from the working class—endure horrific conditions under capitalism. Those who are unemployed, for example, live exceptionally precarious lives and may resort to criminal activities in order to survive. Marx, however, downplays the political potential of the so-called *lumpenproletariat,* favoring instead the revolutionary potential of the working class.

Marx postulates that the struggle between those who own the means of production and those denied access to the means of production is most salient in the analysis of revolutionary transformation. The central idea of Marx's "revolutionary theory" is self-liberation by the masses through political *praxis,* a term Marx conceives as "consciously guided revolutionary practice, as distinct from practice, meaning simply carrying out an action."[20] It is important to stress that praxis is an idea not unique to but rather radically reconceptualized by Marx. In the early nineteenth century throughout Europe, the relationship of philosophy to social and political issues became increasingly fraught and, accordingly, the relationship between knowledge and action became an ever more contentious issue.[21] The Polish aristocrat and philosopher August von Cieszkowski (1814–1894), for example, forwards a positive notion of freedom, defined as the ability to realize "the good" through human praxis.[22] For Cieszkowski, philosophy could no longer contend with theoretical knowledge but must give rise to real action.[23] Notably, Cieszkowski opposed revolution—understood as violent insurrections—opting instead for social and political transformation realized through the self-emancipation of the people and legal reform.[24] Indeed, Cieszkowski insists that "for a holy end, the road must be holy," for whenever unholy means are applied to a holy end, "it is evident that you do not sanctify the means, but debase the end itself."[25] To Cieszkowki, one can add the likes of Bruno Bauer (1809–1882), Ludwig Feuerbach (1804–1872), Johann Fichte (1762–1814), and Friedrich Schelling (1775–1854).[26]

Marx's contribution was to make concrete the idea of alienation in the terms of political economy.[27] As Andrew Bowie contextualizes, the employment of labor in nineteenth-century capitalism involved the most appalling brutality and impoverishment, both material and spiritual, of the working classes.[28] For Marx the essential task was both to properly understand how these conditions materialized under capitalism and to work toward the transcendence of these conditions. Thus, when Marx writes, "The philosophers have only *interpreted* the world in various ways; the point, however, is to *change* it," he is not saying that knowledge is unimportant or inconsequential.[29] Instead, Marx directs attention to the necessity of consciously driven political activities born of material realities. Through solidarity—made possible through the spatial proximity of workers in the modern, capitalist factory—Marx insists that the proletariat, through self-awareness and collective determination, can achieve *human emancipation.* However, to achieve a thorough, human form of emancipation, the exploited and alienated subjects would need to engage in informed direct action on the basis of a critical understanding of their own plight and of possible alternatives.[30] Simply being a member of the so-called working class does not express revolutionary potential or praxis. The working class in-and-of itself does not designate a subjectivity grounded in self-consciousness. Indeed, the so-called working class under capitalism appears as simply the aggregate of alienated subjects denied access to the means of production. And therein lies the problem—and limitation—of an exclusive focus on the emancipatory potential of the working class *in the abstract.*

Conventionally, alienation is rooted in and emanates from exploitation systemic to the capitalist mode of production. Indeed, Marx's critique of capitalism is based on the fact that as a mode of production, it is an inhuman system that prevents or distorts human flourishing. As such, the possible transcendence of alienation *begins* at the moment of production, when workers realize the source of their immiseration and suffering. The alienated subject, however, is not confined solely to the factory floor and, consequently, its self-awareness and *potential* revolutionary consciousness is mediated through social interactions formed elsewhere. Marx was aware of this problem. In the *Economic and Philosophic Manuscripts of 1844* Marx writes, "The worker therefore only feels himself outside his work, and in his work feels outside himself. He is at home when he is not working, and when he is working he is not at home."[31] Here, Marx alludes to the alienation inherent to waged work, of the emptiness of laboring at a boring, repetitive job that affords no joy but is necessary simply to survive. Consequently, if work no longer exists as a creative, productive activity, a flourishing life must be sought elsewhere. In other words, the alienated subject seeks meaning in life beyond its place of employment and, in so doing, renders negligible the potential for workplace emancipation.

Self-emancipation of the alienated subject is a necessary condition for the transformation and eventual overcoming of capitalism. However, as the human species-being is inherently a social and spatial being, this means that self-emancipation—although individually experienced—is itself mediated by the concrete social and spatial relations in which the alienated subject is embedded. For this reason, it is necessary to locate the alienated subject in the everyday geographies of its existence, not as an isolated (liberal) subject but instead as a living being dependent on other living beings for its own survival.

In *The Sane Society,* Erich Fromm provides an evocative snapshot of alienated life from the vantage point of factory workers in the abstract:

> Men work together. Thousands stream into the industrial plants and the offices—they come in cars, in subways, in buses, in trains—they work together, according to a rhythm measured by the experts, with methods worked out by the experts, not too fast, not too slow, but together; each a part of the whole. The evening stream flows back: they read the same newspaper, they listen to the radio, they see the movies, the same for those on the top and for those at the bottom of the ladder, for the intelligent and the stupid, for the educated and the uneducated. Produce, consume, enjoy together, in step, without asking questions. That is the rhythm of their lives.[32]

In this passage, Fromm provides a dystopian reading of mindless production and consumption; an interminable monotony of meaningless activities, repeated day after day until retirement or death, whichever comes first. However, Fromm's alienated society is a homogenous society, seemingly populated with nondescript *men.*

To seriously challenge the alienated conditions inherent to the capitalist mode of production, it is necessary to challenge both scholarly and popular accounts of the homogeneity of the so-called working class. As Sandro Mezzadra writes, efforts are needed to "politicize the analysis of the proletarian body, which means to carefully investigate the ways in which the construction of that body as a racialized or sexualized body facilitates forms of domination and exploitation that acquire a differential character."[33] To this end, I provide a scaffolding upon which to argue that the alienated subject assumes myriad forms and its embodied form remains always a contested field of struggle and subjectivation that is manifest in the deleterious attitudes of indifference and intolerance, and the capacity to hurt, both within and between classes. Racism, patriarchy, and other prejudices inform the alienated social relations inherent to capitalism; accordingly, emancipation from class exploitation requires a direct engagement with, but not exclusive of, feminist and antiracist practices.

In the first volume of *Capital,* Marx invites his readers to enter "the hidden abode" of production, that is, the industrial factory, to see concretely the source of exploitation and alienation inherent to the capitalist mode of production. In this hidden abode capitalists combine the means of production (machinery and raw materials) with labor power (purchased on the labor market) in order to create commodities for exchange. And here, in graphic detail, Marx lays bare the inner workings of especially industrial capitalism and the transformation of once-vital, creative, productive human beings into mere appendages of heartless, soulless machines. However, in order to fully realize the alienated subject in its totality, that is, through its lived experiences beyond the factory, I invite readers to meet the workers prior to their clocking in at work, that is, at the bus stop before going to work.

Waiting at Sartre's Bus Stop

Unlike more canonical accounts of the liberal subject *as an individual,* I premise the everydayness of the alienated subject as always and already mediated by its position within myriad and even contradictory *social collectives.* For this reason, I find tremendous purchase in Sartre's theory of groups.[34] In his *Critique of Dialectical Reason,* Sartre distinguishes several "forms" of social collectives that are grounded in concrete examples of everyday life.[35] Accordingly, in his general orientation toward social relations, Sartre accepts the Marxist principle that the mode of production of material life mediates the development of social, political, and intellectual life.[36] Thus, Sartre proposes a critical dialectics that understands human activity in terms of reciprocal interactions between and among individuals and groups.[37] This is significant insofar as the alienated subject, unlike the liberal subject, is premised as always positioned within a complex social ensemble of myriad groups that continually form and transform. As Iris Marion Young explains, "the discourse of liberal individualism denies the reality of groups" in that "categorizing people in groups by race, gender, religion, and sexuality and acting as though these ascriptions say something significant about the person, his or her experience, capacities, and possibilities, is invidious and oppressive."[38] However, for Young, the privileging of the liberal subject—as an individual—obscures an understanding of structural oppression. Young elaborates:

> Without conceptualizing women [for example] as a group in some sense, it is not possible to conceptualize oppression as a systematic, structured, institutional process. If we obey the injunction to think of people only as individuals, then the disadvantages and exclusions we call oppression reduce to individuals in one of two ways. Either we blame the victims and say that disadvantaged people's choices and capacities render them less competitive, or we attribute their disadvantage to the attitudes of other individuals, who for whatever reason don't "like" the disadvantaged ones.[39]

A theoretical deference to the liberal subject, subsequently, contributes to the fallacy that poor people are poor primarily, if not solely, because of bad decisions, or that racism exists because a "few bad people" harbor racist attitudes. Either way, the salience of social and structural relations of prejudice, discrimination, and oppression are elided. A focus on group formations, conversely, highlights the ways in which individuals benefit or suffer from the privileges or drawbacks associated from concrete categorical types. White privilege in the United States, for example, expresses the gains white people derive, not through individual merit or accomplishment, but simply through their identification as members of the dominant social group.

To begin, a group can be defined simply as a collection of persons who recognize themselves and others, however loosely, as being in a unified relation with one another. This identification may be exceptionally banal, in the sense of expressing a mutual affinity for a sports team or activity, such as running or biking. Conversely, one may associate with a particular political party or labor union. In both examples, however, in self-identifying as a participant of a group, an individual acknowledges themselves as oriented toward the same goals as the others in the group.[40] Indeed, on this basis, even standing in line at the grocery store constitutes a group—and it is this insight, of the spectrum of *everyday* group formations, that Sartre underscores.

It is common to conceive of the everyday as comprising the most banal of activities that occupy our daily lives: the dull routine of simply being. On any "normal" day we eat breakfast, go to work, grab a quick lunch, go shopping, exercise at the gym, eat dinner at a restaurant, take the dog for a walk at a nearby park, catch a film at the local theater, and go to sleep, only to repeat with slight variation many of these same activities day after day after day. And when we stop and reflect upon our days, we wonder where the time went. Our lives seem busy—too busy—packed with a motley mixture of tasks and chores. Our days are filled yet seem unfulfilled.

There is a quantitative sameness to our everyday life, notably under the capitalist mode of production, as our lives become ever more abstracted. Highmore explains that "the phrase 'marking time' brings with it some of the flavor of the everyday modernity in its ambiguous play on the literal process of 'marking' (differentiating, discriminating) and its everyday meaning of dull waiting, of boredom."[41] For Highmore, this ambiguity materializes in the standardization of time—as evidenced by our submission to bus and train schedules—and the routinization of daily life, such as having to clock in at work at a certain time or waiting for a doctor's appointment.[42] Thus, Susan Stewart writes: "The pages falling off the calendar, the notches marked in a tree that no longer stands—these are the signs of the everyday, the effort to articulate difference through counting. Yet it is precisely this counting that reduces differences to similarities, that is designed to be 'lost track of.' Such 'counting,' such signifying, is drowned out by the silence of the ordinary."[43]

Marx writes at length on the monotonous existence of factory work, of the men and women reduced to nothing more than being "living appendages" of a heartless machine. However, as Highmore explains, "What makes continuous production register so vividly is the regulating of time within the widespread conditions of industrialization. From the point of view of the everyday, industrialization is not something limited to factory production, but something registered in nearly all aspects of life."[44] In short, everyday modern life has become fully conditioned to the market logic of capital: societal values are part and parcel of the production, distribution, and consumption of commodities. This, in turn, has tremendous importance for our understanding of the modern alienated subject, for no longer are we seemingly in control of our lives. Rather, capital itself has taken control.

When Cole and Ferrarese ask how capitalism forms our lives, they ask us to reflect on how we would like to live and, importantly, to consider how our form of life delimits or forecloses certain prospects by excluding other forms of life.[45] They stress that "the notion of 'form of life' always seeks to grasp the articulation of the 'social' and the 'vital' on which the institutions of the human world rest."[46] Capitalism, as a form of life, is conditioned by particular social and structural relations oriented around the valorization of capital. Dominated by the market logic of exchange-value, for example, a flourishing life appears in the act of consumption, where the opportunity to choose among dozens of brands of bagels or breakfast cereals passes for freedom. It is no surprise, therefore, that many people who protested against shelter-in-place mandates during the Covid-19 pandemic expressed dismay that meaningful activities, including the ability to shop at Wal-Mart or eat at Applebee's Restaurant, were being taken away by un-American liberals.

As a formative aspect of society, capitalism appears ossified, sedimented into the sutures of everyday life. However, appearances are deceiving and, as Marx and Engels premise, "all that is solid melts into air."[47] Zygmunt Bauman captures this fluidity in his concept of *liquid modernity.*[48] For Bauman, modern capital has the illusion of solidity, of permanence, in part because of the centralization of institutional power and the bureaucratization of everyday life. However, as industrial capital gives way to alternate forms—advanced capitalism, flexible capitalism, finance capitalism—the illusion of modernity's solid foundation dissipates. As Raymond Lee writes, "In a world of shape-shifting capital and labor, modernity is best defined as amorphous—in short, liquid."[49] To that end, what distinguishes liquid modernity from early modernity is the lack of stable institutions.[50] Accordingly, liquid modernity is a concept of "social change that attempts to uncover the consequences of advanced social differentiation and alienation" within the vicissitudes of "late" capitalism.[51] It is a warning that everyday life under capitalism is increasingly defined by "unbearable human suffering and injustice, characterized by increasing social and economic polarization."[52]

To render the everyday as the locus of alienation is not to succumb to nihilism, for the social and spatial relations that condition alienation also contain the seeds of salvation. As Lefebvre writes, it is in the everyday that "people are born, live and die. They live well or ill; but they live in everyday life, where they make or fail to make a living either in the wider sense of surviving or not surviving, or just surviving or living their lives to the full. It is in the everyday life that they rejoice and suffer; here and now."[53] The everyday, in other words, is where (and when) we construct and experience meaning in life. It is thus an ambiguous space-time configuration that mediates the contradictions of alienation and emancipation.

Sartre's theory of groups captures much of this ambiguity, for he recognizes that individuals who are engaged in their day-to-day activities are embedded in myriad concrete social situations inhabited by other individuals engaged in their own activities. In other words, throughout our daily routines, we enter and exit many group formations, and it is this dynamic that conditions both our sense of alienation and of meaning in life. This was dramatically brought to the fore during the Covid-19 pandemic. Compelled to shelter in place, our daily activities were abruptly altered. No longer was it possible to *simply* go to the store and buy groceries, or *merely* go to the barber shop for a haircut, or *only* go for a walk through the park. Day-to-day activities and mundane tasks that once mattered little now mattered a great deal. So connected have we become to the spatiotemporal rhythms of capitalism that our physical separation from its comforting *but alienating* routine itself becomes a source of alienation. To that end, going to Wal-Mart or Applebee's *does* for many people provide meaning; these *are* places of comfort and security, evocative perhaps of simply spending time with family and friends. Effectively, under capitalism, alienation can and often does provide meaning, and paradoxically our emancipation—however ephemeral—becomes alienating.

Why this is so is rooted in our formation of, and participation in, myriad spatially bound social collectives, or groups. Often, when we study groups, we begin with obvious but superficial characteristics that mark everyday subdivisions between people: ethnicity, nationality, gender, occupation, and so on. Sartre, conversely, begins with the *gathering* of people at particular times and particular places, related to some object of common concern, such as waiting at a bus stop.[54] In other words, there is often a time-space context to group formation. Bus stops, for example, are ordinary features of the human landscape. At specified times and concrete locations, people come together and wait for the bus, whether their personal destination is work, a retail store, or a friend's house. And beyond their shared concern for the on-time arrival of the bus, the people who wait for the bus are largely unaware and unconcerned with everyone else who is waiting. I say "largely" for the fact that, in reality, some people are very much aware of those around them. For example, as the work of feminist geographers documents, women take very seriously the threat of sexual harassment or physical violence.[55] In particular, research into the geography of women's fear reveals a pervasive awareness of vulnerability to sexual assault and an array of self-protective strategies and behavioral constraints, such as travelling with an escort or avoiding certain places at certain times.[56] In the abstract, however, the bus stop is just a place, that is, a place where "we simply become ciphers, interchangeable parts in an undifferentiated, functioning plurality: waiting for a bus."[57]

Those waiting for the bus, Sartre explains, may differ in age, sex, class, and social milieu, and they wait in relative isolation joined together—that is, unified—by a particular albeit mundane activity, that is, waiting for the bus to take them to their destination. This passive activity Sartre terms the *practico-inert,* that is, "those aspects of social reality that are the consequences of human action, but that oppose, or set limits to, the pure freedom of individual action."[58] For example, the people waiting for the bus are free to wait for the bus, and they are free to choose not to wait for the bus. Their freedom, however, is limited, on one hand, by the bus schedule and, on the other hand, by the actions of the bus driver. Indeed, as we expand our understanding of the situation, we realize that the bus driver is also circumscribed, for example, by her adherence to a schedule determined by someone else, by the proper maintenance of the bus so that it does not break down, by the congestion of the road that might lead to delays, and so on. Here, the practico-inert is the spatiotemporal realm of alienation, a realm marked by the ambiguous interplay of free will and determinism, of discipline and resistance.

Within the capitalist mode of production, everyday human existence produces a geography "of passive being, formidable in its inertia, which in turn produces a definite kind of social grouping Sartre calls a 'series.'"[59] For Sartre, a series comprises a form of human gathering and alienation as a mediated relation to the other.[60] Stated differently, a series is a contingent assembly of unrelated subjects united only by a common object, such as waiting for a bus.[61] As Peter Caws elaborates, "Serial relations abound in daily life—customers in the market, spectators in the theater, listeners to the radio or watchers of television, voters in an election, drivers on a highway, all constitute series whose members share a connection to an external object but have no internal connections between themselves."[62]

As we move about in our day-to-day activities, we subject ourselves to innumerable series, and we do so unreflexively. Indeed, so common is the practice that we fail to think of these mundane activities as forming any meaningful part of our lives. If asked, at the end of the day, how many times we "gathered" in a series, we would be hard pressed to remember, let alone say anything substantive about the experience. This is not to say that series are unimportant in our everyday lives, but rather to suggest we are largely indifferent to these groupings. We would obviously *prefer* not to wait, but since it is so much a part of our day-to-day lives, we usually just take it in stride.

Series give structure to our routines even as they may be the source of boredom or frustration. Knowing that we will have to wait for a bus, for example, we adjust our schedules so that we arrive at the bus stop at an appropriate time. In anticipation of a long line at the bank, we leave earlier, in an attempt to avoid the crowd. In short, our awareness of series conditions other activities that do provide meaning. Thus, we stand in line at the bus stop, in order to catch the bus and so arrive on time at work; and we avoid the crowded bank so that we won't be late when meeting friends to watch a film at the local theater.

There is an element of randomness to series formations, in that many people on any given day might arrive at the bus stop. That said, there also is an element of regularity, for some people take the bus every day and come to recognize those who routinely take the bus and those who do not. In fact, some people may informally claim particular seats as their own when riding the bus. In addition, a series may be more formally ordered in such a way as to establish external connections between its members.[63] At the bank or movie theater, for example, people are often expected (required) to stand in line. Similarly, at sporting events, spectators behave in a more or less coordinated fashion, alternately cheering and booing in unison, depending on the course of the game.[64] Ultimately, though, behind the façade of solidarity, the members of a series remain isolated, assembled together only until the object of their coming together dissolves.

This, again, is not to imply that series are inconsequential. As George Stack explains, despite its weakness as a social force, the seriality is anterior to group formation and is thus the social structure out of which groups emerge.[65] In other words, it is the coming together of disparate people, at a particular time and place, that is necessary for the emergence of more cohesive social formations. To this end, a more cohesive group formation occurs when the members of a series become aware of one another not merely as accidental participants having no internal relations to one another, but as sharing a common interest that engages a common emotion.[66] In Sartre's example, a late bus draws the series together in a more emotional way. People waiting for the bus begin to grumble about being late to work or meeting their friends. A shared inconvenience brought about through an external object—the tardiness of the bus—provides a source of solidarity beyond the physical act of waiting at a bus stop. Now, the members experience a common bond that provides a deeper sense of meaning, indeed, an experience that becomes more memorable. The series, at this point, transforms into a *group-in-fusion.*

The group-in-fusion is the *negation* of seriality, that is, the coming together of individuals to potentially act as a collective.[67] In other words, there is a latent power inherent in the group-in-fusion, a possibility for direct action that transcends a sense of shared frustration. Sartre uses the example of the peasantry storming the Bastille during the French Revolution. We don't have to posit anything so grand as this to realize that a group-in-fusion can be an effective *political* force. Indeed, any spontaneous coming together of people who share a common objective or purpose can be considered a group-in-fusion. Crucially, people who "belong" to groups-in-fusion are not indifferent to the object of concern. The people waiting at Sartre's bus stop are no longer disinterested bystanders but active agents who express their intolerance of the situation.

Within the group-in-fusion, individuals act as a collective subject and, in the process, undergo a personal transformation of self-realization. While as members of a series, people exist in isolation, that is, as alienated subjects, participation in a collective creates a communal sense of meaning and purpose. Individual emancipation is made possible through collective determination. And, in fact, this gets at Marx's notion of *social* revolution, for Marx held that workers individually would realize through their collective labors the source of their exploitation and thus join in solidarity with other like-minded workers to overthrow capitalism. However—and this is a point that cannot be overemphasized—the group-in-fusion is neither inherently revolutionary nor reactionary; it is, in the abstract, politically neutral. On the one hand, we often think of social movements as progressive, of people marching against unjust and discriminatory policies or institutional racism. Thus, the spontaneous protests that erupted in opposition to Trump's anti-Muslim ban in 2017 can be considered groups-in-fusion. On the other hand, there are innumerable instances of people coming together to express their support for racist or misogynist ideals, in opposition to progressive movements. Counterprotestors, such as the Proud Boys who decried shelter-in-place orders, for example, are also examples of groups-in-fusion.

It is worth pausing for a moment on the importance of external objects as the source for groups-in-fusion. The object in question may have a concrete reality, such as a late bus or a virus, but it may also be ideological or otherwise immaterial. Indeed, the "object" that unites a group of people may only exist discursively, as in Trump's incessant attacks on supposed threats to the United States. For example, in his effort to build a wall along the U.S.–Mexico border and to deny entry of persons from Central and South America, Trump routinely—and falsely—claimed immigrants, legal or otherwise, commit crimes far in excess of so-called U.S. citizens (meaning, of course, *white* citizens). On March 2, 2019, to highlight one instance, Trump cited a study by the anti-immigrant hate group Federation for American Immigration Reform and claimed that "illegal aliens are incarcerated at three times the rate of legal residents."[68] The myth of the criminal immigrant—a stalwart trope of Trump's rhetoric—has long served anti-immigrant hatred in the United States; under the Trump administration, however, the discourse was elevated to new heights. Not only did Trump regularly cite fallacious figures about immigrants committing crimes, he also orchestrated public spectacles to both incite hatred against persons of color and generate sympathy among otherwise indifferent white people. In June 2018, for example, Trump met with family members of individuals killed by undocumented immigrants, a group he calls "angel families." In attendance were members from Advocates for Victims of Illegal Aliens Crimes, a splinter group from the anti-immigrant hate group Remembrance Project.[69] In its totality, Trump's rhetoric of hatred and fear serves to galvanize (mostly white) people who may otherwise be indifferent to political issues such as immigration policy. In doing so, Trump effectively created the conditions whereby disparate groups of people came together, both in person and virtually through social media, to register their intolerance and hostility to an imaginary threat.

The group-in-fusion is necessarily unstable. As Young explains, social life consists of constant ebbs and flows of groupings out of series; most groups dissipate soon after they materialize—such as the people waiting impatiently for the late bus—but other groups transform yet again and assume a more substantive form.[70] Now, members of a group-in-fusion may decide that a more sustained commitment is necessary to confront the threat. For example, what if the people waiting at the bus stop learn that some policy exists that results in the bus being late on a regular basis. The external threat, of being late for work or of meeting friends, is no longer understood as a random inconvenience but instead a systemic problem that demands more concentrated action. The bus riders, at this point, establish a more formal committee and members pledge their support to challenge the delinquent bus company. In Sartre's terminology, the group-in-fusion transforms into a "sworn" group.[71]

While the group-in-fusion is a spontaneous organic unity, the pledge of the sworn group mediates between the members of the group and binds one to the other; in turn, this creates a semipermanent structure that is maintained by each individual's promise to all its members that they will protect the other from the external threat.[72] In practice, the "swearing" or "pledging" loyalty can assume many different forms. Potential members, for example, may have to sign a written document or to perform a particular (and ritualistic) action; dues may be required and uniforms or some other visible marker might be displayed. Regardless, the pledge, symbolically, allows each member to promise to other members that they will act in a way that advances their chosen cause.

The act of swearing or pledging to one another introduces a solemnity that may have far-reaching consequences.[73] Within the sworn group, each individual affirms that they will care for and affirm the other's practical freedom, that is, their freedom to confront the threat. However, as pledged members, each person vows to fulfill specific obligations and to perform necessary functions within the group. In this way, people's individual freedoms are effectively limited within the sworn group. The individuals of the group-in-fusion support one another as they each act together to confront the same external threat; as members of a sworn group, however, people are willing to relinquish a certain amount of freedom in return for the opportunity to participate in something that gives them meaning. If alienation is a disorienting feeling of existential exclusion, membership in a sworn group provides something more than an emotional antidote. Consequently, when the alienated subject experiences little or no meaning through work, that is, productive labor, the alienated subject may find meaning through membership in a "sworn group." Here, group identification transcends that of the hobbyist. The alienated subject is not merely following a favorite sports team but is actively and consciously working toward some objective in concert with other like-minded individuals. As a member of a sworn group, the alienated subject may be intensely loyal and emotionally invested both to the leadership and to the greater purpose. This effectively captures the cultlike qualities of many Trump supporters who faithfully followed the former president from rally to rally.

Here, Eduardo Bonilla-Silva forwards a conception of "racialized emotions" that has a direct bearing on the generative meaning-making of the alienated subject.[74] Bonilla-Silva explains that racialized emotions are anchored in our subjectivity as social collectives. Accordingly, the racial subject should also be understood as an emotive subject who "feels" race.[75] Building on this notion, the alienated subject is also and already an emotive subject who feels race, gender, and so on. This in fact strikes at the ambiguity of the alienated subject *in the abstract,* for alienated subjects embody complex and indeed contradictory beliefs and behaviors, depending on their situated contexts. As developed more fully in chapter 4, the *white* alienated subject (in the abstract) may attempt to transcend (or mollify) class-based exploitation through racist or sexist attitudes, including intolerance toward those viewed as the cause of its exploitation. Consequently, it is but a small step for the intolerant, alienated subject to take direct action against those who are perceived to embody the threat. For example, as Bonilla-Silva muses, "when a white worker is happy with the idea of building a wall, or a Muslim ban, or with wars and interventions all over the world, they are defending emotionally a racial regime as they see it and understand it."[76] On this point, we can turn now to Sartre's concept of "fraternity-terror," that is, of being faithful to one's sworn group to the point of doing harm toward a perceived enemy.[77] Sartre writes of the violence enacted:

> It is a bond of fraternity aroused and accentuated amongst the lynchers, in so far as it is a brutal reactualization of the pledge itself and in so far as every stone that is thrown, every blow delivered, is a new affirmation of the pledge: whoever participates in the execution of the [enemy] reaffirms the untranscendability of the group-being as a limit of his freedom and as his new birth, and he affirms

> it in a bloody sacrifice which, moreover, constitutes an explicit recognition of the coercive right of all over every individual and everyone's threat to all.

The violent act, in other words, becomes a statement and an affirmation of one's loyalty to a cause; physical violence directed toward a perceived enemy *provides meaning* for the alienated subject living in fear. We see this especially in the attitudes and actions of far-right extremists.[78] On June 17, 2015, for example, a twenty-one-year-old white man, Dylann Roof, shot and killed nine African Americans at a Bible study meeting at Emanuel African Methodist Episcopal Church in Charleston, South Carolina. Prior to the attack, Roof reportedly said he was there "to shoot black people."[79] On August 3, 2019, Patrick Crusius, a twenty-one-year-old white man, entered a Wal-Mart in El Paso, Texas, and opened fire with an automatic rifle. Just prior to the shootings, he posted online a four-page manifesto to make clear his reasons.[80] Here, Crusius referred to immigrants to the United States as "invaders" and parroted many white supremacist talking points, including fears of "ethnic displacement" and "race mixing."[81] During the shooting, Crusius explicitly and self-consciously targeted Hispanics. Within minutes, twenty-two people lay dead or dying, with more than two dozen others injured. On October 27, 2018, a neo-Nazi attacked the Tree of Life synagogue in Pittsburgh, Pennsylvania, killing eleven at Shabbat morning services. According to eyewitnesses, he shouted "All Jews must die" as he walked in.[82] And on April 27, 2019, nineteen-year-old John Earnest entered the Chabad of Poway synagogue in Poway, California, during Passover celebrations and opened fire with an AR-15, killing sixty-year-old Lori Kaye and injuring three others. Prior to the attack, Earnest posted an open letter on the white supremacist–friendly online forum 8Chan; his statement was steeped in white supremacist tropes, replete with false claims of a global conspiracy to replace white people.

Although the causes of mass shooting events are complex, we would be remiss to ignore the vitriolic rhetoric of Trump and his supporters as contributing factors. Trump's dehumanizing language; his repeated assertions of Muslims and Hispanics as invaders, of Mexicans as "criminals and rapists"; and his implicit (but at times explicit) calls for direct violence are echoed in the words of far-right shooters. Crusius, for example, repeated Trump's hateful statements against immigrants and persons of color and his frequent allusions to "invasions" and "infestations." Indeed, Crusius explains in his manifesto, "This attack is a response to the Hispanic invasion of Texas."[83] This illustrates Sartre's fraternity-terror, in that far-right extremists, through their violent actions, express their loyalty to hateful causes and in doing so claim membership to a larger group.

We should consider also the oft-repeated explanation of these violent acts as being perpetrated by "lone wolves," that is, by individuals acting on their own accord and not in response to the racist rhetoric expressed, for example, by the president. Framed as a deviant individual or the victim of circumstances (such as bad parenting or alienation), and redolent of the liberal subject, the lone wolf enables pundits and politicians to sunder racist violence from the persistence of racial and gendered inequalities in society. However, as Gavin Rae explains, the sworn group is an example of the sort of organized, democratic, and fundamentally open group formation that affirms rather than constrains individual's practical freedoms; in turn, the pledge of the organized group provides a standing promise that each member will protect and care for the freedom of the other.[84] In short, through one's identification with, for example, white supremacy, a person can commit individual and isolated acts of violence *in the spirit of the overall group.* The aforementioned mass shooters, in other words, did act alone, but only insofar as they recognized a common purpose—a meaning in life—with other like-minded individuals. As Sartre concludes, the "pledge, whether implicit or explicit, defines everyone as a common individual, not only because it concerns his being-in-the-group, but also because it is only through the mediation of all that it can take place in everyone."[85] In other words, in a white supremacist society in which white people claim allegiance, either directly—as in membership in hate groups—or indirectly—through one's acceptance of white privilege—there is no exteriority, and thus "lone wolf" violence does not exist. Individual acts of violence are symptomatic of structural forms of racist ideologies.

Over time, sworn groups may dissolve, perhaps fractured by internal dissent, or they may harden into more formal structures, such as "statutory groups" or "institutions." Sartre's argument, at this point, is not that there is necessary progression of, for example, sworn groups into more permanent structures, but instead that groups, under the right conditions and leadership, continually form and transform. As Caws concludes, "What they have in common is the potential for totalization, the uniting of multiple individuals into a totality, which from the outside takes on solidity and objectivity."[86]

In summary, Sartre provides a useful framework to evaluate the intricacies of group formation and, in so doing, directs attention toward the myriad social and spatial groupings in which the alienated subject enters and exists. In addition, it is important to recognize that the myriad social formations identified by Sartre and elaborated on by subsequent scholars do not constitute successive stages of historical development but instead coexist, clash, and coalesce. In its everyday existence, the alienated subject participates, to a greater or lesser degree, in myriad and even contradictory group formations and, consequently, embodies and inhabits multiple subject positions.

Marx writes of the emancipatory potential of the proletariat, and many who follow Marx continue to privilege a class-based agenda to overcome the exploitation and alienation that is systemic to capitalism. In the process, antiracist and antisexist agendas, for example, are seen as secondary. However, as Sandro Mezzadra asks, "Is it possible to think of class formation while emphasizing the deep heterogeneity of contemporary living labor?"[87] This is a crucial question, one that is fundamental to the work of Kimberlé Crenshaw, Patricia Hill Collins, Martha Gimenéz, Holly Lewis, and many other scholars working at the intersection of Marxism, feminism, queer studies, and critical race studies. It is a question, also, that remains essential to my overall project, given the profound heterogeneity of the alienated subject.

The Intersectionality of Alienation

The working class assumes a central place in Marx's thinking precisely because of its potential for revolutionary self-emancipation. That said, Marx frequently tempers his optimism, conceding that the development of a proletarian class consciousness is a *tendency* grounded in the material existence of the worker.[88] In other words, the peculiar and particular social and structural relations produced and reproduced under capitalism bring about concrete contradictions that, in their resolution, hold the possibility of self-emancipation and, through solidarity, the subsequent transformation and transcendence of capitalism.

On the occasion of Marx's 200th birthday, Peter Goodwin asks: "Is it possible to be a Marxist without accepting the self-emancipation of the working class as an integral part of Marxism?"[89] Goodwin's question weighs heavily on our excavation of the alienated subject, not least because, conventionally, the alienated subject is positioned as a member of the working class. This of course is a misreading of Marx, for under the capitalist mode of production, even capitalists are alienated. However, as we have seen, Marx insists that "the capitalist can live longer without the worker than can the worker without the capitalist."[90]

Throughout this project I return frequently to Marx's axiom because it speaks directly to the uneven vulnerability and susceptibility to a truncated life. All human beings share a biological mortality, but this commonality is tempered by unequal access to employment opportunities, health care, criminal justice, and so on. When claims are made for social justice, the demand isn't to privilege one group over another; rather, the point is to underscore the inequity of social and structural relations that impede the capability of some people to not only live a flourishing life but to avoid a truncated life through premature death. To remain indifferent to the vast gulf that separates the life chances among people is itself a hallmark of privilege. Self-emancipation—and I think Marx implies this—requires an awareness of the decided unfairness of life conditioned by the capitalist mode of production.

The alienated subject *in the abstract* is not a member of the working class but instead is a subject whose life is mediated by, or subsumed under, the ideology and material relations of capitalism. The alienated subject we see waiting at Sartre's bus stop is not de facto a white cis heterosexual man who labors in an automobile factory in Ohio. Instead, the alienated subject occupies multiple subject positions. The alienated subject is the unmarried Filipina domestic worker in Hong Kong, the divorced Romanian man washing dishes in Barcelona, the Mexican lesbian working in a maquiladora in Ciudad Juarez, the Black transgender woman who operates a small publishing house in London. To this end, recognition of the multiple subject positions of the alienated subject raises difficult questions for a reconstructed theorization of alienation, notably the relation between exploitation and myriad other structures of oppression, such as racism, patriarchy, trans- and homophobic prejudice, xenophobia, nationalism, religious bigotry, and so on. How are we to proceed? How, precisely, should we understand the subject that is the alienated subject and may become the emancipated subject?

An obvious starting point is the concept of the subject. Notably, I do not employ the terms *individual, person,* or *body,* nor do I frame alienation as an *identity.* Each of these terms carries their own intellectual baggage and are equally fraught with potential misunderstanding.[91] Here, I follow Catherine Belsey in my adoption of *subject* as a more capacious way of thinking about issues.[92] On the one hand, as a grammatical term, *subject* places the emphasis on the language we learn and from which we internalize the meanings. We see this, for example, in the ways in which we conceive "man" or "woman" or "white" or "black." Indeed, one critical thematic of feminism is the important question of what it means to be a woman under different historical and geographical circumstances.[93] On the other hand, *subject* calls out the ambiguity and contestation surrounding who—and what—we are. We may, for example, subject ourselves to dominant discourses of societal-specific meanings of "man," "woman," and so forth. Thus, a white man may internalize the hegemonic power of "whiteness" and "manliness" in the United States, thereby enjoying the privileges of his exalted position. Alternatively, we can resist prevailing norms and challenge accepted meanings. That said, one's ability to "freely" subject oneself to any particular discourse is not guaranteed. To be a subject entails also the possibility that one is subjected to intolerant views and stereotypes.

One does not choose to be categorized as an inferior subject, but that is precisely what racism does: it categorizes specific racialized groups as inferior and thus undeserving of empathy or justice. When Trump uses inflammatory rhetoric to describe Mexicans as criminals and rapists, he is subjecting an entire population to his racist bigotry. This is a crucial element of any subject position, for the process of subjectivization, that is, of being subjected to particular discourses, impacts greatly our exercise of free will. Indeed, simply being *aware* of how others frame ourselves is sufficient to modify our everyday behaviors and impacts our ability to live a meaningful life, free from the fear of violence. In a key passage of *Black Skin, White Masks,* Frantz Fanon describes the experience of being called out as a "nigger." Fanon writes:

> My body was given back to me sprawled out, distorted, recolored, clad in mourning in that white winter day. The Negro is an animal, the Negro is bad, the Negro is mean, the Negro is ugly; look, a nigger, it's cold, the nigger is shivering, the nigger is shivering because he is cold, the little boy is trembling because he is afraid of the nigger, the nigger is shivering with cold, that cold that goes through your bones, the handsome little boy is trembling because he thinks that the nigger is quivering with rage, the little white boy

> throws himself into his mother's arms: Mama, the nigger's going to eat me up.[94]

Here, Fanon describes in unadulterated language his subjectively experienced response to a hateful, racist epithet.[95] Moreover, Fanon captures the efficacy of subjectivization, for physical force is not required when the coercive violence of being seen and being labeled is sufficient to exert dominance over another. As Michel Foucault writes, "There is no need for arms, physical violence, material constraints. Just a gaze. An inspecting gaze, a gaze which each individual under its weight will end by interiorizing to the point that he is his own overseer, each individual thus exercising this surveillance over, and against, himself."[96] In short, adherence to the term *subject* reveals the contradictions associated with simply *being*: of who we are, but equally important, to what degree are we safely able to determine who we are.

There is an additional motivation to my employment of the term *subject*. As Paola Rebughini notes, "The concepts of subject and subjectivity have been important in social science debates since the turning point of 1968, when they ceased to be an object of abstract philosophical reflection and became a matter of political and sociological theory."[97] She explains: "This politicization of the subject concerns not only its demolition as ontological representation of the white, male, bourgeois and European emancipated subject, but it also concerns the renewal of the reflection on the status of the subject as citizen entitled to rights."[98] As Sylvia Wynter writes, the liberal subject as rational, political subject exists always in opposition to its secret twin, that is, "its negation, the nonrational subject."[99] To this point, anti-Black violence is a necessary function in the production of whiteness and white subjectivity. As Orisanmi Burton explains, "Whiteness [is] a structural position atop the racial order and blackness [is] that which must always be policed." Within the racial capitalist systems, Burton elaborates, "Whiteness extols capital accumulation over all other objectives and it afflicts its proprietors with a twin condition of blindness and aphasia, inhibiting their capacity to recognize the discriminatory public policies, or name the forms of genocidal violence that make whiteness possible. And because it requires public recognition and acceptance of its norms and values, whiteness places a premium on social homogenization. Whiteness is simultaneously produced by and productive of the hegemonic structure of white supremacy—a racially ordered regime of dominance."[100]

In calling for the negation of the liberal subject, I postulate the figure of the alienated subject. Under the capitalist mode of production, the alienated subject *in the abstract* is impeded in its ability to lead a flourishing life through the realization of its creative, productive potential. Even the alienated *bourgeois* subject, abstractly, is hindered in fulfilling its creative, productive potential. However, to critically interrogate the concrete realities of the alienated subject as a *lived being* requires an *intersectional* epistemology that takes seriously the multiple and contradictory subject positions that condition its life and gives it meaning.

Intersectionality, and the subsequent metaphor of intersecting categories of discrimination, was introduced by the Black feminist legal scholar Kimberlé Crenshaw to underscore the inadequacy of approaches that treat race and gender as exclusive or essentially separate categories.[101] Crenshaw's objective, she explains, was "to illustrate that many of the experiences Black women face are not subsumed within the traditional boundaries of race or gender discrimination . . . and that the intersection of racism and sexism factors into Black women's lives in ways that cannot be captured wholly by looking at the race or gender dimensions of those experiences separately."[102] In doing so, Crenshaw builds upon over a century of Black feminist thought in an effort to more fully interrogate the concrete realities of Black women living in the United States and other settler societies. Indeed, elements of intersectionality as a concept, Elena Ruíz notes, is seen in Black feminist writings since the nineteenth century and includes the works of Maria Stewart, Sojourner Truth, Anna Julia Cooper, Ida B. Wells, Elise McDougald, Sadie Alexander, and Francis Beale.[103] Collectively, Ruíz explains, their contributions are "based on critical examinations of lived experience in light of the systemic racism, sexism, and classism that permeated all aspects of their lives" and "disclose the existence of compound structural oppressions in society, since Black women were at the crossroads of gendered bias in patriarchal society, racial bias in racialist republics, and class bias in stratified public life."[104] Crucially, these writings display also a sensitivity toward, and awareness of, the finitude of life, for one's vulnerability to a truncated life through premature death is conditioned by one's exposure to multiple and intersecting oppressions.

To this end, a key moment in the history of the Black feminist intellectual tradition was the appearance in 1978 of "A Black Feminist Statement" authored by the Combahee River Collective.[105] In this brief but powerful document, they write, "Our politics initially sprang from the shared belief that Black women are inherently valuable, that our liberation is a necessity not as an adjunct to somebody else's but because of our need as human persons for autonomy."[106] This is a critical declaration, in that it calls out the hypocrisy of so-called universal declarations of rights and social justice, for historically such rights were understood from the vantage point of property-owning, heterosexual white cis men. Conversely, the Combahee River Collective, as Black feminists and lesbians, demanded their right "to be recognized as human."[107] Fundamentally, members sought to affirm unequivocally that "Black women's lives were valuable and worth saving."[108]

To be recognized as human, however, requires one to be recognized as a complex *human being,* that is, to not be reduced to a singular attribute in isolation. Subject formation is both relational and contextual; who we "choose" to be—and how others view us—is informed by preexisting structures, institutions, and norms. As Amartya Sen explains, in terms that resonate with Sartre's conceptualization of group formations:

> In our normal lives, we see ourselves as members of a variety of groups—we belong to all of them. A person's citizenship, residence, geographic origin, gender, class, politics, profession, employment, food habits, sports interests, taste in music, social commitments, etc., make us members of a variety of groups. Each of these collectives, to all of which this person simultaneously belongs, gives her a particular identity. None of them can be taken to be the person's only identity or singular membership category.[109]

That said, there are those who seek to restrict and constrain our subjectivity, through various means of physical and symbolic violence. Thus, the Combahee River Collective explains, "The mere names of the pejorative stereotypes attributed to Black women (e.g., mammy, matriarch, Sapphire, whore, bulldagger), let alone cataloguing the cruel, often murderous, treatment we receive, indicates how little value has been placed upon our lives during four centuries of bondage in the Western hemisphere."[110] Accordingly, members of the collective recognized that traditional accounts of oppression erased their lived experiences in favor of essentialized constructs—woman, Black, poor. They write: "Our situation as Black people necessitates that we have solidarity around the fact of race, which white women of course do not need to have with white men, unless it is their negative solidarity as racial oppressors. We struggle together with Black men against racism, while we also struggle with Black men about sexism."[111]

To this end, intersectionality provides an analytical tool for open-ended investigations of the overlapping and conflicting dynamics of race, gender, class, sexuality, and other potential sites of inequalities and injustices.[112] Indeed, the intersectional arguments foreshadowed by the Combahee River Collective are indispensably important toward our theorizing the negation of the alienated subject by an emancipated subject. Members of the Collective, for example, affirmed that, while the liberation of all oppressed peoples necessitates the destruction of the political-economic systems of capitalism and imperialism, such a revolution must necessarily, among other things, also be feminist and antiracist.[113] As Taylor explains, "Because Black women were among the most marginalized people in [the United States], their political struggles brought them into direct conflict with the intertwined malignancies of capitalism—racism, sexism, and poverty."[114] Taylor continues: "The women of the C.R.C. believed that, if Black women were successful in their struggles and movements, they would have an impact far beyond their immediate demands. As they put it, 'If Black women were free, it would mean that everyone else would have to be free since our freedom would necessitate the destruction of all the systems of oppression.'"[115]

Marx, I believe, is correct to underscore the emancipatory potential and revolutionary power of the alienated proletariat, that is, those separated from the means of production. His hope that self-awareness mediated by collective determination can unleash a social movement capable of transforming capitalism in such a way to permit the flourishing of meaningful life for humanity as a whole is not entirely misguided. However, as we move forward, we must acknowledge that the profit logics of capitalism produced myriad subject positions who might alternately benefit or suffer from its workings. As Bohrer concludes, "That capitalism requires multiple kinds of exploitation, multiple forms of dispossession, and multiple kinds of subjects in order to gain global hegemony is corroborative evidence for Marx's fundamental diagnosis of the system's simultaneous resilience and its ultimate fragility."[116] Given this admission, Marx's analysis of alienation must simultaneously be stretched to account for the contradictory subject positions that enable some to remain indifferent to, or intolerant of, others. Alienated subjects do not constitute a homogenous group but instead comprise a multitude of people who experience exploitation and alienation in vastly different ways. Alienated subjects occupy multiple subject positions that, in turn, condition their experiences of, and responses to, class alienation. Exploited and alienated white workers, for example, may find meaning in their privileged whiteness and so remain indifferent to the suffering of racialized Others deemed inferior or undeserving. In the end, the Combahee River Collective concludes, "We need to articulate the real class situation of persons who are not merely raceless, sexless workers, but for whom racial and sexual oppression are significant determinants in their working/economic lives."[117]

Conclusions

The hope and purpose in life for Marx was the overcoming of the stultifying effects of the capitalist mode of production. For not only does capitalism impede one's ability to cultivate a flourishing life, capitalism inheres a gross violation of those conditions that for many people make life itself possible. We all share the fact of mortality, but how this is experienced is far from equal under the logics of capitalism. On this point, Marx believed in the revolutionary potential of the proletariat, for it was this group, Marx surmised, that would develop its consciousness and become capable of building a new society that would lead to the betterment of all humankind.[118]

That said, many scholars and activists question the relevancy both of Marx and of the central role afforded to the working class toward the abolition of structures and social relations of oppression. David Lovell, for example, concludes that Marx's theory is incidental to radical social change and that it no longer has the power to convince us that the working class is the class of the future.[119] And while Lovell concedes that Marx was too honest and intelligent to ignore evidence of the proletariat's passivity and susceptibility to "bourgeois prejudices" such as racial intolerance, when Marx does address these, he too often considers them transient or isolated. In other words, racism, sexism, and other forms of structural oppressions are mostly rendered impotent and appear as epiphenomenal to the primacy of class subjectivity and struggle. Consequently, for Lovell, the transcendence of exploitation, alienation, and other forms of oppression must be found elsewhere.

Lovell, I believe, overstates the case; there is a continued relevancy. Marx's conception of revolution, that is, the philosophy of praxis and its accompanying notion of workers' self-emancipation, remains a useful compass toward the abolition of injustices systemic to capitalism. As Löwy remarks, however, this does not mean that one can find in Marx the answers to all our problems, or that there is nothing to be reconsidered or criticized in the complex body of his economic or political views.[120] Indeed, the limitations inherent to Marx's writings should serve as a guide in our way forward. To this end, a principle corrective is the dismantling of the privileged role of the (white, male) alienated subject.

In this chapter I make the case for an intersectional epistemology for the study of alienation. This follows from an awareness that the extraction of surplus labor, as San Juan Jr. writes, always involves conflict and struggle.[121] We readily understand, for example, how the social relations of production condition the way in which subjectivities are mediated by the capitalist form of life. And yet, workers are not spatially confined to their place of employment. While alienation may be rooted in the exploitation of waged labor, meaning in life is often developed elsewhere, as workers and capitalists alike form and reform complex and contradictory groupings. Indeed, subject positions—including class consciousness—are articulated in myriad group formations, some formally organized, others more ephemeral. To this end, the particular subject positions of race, gender, sexuality, and so on enter into the totality of contradictions that define a specific conjuncture.[122]

Conjunctures, much like intersections, are crossroads. And as Bauman cautions, "Crossroads call for decisions about which way to go, but the first crucial, and not at all obvious decision to be taken is to recognize the crossroads as a crossroads—to accept that more than one way leads from here into the future, and that sometimes pursuing the future—any future—may require sharp turns."[123] The Covid-19 pandemic marks one such crossroad. As Heather Brown writes, each passing day illustrates the need to uproot a vicious and vile capitalism that places value on human life only as far as it can profit from it and replace it with a society that values all of its members as living embodiments of our species, regardless of race, class, gender, sexuality, gender identity, or ability.[124] For the pandemic underscores the persistent indifference to life inherent to the capitalist mode of production and not simply because markets are unable to effectively respond to human needs. Rather, as Brown clarifies, the Covid-19 pandemic brings into sharp focus the inequalities intrinsic to and necessary for capitalism. In the United States, for example, millions of people—but especially the poor and people of color—lack adequate health care and thus are less likely to seek or to receive treatment.[125] In addition, as epidemiologist and former director of the Detroit Health Department explains, too many Americans work gigs—like waiting tables or driving Uber or Lyft—that leave them uniquely vulnerable to the economic interruptions caused by Covid-19. Economic losses, in turn, may leave millions at risk of eviction and becoming unhoused, thereby exacerbating their vulnerability to illness and lack of adequate health care.[126]

And the grave consequences are anything but shared equally within society. Indeed, the deaths attributed to Covid-19 document in grave ways the inequalities systemic to *racial* capitalism in the United States. As Whitney Laster Pirtle writes, "Those with high socioeconomic status secure a superior set of knowledge, power money, power, prestige, and beneficial social connections, all of which can alleviate the consequences of the disease."[127] Given the stark racial disparities among wealth, this translates into an increased vulnerability especially among Blacks, Latinx, and Indigenous peoples in the United States. Indeed, with respect to unemployment, morbidity, and mortality, Black, Indigenous, other people of color, and women have suffered disproportionately during the pandemic.[128] In this way, the Covid-19 pandemic intensified the vulnerability of an already precarious population, for as El-Sayed affirms, "When you look at communities that are suffering the most, they're communities on which environmental injustice, structural racism, and their implications on poverty, have already softened the space for the incoming of this virus to devastate people."[129]

It is not simply that capitalism benefits from racial divisions. More directly, racial solidarity trumps class solidarity in the sense that attitudes of racial superiority provide a sense of meaning not found elsewhere. The alienated subject, for example, may affirm its meaning in life through an intolerance directed at those perceived as the Other, that is, toward those whom the alienated subject believes is the source of its own alienation. That this lack of solidarity is possible emanates from the power of myriad and intersectional structures and relations of oppression. As Michael Yates writes, despite—or maybe because of—the conditions workers encountered during the pandemic, many protested and struck. Yates recounts that there were "strikes and threatened strikes at Amazon warehouses, a Barnes and Noble warehouse, Whole Foods, automobile plants, food delivery services like Instacart, transit companies, restaurants, sanitation companies, farms, and food processing plants. In fact, between March and early July 2020, there were more than 800 wildcat strikes, varying in size and duration, across the United States.[130]

For Yates and many other commentators, the protests staged in support of vulnerable members of the working class—the meatpackers and bus drivers, the nurses and caregivers, the farm laborers and sanitation workers—offered hope for charting a path toward a society that promotes the flourishing, rather than sacrificing, of life. This hope, however, was only dimly perceived until the state-supported premature death of an alienated Black man.

4

Whose Lives Matter?

He was known to many of his friends as Big Floyd. Born on October 14, 1973, in Fayetteville, North Carolina, George Floyd grew up in public-housing projects of the Third Ward, an impoverished Houston neighborhood called the Bricks. In high school, Floyd excelled in sports. He received a basketball scholarship from South Florida Community College and became the first of his siblings to attend college. He later transferred to Texas A&M University's Kingsville campus, but never earned his degree. A series of bad decisions plunged Floyd into a dark period of his life. He was arrested multiple times and, beginning in 2004, Floyd served ten months in jail for a $10 drug deal. Four years later, Floyd pleaded guilty to aggravated robbery with a deadly weapon. For this, he served an additional four years in prison.[1]

At forty years old, Floyd's once promising life appeared all too predictable: another Black man on the brutal carousel of America's carceral system. But Floyd wanted to follow a different path: he wanted to help others, and to help others learn from his experience, of his struggle with drugs and depression and violence. As Patrick Ngwolo, a lawyer and pastor of Resurrection Houston, describes Floyd, his story was one of redemption.[2] Released in 2013, Floyd committed his life to church and to the uplifting of other men broken down by drugs, poverty, and violence. Floyd acknowledged the mistakes he made, the poor decisions. In a video he posted on social media aimed at convincing young people to put down their guns, he explained: "I got my shortcomings and my flaws. I ain't better than nobody else."[3] But Floyd also acknowledged the lack of opportunities available for Black men such as himself. And through his selfless dedication to others, Floyd found meaning in life. Moving between Houston and Minneapolis, Floyd immersed himself in a Christian program that provided drug rehabilitation and job placement services for men like himself.

Sometime in April 2020 Floyd contracted Covid-19; while he recovered physically, the economic costs were difficult. Like so many other people throughout the United States, Floyd found himself unemployed and struggling to survive.

On May 25, 2020, Floyd bought a pack of cigarettes at Cup Foods, a small grocery store in Minneapolis. According to the store owner, Mike Abumayyaleh, Floyd was a regular and never caused any problems. However, on this day, Abumayyaleh wasn't at work and the store employee did not recognize Floyd. During the transaction, the employee suspected Floyd was using a counterfeit $20 bill and, following protocol, called the police. Shortly thereafter, two police officers arrived. Floyd was sitting with two other men in a car parked nearby.[4]

The two officers approached Floyd and ordered him to show his hands. For reasons unclear, one of the officers, Thomas Lane, had his weapon drawn. Floyd, unsure why he was being detained and fearful of being killed, didn't move. The officers then forcibly removed Floyd from the car and handcuffed him. Now, secured in custody, Floyd apologized repeatedly and asked why he was being arrested. The officers informed him he was suspected of passing counterfeit bills. It was then, as the officers attempted to place Floyd in the police car, that the struggle ensued. Floyd claimed that he was claustrophobic. Other officers arrived, including Derek Chauvin, who pulled Floyd—still handcuffed—to the ground, pinning him on his stomach. For nine minutes and twenty-nine seconds, Chauvin kneeled on Floyd's neck. And more than twenty times, Floyd cried out that he couldn't breathe. Slowly suffocating, Floyd pleaded; he begged; he called out to his dead mother. All the while, Chauvin—assisted by three other officers—kept the pressure on Floyd's neck. Floyd struggles to say, "You're going to kill me." Chauvin replies: "Then stop talking, stop yelling. It takes a heck of a lot of oxygen to talk." Floyd says again, "Can't believe this, man. Mom, love you. Love you. Tell my kids I love them. I'm dead."[5]

In the aftermath of the police killing of George Floyd, demonstrations sprang up in Minneapolis and numerous cities across the country.[6] According to data provided by the Armed Conflict Location & Event Data Project (ACLED), between May 26 and August 22, 2020, an estimated 7,750 demonstrations in more than 2,400 sites in all 50 states arose in peaceful outpourings of grief and anger.[7] In total, more than 26 million people participated in protests throughout the United States, standing side-by-side in solidarity for justice. It is significant, also, that these protests occurred during a period of *marginal* labor revival.[8] Both 2018 and 2019, for example, witnessed a small and significant uptick in major strikes. Thus, whereas in 2017 the United States experienced only seven major strikes—the second lowest number of such occurrences since records were first kept in 1947—in 2018 there were twenty such strikes and in 2019 there were twenty-five. Remarkably, there were major strikes by public school teachers, health-care providers, and social assistance workers, such as those providing child care and home health assistance, and these were held in many "unexpected" locations, such as Arizona, Oklahoma, West Virginia, Kentucky, and North Carolina.[9] Certainly, as Michael Yates explains, these numbers are a far cry from the heyday of labor activity. Between 1947 and 1982, by way of illustration, the number of major strikes per year never fell below 145, with a high of 470 strikes registered just in 1952.[10] Yates's point remains valid, however: the taking to the streets of workers across the country is not inconsequential. Tellingly, this is the face of the working class in the twenty-first-century United States. As Peter Hudis writes, the protests did not detract from the class struggle but instead enhanced it, by bringing into view the deadly ramifications of life under capitalism. Indeed, Hudis concludes, that is why so many people from diverse backgrounds joined the protests, including working-class whites.[11]

The protests that emanated from the brutal killing of Floyd resonated also with broader social justice movements beyond the United States. The protests surrounding the violent death of Floyd must be understood in the centuries-long and brutal history of white supremacy and racial capitalism, a *global* history in which the lives of Blacks and so many other people of color have—in the words of Martha Biondi—become characterized by a social condition of disposability.[12] Indeed, reflective of the political economic pandemic known as capitalism, hundreds of thousands of people engaged in solidarity protests around the world.[13] Spanning six continents, protests erupted in over fifty countries and territories. In Chile, for example, *La Primera Línea,* a collective of people dedicated to challenging police violence in that country, issued an open letter in solidarity against police violence and white supremacy. "We are a group of friends," the letter affirms, "writing to all of you in the US about our experience of what such a revolt can look like as it stretches on for months."[14] The letter continues: "When the governments declare [a] state of emergency and call on the military and citizens alike in an attempt to force a return to normalcy . . . [they] attempt to portray a world of clear divisions—between peaceful protestors and criminal delinquents, between normalcy and crisis, between human rights and national security, between good cops and bad apples."[15] Similarly, in Kurdistan, the Kurdistan Women's Communities (KJK) released a detailed statement on the murder of Floyd and expressed solidarity in the face of racism and nationalism.[16] Drawing parallels with ongoing violence directed toward Kurdish communities, the statement reads, in part:

> We unequivocally condemn this blatant racially motivated violence perpetrated by the state and express our deepest condolences to the family and friends of George. This crime is neither the first nor, unfortunately, will be the last of its kind. . . . Not a day passes when Kurdish people are not attacked and murdered for simply being Kurdish. Everywhere, particular communities are declared as enemies and attacked. We must not dismiss these kinds of atrocities as individual acts. We have to look at them in the overall context of social conditions. Nationalism and racism must be challenged critically and fought effectively in the context of the nation-state and capitalism realities. Racism and nationalism are an extremely efficient ideological instrument of state, power and domination systems.

These two statements, and dozens more, issued separately but in solidarity across the continents, exemplify the connections made by those who dare to say "enough" to ongoing injustices wrought by racial capitalism on a global scale. The KJK, for example, affirm that "the main issues of our time are, climate catastrophe, environmental destruction, war, poverty, flight displacement, pandemics and many more have their origin in power and domination."[17]

The brief but meaningful life of Floyd was conditioned by a lifetime of systemic racism. It is notable that not only disenfranchised and precarious Black people in the United States, such as George Floyd, but marginalized peoples the world over are portrayed especially within far-right, conservative quarters as *disposable* and, by implication, undeserving of care. On this point, Blacks are rarely members of the *working class* but instead inhabit the ranks of the *underclass.* As such, Black men such as Floyd are almost invariably portrayed as irresponsible, work-shy freeloaders and/or violent thugs and criminals who refuse to abide by the law. Rarely are Black men such as Floyd portrayed sympathetically, as alienated subjects struggling against racism and class exploitation, struggling to achieve and to provide a meaningful life for their families in a precarious economy.

To this end, the objectives of this penultimate chapter are twofold. First, I excavate the ideological construction of the *white* alienated subject within the context of white supremacy and racial capitalism.[18] This is a necessary step, for notions of the working class "go to the heart of our conception of the socialist idea."[19] By extension, the emancipatory potential of the *alienated* working class remains central to the transformation of capitalism into something else, something more meaningful, that is, something that facilitates those actions which advance and do not inhibit the life and well-being of others. And yet, alienation is frequently discussed *in the abstract,* as a condition of particular social conditions unique to the capitalist mode of production. On this point, the scholarship on alienation frequently fails to adequately engage with racism, or does so only as an addendum. For example, we speak of alienation but, in the context of Black workers, we qualify Black alienation. Alienation in and of itself remains marked by an uncritical and unchallenged whiteness and, subsequently, "acts as the unseen, normative category against which differently racialized groups are ordered and valued."[20] Simply put, an uncritical deployment of alienation operates as a fundamentally *white* concept.[21]

In practice, the *white* alienated subject (as an abstract figure) is called upon to do some heavy lifting for the maintenance of white supremacy. Here, as the argument goes, economic hardships experienced by members of the *white* working class emerge from a constellation of factors tied directly to the legislation and institutionalization of "reverse racism," that is, practices such as affirmative action and liberal immigration policies. In actuality, the conservative agenda does not redress the economic challenges of the working class, white or otherwise, but instead privileges the exceptionally wealthy. However, symbolically, the concern expressed by these commentators over the plight of the mythical "blue-collar" worker who desires nothing other than to receive a fair wage for a fair day's work belies a countermovement enacted to push back political, economic, and social gains achieved by the broader civil rights movement. Deliberately ignored by these commentators is the heterogeneity of the working class and especially the existence of Black and Brown exploited and alienated subjects.

To this end, the racial formation of the *white* alienated subject must be understood in a dialectic relationship to its Other, for the alienated white worker has always been framed and has derived meaning from its racialized position in society—for no matter how bad life may be for the alienated white subject, it was always valued above that of the nonwhite.[22]

This brings us to the second objective of this chapter, that is, to consider the emancipatory potential of the Black Lives Matter movement as a challenge to the idolatry of the *white* alienated subject.[23] My intention here is not to provide a chronology of the movement; for this, I defer to the insightful accounts provided by Barbara Ransby and Keeanga-Yamahtta Taylor, among others. Rather, I consider the Black Lives Movement—and the racist All Lives Matter countercampaign—as paradigmatic of the wider struggle for social justice and emancipation under conditions of neoliberal racism. Accordingly, I forward the argument that the Black Lives Matter movement illustrates the promise and potential of emancipatory struggles centered on the belief that meaningful life is possible, but this requires a collective engagement with the alienating structures and social relations of oppression that foster indifference, intolerance, and capacity to hurt.

Neoliberal Racism in the United States

Neoliberalism, broadly understood, refers to a set of political-economic ideas and practices that emerged in the late 1970s with the intent to restore and consolidate elite class power.[24] As David Harvey explains, neoliberalism "is in the first instance a theory of political economic practices that proposes that human well-being can best be advanced by liberating individual entrepreneurial freedoms and skills within an institutional framework characterized by strong private property rights, free markets, and free trade."[25] Notably, neoliberalism entailed also shifting the balance of power and interests within the bourgeoisie from production activities to institutions of finance capital. In this way, financial power could be used to discipline working-class movements.[26] Effectively, neoliberalism constitutes an explicit attack on the working poor through the dismantling of welfare programs, job-protection legislation, trade unionism, and worker collective action.[27]

The consequences have been shocking. In 1968, the top-earning 20 percent of households accounted for 43 percent of the country's income, while those in the lower four income quintiles accounted for 56 percent. In 2018, however, households in the top fifth of earners brought in 52 percent of all income, more than the lower four-fifths combined. And among the top 5 percent of households—that is, those with incomes of around $250,000—their share of all income rose from 16 percent in 1968 to 23 percent in 2018.[28] Crucially, there is also a value gap between whites and Blacks in the

United States. In 2020, for example, the median net worth of white households ($170,000) was about 10 times the median worth of Black households ($17,600). In addition, the median income for Black households ($41,000) was about 60 percent less than that of whites ($71,000); the poverty rate for Blacks (21 percent) was more than double that of whites (8 percent); and Black workers were 60 percent less likely than whites to have health insurance.[29]

Bluntly, neoliberalism at its core is a class-based project engendered to redistribute wealth from lower classes to economic elites.[30] And to this end, neoliberalism has been grievously successful. Indeed, since 1975, an estimated *$50 trillion* have been redistributed upwards. As Nick Hanauer and David Rolf explain, the top 1 percent's share of total taxable income has more than doubled, from 9 percent in 1975, to 22 percent in 2018, while the bottom 90 percent have seen their income share fall, from 67 percent to 50 percent; this represents a direct transfer of income from the vast majority of working Americans to a handful at the very top.[31]

That said, neoliberalism is not monolithic and, indeed, one of neoliberalism's enduring features is that it can be applied selectively and tailored to fit specific sociospatial conditions.[32] To that end, I heed the call of David Roberts and Minelle Mahtani who argue that current conceptualizations of neoliberalism require more precise articulations that move beyond simply citing the eruptions of, for example, race/racism, that result from neoliberal practice, toward actually shaking the racist foundations that saturate neoliberalism.[33] In other words, racism is neither epiphenomenal nor ancillary to neoliberalism but instead foundational. This holds tremendous importance for our subsequent interrogation of the white alienated subject, if only because members of the so-called white working class often vote against their own economic interests. Why is this?

To begin, we need to acknowledge that subjects in a purely capitalist society must be capable of participating in at least some components of capitalist market, since survival depends on being able to buy at least the basic necessities.[34] In the United States, for instance, to be jobless is effectively a death sentence, for without a job the likelihood of obtaining adequate housing and health care is nearly impossible. Indeed, even with a job—given the paltry minimum wages paid to workers in this country—one's vulnerability to premature death remains higher than that of workers in other so-called advanced economies. Adam Shah, for example, writes, "The long-term systemic reason that working people are willing to accept jobs that cannot provide enough income to cover basic needs is because they are unable to organize and demand higher wages." He explains: "Unionization is clearly tied to higher and more equal wages. The real disincentive working people face is that if they try to assert their right to collective bargaining, they often are quickly fired even though such firing is technically illegal."[35] And the consequences of losing one's job—for simply demanding better wages and working conditions—are devastating: loss of income, loss of housing, loss of health insurance, and food insecurity.[36] However, as the aforementioned economic indicators suggest, white workers, while still grossly exploited, are relatively better off than most Black people and other minority populations. White workers, effectively, stand to benefit under the present system of racial capitalism and, for reasons discussed later, actually tend to vote against their class interests. In fact, that there is no sustained class struggle in the United States is not happenstance.[37] As Jeffrey Reiman and Paul Leighton explain, "For the vast majority, the many millions struggling hard to satisfy basic needs, to acquiesce to the vast wealth of a small minority, it is necessary that the majority come to believe that these disparities are justified, that the present order is the best that human beings can accomplish, and that they are not being exploited by the have-plenties. In other words, the system requires an effective ideology to fool enough of the people enough of the time."[38] That ideology is white supremacy.[39]

Although often associated with hood-wearing members of the Ku Klux Klan or skinheads affiliated with neo-Nazi hate groups, white supremacy—especially among critical race scholars—has a more expansive meaning. For Frances Lee Ansley, for example, white supremacy refers "to a political, economic, and cultural system in which whites overwhelmingly control power and material resources, conscious and unconscious ideas of white superiority and entitlement are widespread, and relations of white dominance and non-white subordination are daily re-enacted across a broad array of institutions and social settings."[40] To this end, white supremacy serves several interrelated functions, paramount of which is the fostering of white privilege. Scholars have long documented the salience of white privilege in U.S. society. As Laura Pulido describes, "In the US in the 1990s, the concept of white privilege emerged as a popular way to explain how white people benefitted simply from being white."[41] Peggy McIntosh, for example, likened white privilege to an "invisible package of unearned assets" that white people can utilize every day, often without even being aware of their privilege.[42] Here, whites derive material—and emotional—benefits from the simple fact that they are defined as white.

The discussion from chapter 3 bears repeating from a broader perspective than Trump's campaign rhetoric. An early and important conception of white privilege is W. E. B. Du Bois's articulation of what he termed the "psychological wages" of whiteness. Writing in the 1930s, Du Bois explained that although white workers historically received low wages, they "were compensated in part by a sort of public and psychological wage."[43] Du Bois elaborates: "They were given public deference and titles of courtesy because they were white. They were admitted freely with all classes of white people to public functions, public parks, and the best schools."[44] In short, white workers were offered the opportunity to cash in on their privilege of simply being white in a society founded upon racial prejudice, discrimination, and violence. This explains, in large part, why even marginalized and impoverished white people continually vote against their economic self-interests and support elite class rule, for exploited and alienated white workers stand to benefit in a racist, capitalist society solely because of their whiteness. As Du Bois well understood,

> the plight of the white working class throughout the world today is directly traceable to Negro slavery in America, on which modern commerce and industry was founded, and which persisted to threaten free labor until it was partially overthrown in 1863. The resulting color caste founded and retained by capitalism was adopted, forwarded and approved by white labor, and resulted in subordination of colored labor to white profits the world over. Thus the majority of the world's laborers, by the insistence of white labor, became the basis of a system of industry which ruined democracy.[45]

Consequently, from this vantage point, white privilege persists, in part, because it operates through collective *inaction,* that is, a society structured around racial domination need only be unopposed to continue. In other words, a shared indifference among a majority of white people is enough to maintain the racist status quo. Martin Luther King Jr. was well aware of this problem. In a speech delivered at the National Cathedral, Washington, D.C., on March 31, 1968, King declared: "And it may well be that we will have to repent in this generation. Not merely for the vitriolic words and the violent actions of the bad people, but for the appalling silence and indifference of the good people who sit around and say, 'Wait on time.'"[46] King was well aware of the power of indifference, that is, of the moral blindness afflicting so many white (and nonwhite) people. One does not have to commit overtly racist acts or pledge membership to a white nationalist group to allow racism to flourish; one needs only to stand in silence.

However, while white privilege remains an important analytic frame to analyze taken-for-granted benefits and protections afforded to whites, the concept of privilege emphasizes the social condition of whiteness, rather than the institutions, practices, and processes that produce this condition in the first place.[47] Accordingly, critical scholars increasingly emphasize white supremacy to capture the reality that racism operates as a *process* that is constantly reconfigured through ongoing struggle.[48] As Zeus Leonardo writes, "In order for white racial hegemony to saturate everyday life, it has to be secured by a process of domination, or those acts, decisions, and policies that white subjects perpetuate on people of color."[49] As such, "white supremacy more precisely describes and locates white racial domination by underscoring the material production and violence of racial structures and the hegemony of whiteness in settler societies."[50] It is for this reason that Ruth Wilson Gilmore powerfully defines racism as "the state-sanctioned or extralegal production and exploitation of group-differentiated vulnerability to premature death."[51]

Crucially, the shifting terrain of the political economy of the United States, namely, the active forwarding of neoliberalism, has been made possible by a deliberate transformation of race and racism. Pulido explains that "in order for neoliberalism to be considered legitimate, the social formation must not be seen as racist."[52] Simply put, the neoliberal order is predicated on the whitewashed liberal subject, the belief that all workers enter the market on a level playing field, and that racist institutions have been relegated to the past. Consequently, observed inequalities—such as the racial wealth gap—are dismissed as the unfortunate outcome of bad decisions by irresponsible people, who just *happen* to be disproportionately nonwhite. As such, Pulido concludes, "there is a refusal to grapple with structural racism to personal prejudice and racial hostility."[53] This is manifest in the widespread belief among many whites that the United States has entered into an era of postracism.

Currently, in the United States, neoliberal racism is marked, first and foremost, by an active suppression of race as a legitimate topic or term of public discourse and public policy.[54] Programs designed to remedy racism, such as affirmative action and desegregation, consequently are themselves the objects of critique, drawing cries of "reverse racism."[55] Likewise, the mass demonstrations against police violence and the affirmation that Black Lives Matter are distorted and reconfigured as part of a nefarious antiwhite agenda promoted by ungrateful Black people and traitorous liberal whites. How this sordid state of affairs has come into existence—and how the figure of the *white* alienated subject factors into the demand that Black Lives Matter—occupies the remainder of this chapter.

Nixon and the Southern Strategy

From the 1940s onward, Keynesian economics guided the U.S. economy and delivered high rates of economic growth. In the aftermath of the Great Depression and the Second World War, the U.S. government assumed a more active and interventionist role in the U.S. economy. Policymakers accepted that the federal government "should focus on full employment, economic growth, and the welfare of its citizens; and that state power should be freely deployed, alongside of or, if necessary, intervening in or even substituting for market processes to achieve these ends."[56] All that was needed for the system to work, Chris Harman explains, was for the government to disregard outdated free market orthodoxies and to intervene in economic life to raise the level of spending on investment and consumption.[57] As a result, a suite of Keynesian regulatory, fiscal, and monetary policies were initiated, thus marking a class compromise between capital and labor, as the government established standards for the social wage by constructing a variety of health, education, and welfare systems.[58]

During these years, investment accelerated, real incomes rose, something like full employment was made possible, and working-class institutions, such as labor unions and left-leaning political parties, exerted a very real influence on policies that led to an expansion of what was called the welfare state of pension, social, and health provisions.[59] Notably, these extended into the public sphere and effected race relations in significant ways. As Joshua Inwood explains, the federal government, for the first time since the end of the Civil War, began to incorporate the labor and political aspirations of Black Americans more fully into the political life of the nation.[60] Consequently, for a brief period in U.S. history overt white supremacy gave way to an ideology of racial liberalism whereupon the federal government shifted from largely ignoring the plight of Black citizens to selectively working to secure basic social and civil rights.[61]

With the passage of a series of civil rights bills in the late 1950s and early 1960s—coupled with the momentous 1954 Supreme Court ruling in *Brown v. Board of Education*—key artifacts of white supremacy were challenged, notably efforts to promote integration in housing and education. However, as Rod Bush explains, economic advances for Blacks were slow and uneven. He explains that economic improvement "accrued only to those Blacks who were able to enter middle-class occupations and thus take advantage of the 'integration' and the liberal employment practices that the turbulence of that era produced. For the lower stratum of the Black population the main benefit was liberal welfare practices, which enabled them to survive despite widespread unemployment and underemployment."[62]

The shift to *racial liberalism*, however minimal in actual, material effect, did result in a sea change in societal attitudes. On the one hand, the rhetoric of political and economic rights raised Black people's expectations while, on the other hand, these same conditions heightened white people's uncertainties regarding their privileged position in society.[63] Wedded to a belief that success or failure is reducible to a zero-sum game, many whites in particular feared that any advance for Blacks would entail also a setback for the white race. In addition, the struggle over civil rights fractured the platform of the national Democratic Party. As Kevern Verney explains, the Northern wing of the party, sensitive to the voting power of growing inner-city Black populations, argued for a more liberal stance on civil rights issues; in contrast, Southern Democrats were strongly opposed to any changes in the status quo. Consequently, this division circumscribed the political agenda of Democratic leaders and shaped the contours of the civil rights movement.

Between 1963 and 1968, the administrations of John F. Kennedy and Lyndon B. Johnson had responded to the Black struggle for equality by pushing important civil rights legislation: the Civil Rights Act of 1964, the Voting Rights Act of 1965, the Twenty-fourth Amendment abolishing the poll tax, and the Open Housing Bill of 1968.[64] In response, however, many white voters—long accustomed to the psychological wages of whiteness and the advantages of white privilege—expressed intolerance and anger toward these legislative actions. As Alexander explains, "Poor and working class whites had their world rocked by the Civil Rights Movement. White elites could send their kids to private schools and give them all of the advantages wealth has to offer. But poor and working class whites were faced with social demotion. It was their kids who might be bused across town, and forced to compete for the first time with a new group of people they had long believed to be inferior for decent jobs and educational opportunities."[65] Indeed, Republican strategists gambled that a perceived growing racial resentment among Democratic voters could be channeled to their political advantage.[66] It was a gamble that paid off.

In the lead-up to the 1968 presidential election, Richard Nixon and his staff devised a racially divisive campaign strategy, known as the "Southern Strategy," to entice poor and working-class whites to switch political loyalties to the Republican Party.[67] Kevin Phillips's well-known political manifesto *The Emerging Republican Majority* (1969) served as a basic point of departure.[68] According to Phillips, the Southern white Democrats had become so angered and alienated by the Democratic Party's support for civil rights reforms, such as desegregation and busing, that those voters could be easily persuaded to switch parties if their racial resentments could be maintained."[69] Of the strategy, Phillips explained: "From now on, the Republicans are never going to get more than 10 to 20 percent of the Negro vote and they don't need any more than that. . . . [But] Republicans would be shortsighted if they weakened enforcement of the Voting Rights Act. The more Negroes who register as Democrats in the South, the sooner the Negrophobe whites will quit the Democrats and become Republicans. That's where the votes are."[70] John Ehrlichman, special counsel to Nixon, was equally blunt, stating unequivocally: "We'll go after the racists."[71]

The Southern Strategy relied on the use of coded language to appeal to, and thus persuade, white voters to support the Republican agenda. More precisely, potent political symbolism was required that played upon cultural conservatism while sidestepping the more volatile issues of employment or wages. Lee Atwater, a Republican political consultant and strategist, explained in an infamous 1981 interview the basis of the Southern Strategy:

> The key is how you handle the race thing. In other words, you start out, you start out in 1954 by saying "nigger, nigger, nigger," [but] by 1968 you can't say nigger, that hurts you, backfires, so you say stuff like "forced bussing," "states rights," and all that stuff. At this point, you're getting so abstract now, you're talking about cutting taxes, by this time you're talking about all these economic things, and the by-product of them is, blacks get hurt worse than whites. What I am saying is, that if it is getting this abstract, and that coded, then

> we're doing away with the racial problem, because obviously sitting around saying, we want to cut taxes, is much more abstract than even the bussing thing, and a hell of a lot more abstract than "nigger, nigger."[72]

In key respects, the Southern Strategy was at its core a blue-collar strategy with an implicit nod to narratives of white alienation. On this point, "it was neither the entire working class nor its material grievances on which the administration would focus; rather, it was the 'feeling of being forgotten' among white male workers that Nixon and his advisors would seek to tap."[73] With the promotion of the Southern Strategy, Nixon recast the ways in which (white) workers appeared in American politics. More precisely, Nixon helped push the concept of worker out of the realm of production, with obvious implications for labor's inability to cultivate a collective proletarian consciousness.[74] In doing so, Nixon effectively transformed the public identity of the working class "from economics to culture, from workplace and community to national pride."[75] No longer confined metaphorically to the spaces of the factory, the (white) alienated subject coalesced to form a group-in-fusion, united in their opposition toward a supposed reverse racism championed by liberals. In the process, Nixon simultaneously marginalized the strength of labor as a political force and greatly foreclosed even further the possibility of solidarity among Black and white workers.

Nixon's approach to the white working class was always more ideal than material, that is, by "making workers' economic interests secondary to an appeal to their allegedly superior moral backbone and patriotic rectitude."[76] As Jefferson Cowie explains, Nixon sought to mobilize their whiteness and their machismo in the face of societal unrest while neglecting ways to improve conditions for the working class.[77] Notably, one of Nixon's fundamental beliefs had always been that the appearance of action was as important, if not more important, than the reality of action.[78] To this end, Nixon was highly adept and skillful in the politics of language. As Murray Edelman explains, "If political language both excites and mollifies fears, language is an integral facet of the political scene: not simply an instrument for describing events but itself a part of events, shaping their meaning and helping to shape the political roles officials and the general public play."[79]

An additional component of Phillips's argument—and thus to the Southern Strategy—was to look beyond the Southern white voter, alienated by the Democrats' commitment to racial equality, and to entice the support of the Northern alienated industrial worker. The problem, Phillips anticipated, "was that working-class voters feared that a Republican administration would do away with popular New Deal programs—from social security to collective bargaining. If Nixon could dispel the notion that his party and his presidency were antiworker, cleverly manipulate the race issue, and peg the label of 'elitism' on liberals, it followed that he could build a post–New Deal coalition that transcended the Southern Strategy. By co-opting the northern blue-collar worker, the Southern Strategy, in essence, would become a national strategy."[80] The genius of the strategy was that "policy and rhetoric would be formulated that did not require federal expenditures or even wage increases—the politics of recognition and status would be enough."[81]

To this end, the Republican Party appealed to the racism of alienated working-class whites, a group long accustomed to the durability of their privileged status and security, through an aggressive and complimentary law and order campaign. Always careful to publicly avoid overtly racist terminology, Nixon declared a "War on Crime," a calculated move that simultaneously negated the economic focus of Johnson's previous "War on Poverty" and underscored the apparent social threat to (white) Americans and their way of life. As such, hand-in-hand with the idolization of the *white* worker was the demonization of all Blacks. Building on centuries of racist caricatures, the Southern Strategy introduced a litany of figures discursively birthed to instill fear, intolerance, and animosity among white voters.

The conservative architects of the Southern Strategy were exceptionally prescient in their evaluation of the (white) American psyche. Kevin Phillips, in particular, understood that the strategy "could point the way toward long-term political realignment and the building of a new Republican majority, if Republicans continued to campaign primarily on the basis of racial issues, using coded antiblack rhetoric."[82] And from Nixon onward, Republican office-holders and candidates have largely remained faithful to the skeletal features of the Southern Strategy: racial polarization, law and order platforms, and the idolization of the white alienated subject. Indeed, this potent mixture would help usher a broader neoliberal agenda designed to crush labor and advance the interests of capital on a scale unimaginable.

By the end of the 1960s, signs of a serious economic crisis of capital accumulation were everywhere apparent.[83] The halcyon days of postwar prosperity were over. Profitability in the major economies began to fall and deep recessions in the 1970s jeopardized the U.S. economy. Capital values were destroyed as old plants in old industries were closed; companies went bankrupt; and mass unemployment reduced labor costs and weakened the ability of trade unions to block reductions in wages and working conditions.[84] In the process, as Cowie and Boehm summarize, "Family income was falling for the first time since the Depression, stagflation unhinged the Keynesian success formula, global manufacturing and competition undermined U.S. economic hegemony, deindustrialization and de-unionization shook the bedrock of working-class success, and a tax system losing its progressive structure justified a revolt against public spending. These factors led to a profound sense of insecurity as the economic structure of blue-collar communities began to crumble."[85]

Many middle- and upper-income white families did experience economic retrenchment; however, that these hardships occurred in the midst of political (but not necessarily economic) gains achieved by African Americans, women, and other minority groups did not go unnoticed. Indeed, for many white families, their worsening economic position was seemingly matched by their declining racial position, that is, their economic status was undermined precisely as their white-privileged and dominant position in the racial pecking order was challenged.[86] In reality, of course, *all* members of the working class were hurting. However, white workers stood to lose not only real income but also the equally valuable psychological wages of whiteness promised by a system of racial capitalism.

Reagan, Racism, and the Neoliberal Turn

As a potential antidote to threats to the capitalist social order, Harvey writes, neoliberalism had long been lurking in the wings of public policy.[87] Since the high-water mark of the antipoverty programs associated with Johnson's Great Society in the 1960s, for example, conservative policy makers had launched attacks on the existence of the economic safety net as a whole.[88] Strongly opposed to Keynesian state interventionist policies, proponents of neoliberalism resented a progressive tax system that financed the government's social contract with the middle and working classes—and the poor—in terms of providing a welfare state set of social programs that gave them both a safety net and educational and other opportunities for social advancement.[89]

The first tentative steps toward a neoliberal agenda did not go unchallenged. As Harvey describes, a wave of labor militancy swept through the advanced capitalist world during the late 1970s and early 1980s, as working-class movements sought to preserve the gains they had won in early decades.[90] In the United States, for example, the biggest strike wave in postwar history rocked the country between 1968 and 1974, including a series of wildcat strikes, democratization and reform movements within the unions, revolts against automation, and new organizing efforts that frequently built upon a promising base of women, minorities, and students.[91]

In response, the Reagan administration drew upon Nixon's playbook and initiated a revanchist political and economic campaign informed by the Southern Strategy. On the one hand, the Republican Party sought an alliance with the Christian Right and, on the other hand, appealed to the cultural nationalism of the white working class.[92] As Harvey explains, this political base, collectively "could be mobilized through the positives of religion and cultural nationalism and negatively through coded, if not blatant, racism, homophobia, and anti-feminism."[93] Hence, the Republican Party intensified the public perception that government-supported social programs enacted by the Democrats unfairly benefited Black people and other minorities and thus kept white voters' anger directed away from Republican federal policy and toward a palpable intolerance of people of color. Seeking to crush labor's organizations and institutions, Reagan disconnected even further Nixon's brand of white, blue-collar identity politics from organized labor's economic demands.[94] Indeed, as Alexander writes, "the late 1960s and early 1970s marked the dramatic erosion in the belief among working-class whites that the condition of the poor, or those who fail to prosper, was the result of a faulty economic system that needed to be challenged."[95] Gorged on a diet of individualism, white privilege, and anti-Black rhetoric, there could be no proletarian-led revolution among white workers.

Effectively, neoliberalists encouraged the white alienated subject to think of itself as an entrepreneurial subject, that is, a subject capable of contributing to the restoration of the United States in the face of frightening social and economic change.[96] Years later, President Donald Trump would echo this strategy, calling upon his supporters to "Make America Great Again" (MAGA). Under Reagan, though, the entrepreneurial subject symbolized an ideal of self-mastery but also embodied the notion of sacrifice of self on behalf of duty, honor, and integrity.[97] To this end, the alienated-cum-entrepreneurial subject exemplified the patriotism, nationalism, and sense of loyalty demanded of the Republican party, that is, vital traits necessary to stem the onslaught of advances made by women, minorities, gays and lesbians, or any other group that didn't conform to their vision of America.

During this period, conservatives gave lip service to the goal of racial equality but actively resisted—and scaled back—desegregation, busing, and civil rights enforcement.[98] In addition, while also paying lip service to the white alienated subject, proponents of the neoliberal agenda effectively dismantled those structures and institutions that provided a modicum of stability and security to the working class as a whole. This was accomplished through a deliberate strategy of coded language and the promotion of a so-called color-blind legislative agenda. Indeed, as Goldfield explains, "Reagan became the respectable proponent of racist populism, all the while claiming that he was merely for fairness, opposing granting of special privileges to women and racial minorities, be it in hiring, college admission, busing, or welfare."[99]

Wielded by conservative neoliberals, modalities of difference such as race do not predetermine one's success, as each individual is ostensibly evaluated solely in terms of his or her economic contribution to society.[100] The neoliberal subject, albeit alienated, is one who takes personal responsibility for its actions, a subject who prioritizes self-sufficiency and eschews governmental assistance. More precisely, the *white* neoliberal subject believes in the infallibility of a color-blind meritocracy; that those who work hard will be rewarded and those who shun their responsibilities will suffer the economic consequences. To this end, conservative (and a growing number of liberal) politicians, pundits, and media outlets manufactured and subsequently idolized the vaunted lunch-box-toting, blue-collar white factory worker as the personification of American exceptionalism: that industrious, square-jawed member of the working class who comes to work every day to provide for his wife and children in the face of a crumbling economy wrought by misguided race- and gender-based policies. If the figure of the industrious white worker was cast in the cauldron of genocide and slavery, its modern features of fortitude and patriotism were polished in the crucibles of neoliberalism.

And the iconography of the white alienated subject was pervasive. Blue-collar themes permeated popular culture, in both film and song, as the neoliberal agenda surged forward. And while the reality of the working class was multiracial, the *idea* of the working class in the popular idiom was, by the 1980s, firmly entrenched as a repository for patriarchy and racism.[101] Indeed, as Jefferson Cowie and Lauren Boehm explain, the idea of the "'working class'—a term that had too long been defined as white and male in popular discourse despite the much more complex reality—had evolved into a label for a hardened form of white, male identity politics. The working class became, in essence, negatively defined: an 'other' dwelling outside of the new politics built by and upon minorities, women, youth, and sexuality."[102] As Alexander concludes, Republicans "repeatedly raised the issue of welfare, subtly framing it as a contest between hard-working, blue-collar whites and poor blacks who refused to work."

Out of the maelstrom of Reagan's revised and revanchist Southern Strategy emerged alongside the figure of the downtrodden but deserving white worker a motley assortment of other racially coded Black figures, notably the "welfare queen" and the "deadbeat dad."[103] Collectively, these figures became as crucial to the neoliberal agenda as the mythology and idolization of the hard-working white American. The welfare queen, for example, was born during Reagan's 1976 presidential campaign. In February of that year, Ann Cammett explains, Reagan called attention to a woman in Chicago who seemed to embody the failings of federal assistance programs. Reagan fumed:

> She has 80 names, 30 addresses, 12 Social Security cards and is collecting veterans' benefits on four non-existing deceased husbands. And she's collecting Social Security on her cards. She's got Medicaid, getting food stamps, and she is collecting welfare under each of her names. Her tax-free cash income alone is over $150,000.[104]

Throughout his campaign and into his presidency, Reagan embellished the narrative of the welfare queen. And although ridden with inaccuracies, "Reagan's anecdotal 'welfare queen' was solidified as the public's stereotype of poor Black mothers."[105] As Cammett concludes, Reagan's tale of the welfare queen resonated with many white Americans who were receptive to the belief that the government was privileging nondeserving loafers over hardworking people like them; in short, the story confirmed many white Americans' common sense of outrage over the deterioration of *their* country.[106]

Conservative politicians recentered the white alienated subject into the core of U.S. politics and, in so doing, "flags, God, guns, heterosexuality, and whiteness had eclipsed the economic politics of labor rights, wages, unions, and working conditions as the focal points for enough of working-class identity to swing the balance of the nation."[107] Here, the importance of the figure of the (white) alienated subject becomes apparent, in that the hardworking *neoliberal* subject is transformed into the downtrodden, (white) alienated subject not because of exploitation inherent to capitalism but instead arising from the actions of irresponsible people of color and of unfair governmental policies that privilege minorities. According to this racial logic, every dollar siphoned off by undeserving (Black) welfare queens is a dollar lost to the more deserving members of the (white) working class. Thus, financial losses experienced by white workers were stoked by members of the Reagan administration to fuel a growing resentment among whites toward Blacks, Hispanics, and other minorities. Indeed, the neoliberal turn was made possible because of racial politics.[108] In turn, however, the racial politics of neoliberalism required the idolatry of a mythical (white) alienated subject who suffered *not* because of structural exploitation inherent to capitalism but because of the alleged delinquency of nonwhites.

In reality, neoliberal policies harmed both white and nonwhite workers; but the former tended to blame neither the (mostly) conservative politicians who advanced the neoliberal agenda nor the capitalists who benefited from the economic restructuring. Rather, white workers regularly blamed (nonwhite) immigrants and Black and Latinx people. Similarly, although the majority of public assistance recipients were white, welfare's association with Blacks in the public imagination drove policy around poverty issues as a whole.[109] Impoverished white workers—including those who benefit from social welfare programs—readily subscribed to the racial and racist coding of poverty. Poor whites were members of the deserving but downtrodden working class; poor nonwhites were nothing more than members of the cheating underclass. By claiming the status of a hard worker, Claudine Pied identifies, poor and working-class whites aligned themselves with the industrious American who faces tough times but picks him- or herself back up and keeps going.[110] Poor white workers in this way can position themselves as victims of deindustrialization and representatives of a national solution (hard work), rather than sources of culture of poverty.[111]

Reagan's highly racialized appeals, targeted to poor and working-class whites, were nearly always accompanied by promises to be tougher on crime and to enhance the federal government's role in combating crime.[112] The racially coded welfare queen, for example, served to criminalize Black mothers as habitually exploiting illegally the welfare program and other government-sponsored programs. To this end, welfare and crime were two pages of the same Republican playbook.

Drug-related crimes were in decline when, in 1982, Reagan initiated the nationwide and federally supported War on Drugs. However, as Alexander clarifies, "from the outset, the war had little to do with drug crime and much to do with racial politics."[113] She expounds: "The War on Drugs proved popular among key white voters, particularly whites who remained resentful of black progress, civil rights enforcement and affirmative action. . . . The War on Drugs, cloaked in race-neutral language, offered whites opposed to racial reform a unique opportunity to express their hostility towards blacks and black progress, without being exposed to the charge of racism."[114] Collectively, the coded images of welfare queens, deadbeat dads, and crack whores provided justification for the expansion of an aggressive law enforcement and the criminal justice system that disproportionately targeted poor people and minorities.[115]

The "habitat" of these racially coded figures was codified by neoliberalists in the racist "broken windows" thesis. Originating in the early 1980s, the broken windows thesis was (and is) part and parcel of the increased "tough on crime" stance long favored by conservative politicians, designed to solicit support among mostly white voters for a suite of right-wing initiatives. Writing in *The Atlantic Monthly,* two conservative pundits, James Wilson and George Kelling, sketched the outlines of a criminological theory that justified an aggressive policing practice.[116] Briefly, the thesis premises that neighborhoods that fail to fix broken windows display a lack of informal social control and thereby unwittingly invite the criminally minded into their midst. Accordingly, the presence of broken windows is symbolic of a degenerative environment that is the breeding ground for increased crime.[117] Tellingly, for Wilson and Kelling, the threat to the general public is embodied by so-called low-level offenders: panhandlers, drunks, addicts, rowdy teenagers, prostitutes, loiterers, and the mentally disturbed. Indeed, Wilson and Kelling concede that these are not necessarily violent people—nor have they necessarily committed a crime. However, and collectively, they constitute "disreputable or obstreperous or unpredictable people" and require a police response equal to that of felony offenders.

Ostensibly focused on the physical environment, the broken windows thesis is in the end about "bothersome" and "disorderly" human behavior.[118] As such, the thesis aligns readily with the moral conservatism and backlash against the myriad social justice movements of the preceding decades. For conservatives, the increased tolerance of divorce, abortion, homosexuality, drugs, sexual promiscuity—all seemingly promoted by the civil rights movements, the women's rights movement, and the gay liberation movement—foretold a catastrophic downfall of American society. Urban decline, as manifest by the presence of broken windows, was but the most visible evidence of societal breakdown. For conservatives, the impoverishment especially of the inner city—coded language for Black communities—stood in stark contrast with an idealized community, that is, a respectable, white, middle-class, nuclear family–oriented society.

The broken windows thesis effectively aligned with and underscored an "accumulated resentment and rage associated with middle-class frustration in the face of severe economic recession and governmental retraction."[119] It justified also a shift in law enforcement away from a historical emphasis on felony arrests and toward misdemeanor offenses that, according to the thesis, if left neglected would spiral into more significant problems.[120] As Bench Ansfield writes, "Through the vector of the broken window, infrastructural decay interlaced with social and racial degeneration, and the two lent meaning to each other. These images called to mind infrastructural failure, death, and dying, an affective repertoire that conjured fears of racial and national degeneration."[121]

The broken windows thesis supported also a new and aggressive policing practice known as *zero tolerance.* The term originated as a component of federal and state drug enforcement practices in the 1980s but, in the 1990s, expanded to "denote a sharp, severe, and highly punitive reaction to any form of behavior deemed illegal, malicious, or anti-social to the surrounding community, even those infractions considered to be relatively minor."[122] New York City served as the model for zero tolerance policing. Under the direction of Mayor Rudolph Giuliani, the police and other authorized entities were given extreme leeway in their attempt to deal forcefully with those people—street peddlers, panhandlers, prostitutes, squeegee cleaners, street artists—who (from the standpoint of conservatives) posed a threat to the quality of urban life.[123] Subsequently, as Katharyne Mitchell identifies, "the state-directed assault on New York's urban disorder between 1994 and 2001 was reflected in increased policing and anti-homeless laws, and also in higher stop-and-frisk incidents and arrest rates for misdemeanors such as unlicensed vending, panhandling, public drunkenness, and other petty crimes."[124] In turn, statistics on arrests and convictions fueled the discourse of Black (and other minority) criminality. Unlike their white counterparts, Black men and women were viewed not as struggling members of the alienated working class but instead as being naturally criminal and prone to violence. Unlike their white counterparts, Black men and women were undeserving of assistance, and their presence required a tough police response. No matter that governmental investigations, judicial findings, anecdotal accounts, and statements by law enforcement officials provided overwhelming evidence of the prevalence of profiling in the day-to-day policing of the United States.[125] The image of the Black *thug* reflected the fears and anxieties of many white people, rich and poor alike, who resented the gains, however minimal, that had been achieved through the civil rights movement.

The War on Drugs, coupled with aggressive policing in predominantly minority communities and harsh sentencing laws, set the stage for the massive expansion of the U.S. prison system and, in the end, the disproportionate incarceration of mostly Black and Brown people.[126] Indeed, as Alexander writes, "In less than two decades, the prison population quadrupled, and large majorities of poor people of color in urban areas throughout the United States were placed under the control of the criminal justice system or saddled with criminal records for life. Almost overnight, huge segments of ghetto criminals were permanently relegated to a second-class status, disenfranchised, and subjected to perpetual surveillance and monitoring by law enforcement agencies."[127] By the turn of the twenty-first century, for example, Black men constituted approximately 12 percent of the U.S. population and approximately 13 percent of its drug users, but accounted for 33 percent of all drug-related arrests, 62 percent of drug-related convictions, and 70 percent of drug-related incarcerations.[128] Similarly, Black women were imprisoned at a rate eight times that of white women, and were ten times as likely to be reported to child welfare agencies for prenatal drug use—even though the same proportion of Black and white women use drugs while pregnant.[129] As of 2018, African Americans continue to comprise a disproportionate share of the prison population. For example, African Americans comprised 33 percent of the sentenced population although they made up only 12 percent of the total adult U.S. population; whites, conversely, accounted for 30 percent of inmates yet comprised 63 percent of the adult population. Black men are especially likely to be incarcerated: in 2018, there were 2,272 inmates per 100,000 Black men; this compares with 1,018 inmates per 100,000 Hispanic men and just 392 inmates per 100,000 white men.[130]

The neoliberal state has an investment in fueling the fear of crime, that is, of convincing the public of imminent danger to self and property by overstating the threat of crime and creating the false impression that all citizens are equally at risk of victimization.[131] In other words, with veiled references to a universal shared mortality—"We are all at risk"—proponents of a revanchist neoliberal policing platform sought to unite the public in its opposition to a common threat, one that was more often than not embodied in the form of Black and Brown criminals. The overall objective, Philomena Mariani makes clear, has been "to sell the public on the idea that policing and punishment are the solution to all social-economic problems."[132] Thus, rather than investing in educational or welfare programs, monies were (and are) directed toward law enforcement agencies and the criminal justice system, notably, prisons. In addition, given the long-standing representation of Blacks and other minorities as criminals, the disparities in arrest and incarceration rates are viewed by many whites as reflecting reality rather than systemic discrimination.[133]

The consequences are far-reaching. As Angela Davis explains, "The prison industrial system materially and morally impoverishes its inhabitants and devours the social wealth needed to address the very problems that have led to spiraling numbers of prisoners. As prisons take up more and more space on the social landscape, other government programs that have previously sought to respond to social needs . . . are being squeezed out of existence. The deterioration of public education, including prioritizing discipline and security over learning in public schools located in poor communities, is directly related to the prison 'solution.'"[134] "Prisons do not disappear problems," Davis concludes, "they disappear human beings."[135] Crucially, Davis concludes, "the practice of disappearing vast numbers of people from poor, immigrant, and racially marginalized communities has literally become big business."[136]

The deleterious consequences of an aggressive and discriminatory system of law enforcement, including racial profiling, surveillance, and detention, both on individuals and collectively within communities of color have been many. Here, though, I want to underscore that the mass incarceration of especially Black and Brown effectively benefits a racial capitalism predicated on white supremacy. As Earl Smith and Angela Hattery neatly explain, though prisons serve several functions, including providing punishment and housing those who are adjudicated as requiring separation from the larger social world, a key purpose of the prison-industrial complex is not the rehabilitation of inmates but the removal of unexploitable labor from the free labor market and the transformation of that labor so that it can be extracted.[137] In turn, white workers—and especially white men—implicitly or explicitly benefit from the incarceration of hundreds of thousands of African American men, for high levels of imprisonment effectively remove African American men from the competitive labor force, and upon release they are disenfranchised in the political system and frequently made permanently unemployable.[138]

However, the economic benefits to racial capitalism in general, and to white workers in particular, extend beyond the lucrative profits accruing from prison labor. As Becky Pettit and Carmen Gutierrez explain, "Mass incarceration, and other forms of criminal justice contact, from police stops to community-based supervision, generate consequences related to employment, wages, political engagement, health, neighborhood stability, and a host of other considerations.[139] Pettit and Gutierrez, for example, detail that the removal through incarceration of a large segment of earners reinforces existing income and wealth disparities; incarceration has damaging effects on the health of families and communities; felony convictions have devastating effects on the level of voting, political engagement, and overall trust in the legal system within communities.[140] Overall, they conclude, "the costs of mass incarceration are not simply collateral consequences for individuals but are borne collectively, most notably by African Americans [and other persons of color] living in acutely disadvantaged communities that experience high levels of policing and surveillance."[141] As Pettit and Gutierrez write, diminished employment opportunities, bouts of unemployment, and lost wages influence economic security and self-sufficiency for individuals who have been incarcerated as well as for their families and children.[142]

In addition, the inherent exploitation of capitalism is augmented in race- and gender-specific ways by a criminal justice system guided by an ideology of white supremacy that mediates one's vulnerability to premature death through physical violence. As Priscilla Bustamante, Gaurav Jashnani, and Brett Stoudt explain, "the implementation of broken windows policing, with an emphasis on low-level arrests and frequent police stops, means that those living in low-income communities of color are regularly exposed to police presence and contract."[143] This in and of itself elevates dramatically the likelihood of confrontations with law enforcement officers and the very real possibility of premature death at the hands of state-sanctioned violence, as demonstrated by the police killings of Michael Brown, Laquan McDonald, Tamir Rice, Walter Scott, Freddie Gray, Philando Castile, Breonna Taylor, George Floyd, and so many others.

In bringing this section to a close, we are mindful of Roberts and Mahtani's premise that, in trying to understand the connection between race and neoliberalism, it is important to examine not just the momentary eruptions of race or racism that seemingly result from neoliberal policy reforms, and instead consider racism as an organizing principle of society that neoliberalism reinforces and modifies.[144] In the decades following Reagan's racist War on Drugs, for example, Alexander relates, "black drug dealers and users became regulars in newspaper stories and saturated the evening TV news—forever changing our conception of who the drug users and dealers are."[145] Now, in the minds of many white voters, crime—and especially violent crime—is equated with Blackness. In turn, this semantic connection enables whites to overwhelmingly support the ongoing militarization of law enforcement and the gutting of social programs. Thus, neoliberalism effectively masks racism through its value-laden moral project: camouflaging race-connected practices in an allegedly color-blind meritocracy, making possible a utopian vision of society that is nonracialized.[146] Simply put, Black people are held to be uniquely and directly responsible for their own poverty and imprisonment and, indirectly, responsible for the financial hardships of demoralized but responsible alienated white workers struggling to survive. From this vantage point, the *white* alienated subject personifies precarity, a condition wrought by racialized welfare cheats and undocumented workers who unfairly take advantage of "liberal" systems that no longer reward hard work and individual responsibility. As such, class solidarity will always be limited until Black people (and other minority populations) are not fictionalized as ontologically criminal.[147]

The Fallacy of Postracial Neoliberalism

On November 4, 2008, millions of people celebrated the election of Barack Obama, the first *Black* president of the United States. However, as Luigi

Esposito and Laura Finley foreshadowed, Obama's victory—undeniably a milestone in U.S. history—further legitimized a problematic discourse on racial relations that emerged in the aftermath of the civil rights movement.[148] Specifically, Obama's success confirmed for many whites the transcendence of racism in society and as such justified the color-blind ideology championed since the Reagan administration.

Context matters. When Obama took office, Blacks in the United States compared to whites were three times more likely to live in poverty; nearly twenty times more likely to be incarcerated for illegal drug use; more likely to receive substandard health care, even among Black patients whose income and health insurance policies were comparable to their white counterparts; twice as likely to be unemployed; less likely to graduate from high school and attend college; six times more likely to be victims of homicide; and more likely to be steered into subprime mortgages and lose their homes.[149] And yet, as Esposito and Finley write, many whites subscribed to the narrative of color-blindness as a means of explaining away these inequalities as products of racially neutral considerations, such as differences in lifestyles, individual determination, financial literacy, personal responsibility, and moral values.[150] Indeed, Smith writes, "the comparatively sanguine perceptions of white Americans about the state of racial equality in the face of yawning racial gaps in income, wealth, and employment is indicative of white privilege's 'scheme of irrelevance' regarding the needs and interests of racial minorities."[151] In other words, many white Americans expressed a profound indifference to the suffering of Black people, choosing either to ignore the obvious inequalities or to blame African Americans for their plight.

Initially, for many white Americans, Obama seemingly personified the can-do attitude of the liberal subject, that hard work and perseverance are the keys to success in the United States. In so doing, Obama was portrayed as a Black man who *overcame* his Blackness. This, of course, presupposes that Blackness is a de facto source of shame and pathology that must be abandoned or transformed to fit the normative standards of acceptability defined and demanded by white society.[152] However, Obama's success heralded another, more disturbing trend among much of the white population. As Juliet Hooker explains, prior to 2008, the presumed whiteness of the presidency had been symbolic reassurance that political power remained in the grasp of white people.[153] For many whites, Obama embodied the symbolic loss of white privilege. To that end, a pervasive explanation for white racial resentment in the Obama era—a narrative that appeared frequently both in far-right forums but also in many mainstream media outlets—is that it was driven by working-class whites who felt left behind economically and alienated from the political process.[154] Hence, according to these accounts, the simmering intolerance of white people—frustrated by a sense of unfilled entitlement—was expressed most directly at the ballot box in subsequent elections.

White backlash, Terry Smith explains, has been a recurring and transformative feature of American politics since the Reconstruction era. However, the Obama presidency generated an unprecedented white voter backlash. Since 2008, Democrats lost 69 House seats, 13 Senate seats, 910 state legislative seats, 30 state legislative chambers, and 11 governorships. As Smith concludes, whites rebelled not just against Obama and his party, but against the ideal of racial equality that Obama's election symbolized.[155] This is, arguably, most apparent in the phenomenal rise of the so-called Tea Party movement during the Obama administration.[156]

The purported genesis of the Tea Party was the economic recession of 2007–2008. Ostensibly, extreme far-right members of the Republican party railed against the expanding national debt, rising taxes, and the specter of universal health care. To this end, the Tea Party positioned itself as a champion on the alienated working class in the abstract. In practice, however, the Tea Party was openly racist in its opposition to the Obama administration. Posters and placards at Tea Party rallies, for example, regularly demeaned Obama in racial terms; often, the president was depicted as a monkey or a half-naked African witch doctor. Confederate battle flags were ever-present and Nazi symbols were not uncommon. Indeed, despite repeated claims of race neutrality, the movement attracted numerous white nationalists and anti-immigrant activists.[157] Effectively, the Tea Party moved many white voters from an attitude of racial indifference to intolerance and outright hostility. As Smith details, in 2008—prior to Obama's election—only 26 percent of whites could recall a specific incident in which they were discriminated against because of their race. In other words, for the vast majority of whites, racial discrimination was a nonissue and, accordingly, they could remain largely indifferent to broader conversations on race relations in the United States. However, by 2014, a majority of white Americans agreed with the sentiment that discrimination *against* whites was a serious problem, even more so than discrimination against Blacks. This attitude was expressed most strongly among many conservative whites but especially those who identified with the Tea Party movement. Indeed, 76 percent of white Tea Party supporters believed that racial discrimination against whites was a significant problem.[158] In addition, Tea Party members were far more likely than other white Americans to reject discrimination as contributing to the economic plight of Black people and to believe that Blacks simply do not try hard enough. In the twisted logic of white supremacy, federal, state, and local programs unfairly benefit undeserving and irresponsible Blacks at the expense of white workers—despite the fact that white Americans, on the whole, are economically better off than Blacks. And it was in this context the Tea Party paved the way for a revanchist white supremacist presidency.

In June 2015 the real estate mogul and celebrity icon Donald Trump announced his candidacy for president of the United States. He began his presidential bid with a polemical speech describing the United States as a failed country beset with innumerable problems. For Trump, these problems were embodied especially by undocumented Mexican workers, whom he described as nothing more than rapists, criminals, and drug dealers.[159] In blunt and blatant terms, Trump's comments revealed in no uncertain terms the nature and strategy of his campaign: over the next 18 months he refined his appeal and extended his racist rhetoric toward Black inner-city residents, Muslims, and other nonwhite immigrant groups.[160] In addition, Trump's campaign slogan of "Make America Great Again" was crafted to appeal to the powerful image of the *white* working class. As Douglas Schrock and colleagues identify, Trump's rhetoric underscored the decline of blue-collar jobs and portrayed (falsely) that the economy was in a precipitous downfall.[161] Indeed, Trump effectively capitalized on the "left behind" thesis, the carefully crafted narrative that supposed advancements experienced by Blacks, Hispanics, and other minority groups came at the expense of white workers. However, under Trump's tutelage, the superior productivity of the white working class would literally make American great again.

Trump to that end repeatedly expressed sympathy for the *white* working class and tapped into existing feelings of alienation, fear, and vulnerability. In the process, however, Trump signaled his commitment to whiteness as a whole.[162] And the mainstream media, knowingly or not, underscored Trump's racist message. As Hugh Gusterson explains, news programs consistently put disproportionate weight on a single narrative thread: the role of free trade and factory closings in alienating a postindustrial white working class; in this respect, the media inadvertently reproduced the discourse of Trump.[163] Throughout the presidential campaign of 2016 and into the Trump presidency, for example, the narrative of the (white) working class was a common refrain among the media and many commentators—both to the left and right of the political spectrum. For conservative pundits especially, the white alienated subject was (and is) called upon to do the heavy lifting of white supremacy, that is, to stand in for all the perceived ills confronting and upending the privileges of whiteness. Media outlets, in turn, reified the mythology of the beaten down blue-collar worker—portrayed almost exclusively as a white man, while the precarious conditions of African Americans and other minority groups were downplayed or disregarded.

However, Trump's message was not directed exclusively or even primarily toward actual *members* of the white working class but instead to the white community in general, for the mythology of the industrious, gritty blue-collar worker is a powerful elixir of white supremacy: The Rust Belt steel worker, the Appalachian coal miner, the Midwestern farmer. That is, Trump had no intention to actually *help* white workers. Rather, Trump capitalized on the value of white supremacist ideology and parlayed the myth of the heroic but embattled blue-collar worker into political victory. As Schrock and his coauthors document, by emphasizing the decimation of blue collar jobs, Trump's rhetoric represented the economy as losing ground in ways that could evoke both anxiety or fear among the (white) working class and sympathy among the less precarious white population for their plight.[164] In short, Trump tapped into the discontent and alienation of the white working class in the abstract, blamed Blacks and other people of color for their problems, and pledged salvation through the restoration of supremacy *for all whites.* Hence, Trump's repeated attacks against Obama reinforced the intolerance and resentment expressed by many whites who steadfastly believed the false narrative that Obama was looking out for African Americans and, in so doing, enacted tyrannical policies that marginalized members of the white working class.

Simply put, modern political conservativism's success—including the rise of Trumpism—is dependent in part on the mobilization of far-right and fringe groups that push the boundaries of the conservative flank of the political spectrum, including anti-immigrant, gun rights, and "patriot" groups.[165] In doing so, the white alienated subject appears as the foot soldier of the conservative agenda, for this figure embodies the idea that members of the white working class are denied the opportunity to live a flourishing, meaningful life because of unfair competition promulgated by liberal and progressive forces. Consequently, any exclusionary focus on the white working class—and especially of the white alienated subject—risks exculpating the much larger portion of Trump's coalition who are white and middle class or white and well off.[166] The primary beneficiary of Trumpism is not the downtrodden white worker, but white supremacy.

From the standpoint of many white people, racism is thoroughly rational and its perpetuation desirable, both for material and meaningful reasons. Indeed, as Eduardo Bonilla-Silva explains, given that white people's subject positions are fundamentally built on notions of freedom and of being self-made, as hard-working people in opposition to racial Others whom they see as lazy and undeserving, their support for Trump makes emotional sense. They love Trump not just because he promised them jobs and a border wall; rather, Trump *relates* to many whites because he offers "emotional appeasement."[167] Thus, as Hooker explains, many Trump supporters, some of whom erupted in outbursts of white rage, expressed feeling empowered by his unequivocal embrace of white nativism and his populist, xenophobic, and racist appeals targeting Latino immigrants, Muslims, and Black Lives Matter protestors.[168]

Evocative of the white backlash of the 1970s and 1980s, the spectacle of Trumpism—from red MAGA hats to patriotic flags emblazoned with the Trump name flown on pickup trucks—pays homage to the mythical white alienated subject as the proud defender of traditional American values. In reality, the Trump administration consistently initiated policies or eliminated those programs that would effectively benefit exploited workers of all subject positions. In fact, Trump and the Republican-led Senate almost exclusively legislated policies that worked *against* the working class, all the while championing the mythology of the (white) alienated subject. To this end, Trumpism was but the latest iteration of neoliberal capitalism, as large corporations sought to ensure that the majority of economic gains are absorbed by executives and shareholders and not employees.[169] Notably, the Trump administration derailed an Obama-era plan to extend overtime protections to workers; undermined efforts to hold businesses liable for wage violations against contract and franchise workers; ended a requirement that contractors meet federal labor standards; sided with corporate interests to let companies force workers into mandatory arbitration agreements; made it easier for employers to eliminate unions;

empowered employer discrimination by revoking civil rights protections; reversed protections against pesticides and chemicals in the workplace; and reduced overall workplace safety enforcement.[170] Collectively, the Trump administration weakened the legal rights of the working class, increased their overall precarity, and gutted health and safety regulations, all of which contribute to their increased precarity and vulnerability to premature death.

That a sizeable portion of the white working class continued to support Trump throughout his presidency and after is indicative of the power of white supremacy and their internalization of the alienated subject. Simply put, many white workers cling to the rhetoric used so effectively by Nixon, Reagan, Trump, and other politicians, namely, that economic losses experienced by hard-working white people are caused by economic gains enjoyed by undeserving Black people and other minorities. The fight against a livable minimum wage, for example, is camouflaged as "a reactionary, anti-Black working-class movement" in that "raising the federal minimum wage would incommensurately benefit Black workers because they are overrepresented among low-wage workers."[171] Consequently, the racism, misogyny, and xenophobia of Trumpism portends a particularly virulent form of racial nostalgia that magnifies symbolic Black gains into occasions of white dislocation and displacement.[172]

From this vantage point, Trump's overt racism—and his popularity among predominantly white voters—is actually a reversal of the Southern Strategy, in that increasingly coded language is discarded in favor of overt racist statements. In other words, Trump normalized overt white supremacy. In addition, the vehemence and virulence on display among many Trump supporters both during and after the election is testimony to how deeply white supremacy is rooted in U.S. society. Indeed, Cheryl Matias and Peter Newlove caution that the United States, under Trump, entered a "moment of emboldened en/whitening epistemology that is characterized by the perverse re-appropriation of civil rights and socially just terminologies and concepts—once used to support the rights of People of Color—to instead strengthen White nationalism."[173] They explain: "By self-aggrandizing and perversely re-packaging Whiteness as an ideology that has been discriminated against or victimized by diversity or political correctness, Trump offered racists a way of justifying discrimination toward women, People of Color, immigrants, and Muslim Americans." And, as we will see, it is this emboldened whiteness that underscored the intolerance and hatred of many whites toward the simple demand that Black lives matter.

Making Black Lives Matter

On February 26, 2012, George Zimmerman shot and killed Trayvon Martin, a seventeen-year-old African American who was visiting his father in Sanford, Florida. Prior to the shooting, Zimmerman—a neighborhood watch captain—called 911 to report a "suspicious person." The dispatcher instructed Zimmerman to not approach the person, but Zimmerman disregarded the orders. What happened next remains unclear. Shots rang out and someone screamed "Help, help!" What is certain is that Martin lay dead on the ground.[174] In response, over the following days and weeks, rallies took place in cities across the country demanding justice for Trayvon Martin. Zimmerman, however, repeatedly claimed self-defense, arguing that Martin had violently attacked him. It was not until six weeks later that Zimmerman was finally indicted and made to stand trial on charges of second-degree murder. The racially charged trial, however, resulted in a six-person jury acquitting Zimmerman on all charges.

When acts of horrific violence go unpunished, Cazenave explains, they have an impact that extends beyond any particular incident.[175] So it was in the aftermath of the Zimmerman verdict, for the acquittal reignited feelings of anger and disillusionment throughout the Black community, which, in turn, inspired action and activism.[176] Alicia Garza, a young and queer African American woman, was one such person. On the day the verdict was announced, Garza was at a bar in Oakland, California. Despite her youth, Garza was a long-time activist in the Bay area. An advocate for domestic workers and for queer and transgender rights, Garza had also engaged in the struggle against police brutality and anti-Black racism. After the verdict came out, Garza explains, she was momentarily at a loss for words. She recalls: "We had nothing to say to each other, so most of us turned to social media for an understanding of what other people were saying to help us form our thoughts and make sense of the emotions that we were feeling that moment. I went on to my Facebook and I saw a whole number of things on my timeline that were related to this verdict, and I saw a whole lot of things that disturbed me."[177] In response, Garza began to express her feelings with posts: "the sad part is, there's a section of America who is cheering and celebrating right now. and that makes me sick to my stomach. WE GOTTA get it together y'all." Later, she continued: "btw stop saying we are not surprised. that's a damn shame in itself. I continue to be surprised at how little Black lives matter. And I will continue that. stop giving up on black life." She concluded with the simple, heartfelt affirmation: "black people. I love you. I love us. Our lives matter."[178]

For Garza, two disturbing trends were all too apparent. On the one hand, she decried the "social justice cynicism" surrounding the Zimmerman verdict—that justice always eludes Black people killed by police or vigilantes in the United States—and, on the other hand, she denounced the "respectability politics" that premised Black people could overcome their oppression by working harder and conforming to white America. She later explained, "I was really tired of this narrative that blames black people for conditions that we didn't create. It felt like a dismissal of the real tragedy: that black life doesn't matter in this country."[179]

In response to Garza's post, her friend Patrisse Cullors created the hashtag #BlackLivesMatter. Cullors, herself a queer African American woman, was a graduate of the University of California at Los Angeles and had been organizing in the LGBT community for many years. Cullors posted: "declaration: black bodies will no longer be sacrificed for the rest of the world's enlightenment. i am done. i am so done. trayvon, you are loved infinitely. #blacklivesmatter."[180] Two days later, Garza, Cullors, and their friend Opal Tometi, through social media, began to transform their emotions into a movement.[181] Hoping to foster meaningful change through peaceful protest, Garza, Cullors, and Tometi issued a call for direct action.[182] As Chase explains, "The importance and significance of the early BLM social media posts reveal much of why the movement became a center-point of traditional and social media coverage in America. The combination of love and anger, and the feeling that racial tensions had reached a breaking point, was shared by people throughout the nation."[183]

It was the killing in Ferguson, Missouri, of Michael Brown, however, that galvanized the nascent Black Lives Matter movement.[184] On August 9, 2014, Darren Wilson, a white police officer, pulled up in his squad car next to eighteen-year-old Michael Brown and his friend, Dorian Johnson, who were walking in the middle of the road instead of on the sidewalk. After the initial stop, Wilson determined that Brown was a robbery suspect who stole cigarillos from a local convenience store. What happened next remains unclear. According to some witnesses, Wilson became aggressive, while others claim that Brown was initially confrontational. Wilson then opened fire, Brown ran, turned around, and Wilson fired again. Wilson later claimed self-defense, arguing that Brown was charging at him. Brown died about 150 feet away from Wilson; the unarmed youth was shot six times.[185] Subsequently, in the aftermath of the shooting, members of the Ferguson Police Department broke protocol and let Brown's body lie visible *for hours* in the middle of the street. For Cazenave, this was symbolic, in that the police seemingly wanted to send a message of terror to other community members.[186]

That the response of law enforcement was predicated on intimidation is hardly surprising. The Ferguson Police Department (FPD), as later investigations revealed, had a sordid history of fomenting racial terror and violence. Indeed, the U.S. Department of Justice concluded in 2014 that the FPD—and the Ferguson Municipal Court—routinely violated the constitutional rights of African Americans. In a review of over 35,000 pages of police records and hundreds of interviews, investigators determined that Ferguson police officers as a matter of practice stopped African Americans without reasonable suspicion, arrested them without probable cause, and used unreasonable force against them.[187]

The death of Brown and, later, the failure of a grand jury to indict Wilson, became the catalyst for weeks of demonstrations and protests in Ferguson and beyond.[188] Initially, community members came together to hold a candlelight vigil both in memory of Brown and in solidarity against continual police and vigilante killings of African Americans. In turn, seemingly looking to provoke a response from the peaceful protestors, police forces routinely arrived in armored vehicles with riot gear, tear gas, flash-bang grenades, sound cannons, and guns equipped with rubber bullets.[189] Members of the Black community, however, refused to be intimidated and continued to demand that Black Lives Matter. As Ransby explains, the "Ferguson uprising, an organic mass rebellion sparked by Brown's death at the hands of a notoriously racist local police force, was a defining moment" in that protestors "defied state power and exposed what many outside the Black community would rather ignore—the violent underbelly of racial capitalism and systemic racism."[190]

Ferguson was a microcosm of the violence of racial capitalism and systemic racism. In 1990, for example, Ferguson was a middle-class community with a population about three-quarters white; by 2010, the population was two-thirds black, unemployment had exceeded 13 percent, and the number of residents living in poverty had doubled in the span of a decade.[191] Thus, according to Ransby, "while Brown's killing was the catalyst, the Black working class of Ferguson was angry about much more, and their anger resonated and reverberated around the country and beyond."[192] Indeed, as Taylor details, Black protestors subsequently unmasked the kleptocracy at the heart of municipal operations in Ferguson, revealing that the FPD expressly and routinely targeted the Black population as the major source of revenue. Black households, in turn, were inundated with fines, fees, citations, tickets, and arrests for minor violations to such an extent that the revenues generated were the town's second leading source of revenue.[193] To this end, vigilante violence and state-sanctioned killings by law enforcement officers worked to uphold a racially unjust system that marginalized and further exploited African Americans.

For many white people weaned on decades of racist War on Drugs rhetoric, Ferguson symbolized yet another example of the inherent criminality of Blacks. As Bryan Adamson documents, in recounting the Ferguson events, the "media hewed to a pro-majoritarian orthodoxy that privileged stability over dissent, and allowed audiences to ignore the role structural racism and bias may have played in Brown's death and the grievances demonstrators sought to surface."[194] Indeed, rather than understanding the protests as a manifestation of economic anxiety experienced by alienated workers, Blacks themselves were blamed for their problems. Taylor elaborates: "Explanations for Black inequality that blame Black people for their own oppression transforms material causes into subjective causes. The problem is not racial discrimination in the workplace or residential segregation: it is Black irresponsibility, erroneous social mores, and general bad behavior."[195] The Black Lives Matter movement emerged, in part, to challenge these explanations.

From the outset, the Black Lives Matter movement was conceived as an intersectional effort to call attention to the vulnerability of being Black in the United States. As Garza explains, "Black Lives Matter is an ideological and political intervention in a world where Black Lives are systematically and intentionally targeted for demise. It is an affirmation of Black folks' contributions to this society, our humanity, and our resilience in the face of deadly oppression"[196] To this end, the affirmation that Black Lives Matter is simultaneously a demand for radical transformation of those structures and institutions that result in the premature deaths of African Americans and a demand to enjoy the right to live a flourishing life and to find meaning in a shared humanity.

Demanding accountability for state-sanctioned violence, Black Lives Matter activists utilize a variety of tactics, including marches, rallies, and "die-ins." However, social struggles are inherently spatial struggles and, to this point, a highly effective technique of BLM activists has been to occupy public spaces: highways, intersections, sporting events, retail stores, malls, campaign events, police stations, and municipal buildings.[197] These techniques are extremely effective in that they literally disrupt the flow of capital, that is, they interrupt the everydayness of the economy. Such disturbances not only force people to take notice; they also visibly demonstrate the connection between police violence and racial capitalism. This, for the supporters of the Black Lives Matter activists, is vital, for the overall message is that the harmful conditions experienced by African Americans are both structural and systemic.

Weeks prior to the killing of Brown, for example, New York City Police officer Daniel Panteleo choked to death Eric Garner, a forty-three-year-old African American husband and father of six; four days before Brown's death, John Crawford III, a twenty-two-year-old, unarmed African American man, was killed in a Wal-Mart in a suburb of Dayton, Ohio, while he talked on the phone with the mother of his children; two days after Brown's murder, police in Los Angeles shot Ezell Ford, a twenty-five-year-old, unarmed African American man after an unprovoked investigative stop; and the following day, in Victorville, California, Dante Parker, a thirty-six-year-old African American man, was detained while riding a bicycle by police on suspicion of burglary and tasered multiple times before dying in police custody.[198] These were not isolated events, activists stressed; nor were these the consequence of a few "bad apples" as conservative pundits would have it. Indeed, it is especially common for white pundits to dismiss police violence as abnormalities—if such violence is even acknowledged. Many whites, for example, will single out a particular case and attempt to either portray the Black victim as somehow responsible—he was *probably* in the act of committing a crime anyway—or claim that the offending police officer was merely a bad apple. Both arguments effectively counter the demonstrable evidence that police violence against African Americans and other persons of color is a systemic problem, rooted in the institutional and legislative structures of the United States. As Cazenave explains, "Such killings are often symptomatic of much larger systemic operations that go way beyond and much deeper than just the attitudes and actions of a few rogue individuals."[199]

Importantly, the Black Lives Matter movement calls attention to the fact that it is not just Black men who are routinely detained, arrested, and killed. Black women and Black trans folk are exceptionally vulnerable to violence, although their plight is too often neglected. As Taylor writes, "Police also view Black women's lives with suspicion and ultimately as less valuable, making their death and brutalization more likely, not less. It is hardly even newsworthy when Black women, including Black transwomen, are killed or violated by law enforcement—because they are generally seen as less feminine or vulnerable."[200] During a Trans Liberation Tuesday demonstration held in San Francisco in August 2015, for example, Garza explained: "We understand that, in our communities, black trans folk, gender-nonconforming folk, black queer folk, black women, black disabled folk—we have been leading movements for a long time, but we have been erased from the official narrative."[201]

The efforts of Black Lives Matter coincide with parallel movements, notably the #SayHerName campaign initiated in 2015. In that year, the African American Policy Forum, a New York-based racial justice think tank cofounded by the Black feminist legal theorist Kimberlé Crenshaw, coined the Twitter hashtag #SayHerName also in an effort to call attention to the voices and faces of the numerous Black women who were recently killed by the police—deaths that were relatively ignored by the public and the mainstream media.[202] #SayHerName makes intersectional mobilization part of its agenda with affirmations of commitment to issues of members of many subgroups within the Black community, including women, LGTBQ members, and the differently abled.[203]

Collectively, movements such as Black Lives Matter and #SayHerName mark concerted efforts to decenter the racial, gendered, and sexual presumptions of the alienated subject, that is, to direct attention to the exploitation and oppression of all persons of color, but especially those of the working class. In doing so, a narrative centered on Black women and trans folk serves as both an antisexist and antiracist effort to illuminate how social issues, such as police violence and the school-to-prison pipeline, impact more than just straight cis Black men.[204] Accordingly, these activists acknowledge the unequal vulnerability to a life cut short by, especially, police and vigilante violence; but it also calls out the structural conditions that contribute to health-related premature death, such as the lack of adequate medical care or health insurance. To this end, these movements must also be seen as part of a long-standing and fiercely contested struggle over the ability of African Americans to lead meaningful lives free from premature death.

Within three years Black Lives Matter transformed into a nationwide movement and, according to Juliet Hooker, marks an "important inflection point" in U.S. racial politics.[205] As Hooker writes, "the protests signaled a potential moment of Black political radicalization, when pragmatic forms of Black politics principally aimed at descriptive representation have been overshadowed by a vocal movement seeking to dismantle some of the key pillars of contemporary white supremacy: mass incarceration, violent policing, a biased criminal justice system, and the pervasive criminalization of Black life."[206] The Black Lives Matter movement, however, should not be seen in isolation from a centuries-long struggle against systemic racism and violence in the United States, but instead as the latest iteration in the effort to "preserve Black life in the face of white supremacist violence."[207] This is a history that includes, among other activities, the anti-lynching crusades of Ida B. Wells, the Negro Silent Protest Parade of 1917, the protests surrounding the Scottsboro Boys case of the 1930s, the 1951 *We Charge Genocide Campaign* petition by the Civil Rights Congress, and the actions of the Deacons for Defense and the Black Panthers during the civil rights era.[208] Garza and her cofounders of Black Lives Matter readily acknowledge this debt—but also underscore how they depart from previous movements. As Garza explains, "We don't see ourselves as a trend, we certainly don't see ourselves as a brand, and of course we don't see ourselves as a hashtag." For Garza, Black Lives Matter is part of an emerging social movement which has "many tributaries." She elaborates: Black Lives Matter is "not the leader of [the] movement for black liberation. It is one contribution to a broader movement for social justice and social transformation."[209] She continues:

> Black Lives Matter is a unique contribution that goes beyond extrajudicial killings of Black people by police and vigilantes. It goes beyond the narrow nationalism that can be prevalent within some Black communities, which merely call on Black people to love Black, live Black and buy Black, keeping straight cis Black men in the front of the movement while our sisters, queer and trans and disabled folk take up roles in the background or not at all. Black Lives Matter affirms the lives of Black queer and trans folks, disabled folks, Black-undocumented folks, folks with records, women

> and all Black lives along the gender spectrum. It centers those that have been marginalized within Black liberation movements. It is a tactic to (re)build the Black liberation movement.[210]

Tometi echoes these sentiments. "Black Lives Matter is often called a 'civil rights' movement," she explains, but hastens to add, "to think that our fight is solely about civil rights is to misunderstand the fundamental aspirations of this movement."[211] For Tometi, the struggle is "for full civil, social, political, legal, economic, and cultural rights." To this end, the Black Lives Matter movement, as Tometi underscores, "is beyond just, 'Stop killing us, we deserve to live.'" Rather, it marks an effort for unconditional emancipation where Blacks and other oppressed peoples are able to live a meaningful, flourishing life—a point effectively captured by Tometi: "We deserve to thrive, and this requires the full acknowledgement of the breadth of our human rights."[212]

To this end, the Black Lives Matter movement is intimately part of a much longer geographic struggle informed by Black radicalism.[213] However, as Cedric Robinson is quick to explain, Black radicalism "is not a variant of Western radicalism whose proponents happen to be Black. Rather, it is a specifically African response to an oppression emergent from the immediate determinants of European development in the modern era and framed by orders of human exploitation woven into the interstices of European social life from the inception of Western Civilization."[214] Personified by Paul Robeson, Claude McKay, Richard Wright, and C. L. R. James, among many others, Black radicalism constitutes a particular way of understanding revolutionary consciousness, one that centrally prefigures Black workers. As Kelley writes, the demands for Black emancipation and self-determination is "not simply a matter of guaranteeing democratic rights or removing the barriers to Black political and economic power."[215] Instead, Black radicalism "is about promoting and supporting an independent Black radical movement that [can] lead the way to a revitalized international working-class assault on racial capitalism."[216]

Accordingly, while a prominent concern of the Black Lives Matter movement is the abolition of state-sanctioned violence, the defunding of law enforcement agencies, and the dismantling of the carceral state, these alone are insufficient. Additional demands—not reforms—are necessary to address the vulnerability of Black and Brown people, women, transgender people, and the disabled. As such, Black Lives Matter activists have called for "investment in solutions like quality education, restorative justice, mental and emotional health support, and job opportunities."[217] For Tometi, at a most basic level, the Black Lives Matter agenda "is for all people" and once achieved "will create an inclusive democracy that guarantees freedom and justice for all."[218] This requires, in turn, the articulation of specific *Black geographies*. Not to be confused with Trump's ham-fisted calls to make America great again, the notion of Black geographies signifies an attempt, as Katherine McKittrick explains, to locate and draw on "black histories and black subjects in order to make visible social lives which are often displaced, rendered ungeographic."[219] Camilla Hawthorne elaborates, noting that "the deadly entanglements of white supremacy, capitalism, settler colonialism, patriarchy, and heteronormativity today call for careful attention to the connections between space, place, and power."[220]

Reflective of these social and spatial goals, the epistemological orientation of Black Lives Matter is explicitly geographic and intersectional. Indeed, for Tometi, "This period in history is a celebration of intersectionality, which mandates that the full breadth of our humanity be acknowledged and embraced. This means that queer, trans, migrant, formerly incarcerated, disabled and all of us who find ourselves unapologetic about our complexity are more committed than ever to champion the scope of the human rights agenda that we deserve."[221] Notably, as Garza explains, "Our work is heavily influenced by [Kimberlé] Crenshaw's theory. People think that we're engaged with identity politics. The truth is that we're doing what the labor movement has always done—organizing people who are at the bottom."[222] Here, it is worth quoting Garza at length:

> When we say Black Lives Matter, we are talking about the ways in which Black people are deprived of our basic human rights and dignity. It is an acknowledgement [that] Black poverty and genocide is state violence. It is an acknowledgement that 1 million Black people are locked in cages in this country . . . is an act of state violence. It is an acknowledgment that Black women continue to bear the burden of a relentless assault on our children and our families and that assault is an act of state violence. Black queer and trans folk bearing a unique burden in a hetero-patriarchal society that disposes of us like garbage and simultaneously fetishizes us and profits off of us is state violence; the fact that 500,000 Black

> people in the US are undocumented immigrants and relegated to the shadows is state violence; the fact that Black girls are used as negotiating chips during times of conflict and war is state violence; Black folks living with disabilities and different abilities bear the burden of state-sponsored Darwinian experiments that attempt to squeeze us into boxes of normality defined by White supremacy is state violence. And the fact is that the lives of Black people—not ALL people—exist within these conditions is [a] consequence of state violence.[223]

Of the vulnerability of Black people to premature death, Garza underscores the supposition that "when Black people get free, everybody gets free."[224] In other words, Garza and members of the Black Lives Movement recognize the emancipatory potential of Blacks and other minorities in a class-divided society mediated by white supremacy. This requires, however, a sensitivity to the world-making and meaning-making potential of the human species-being. She explains: "#BlackLivesMatter doesn't mean your life isn't important—it means that Black lives, which are seen without value within White supremacy, are important to your liberation. Given the disproportionate impact state violence has on Black lives, we understand that when Black people in this country get free, the benefits will be wide reaching and transformative for society as a whole."[225]

Notably, Garza affirms the revolutionary aspirations—and potential—of the Black Lives Matter movement in terms not unlike the proletarian revolution of Marx and his interlocutors. However, the central figure is not the lunch-box-toting factory worker but instead the undocumented Latinx workers harvesting crops in California, the second-generation Haitian man driving a bus, and the queer Black woman teaching in an inner-city school. As Taylor identifies, "the Black Lives Matter movement has the potential to make deeper connections to and create relationships with organized labor."[226] She elaborates that "Black workers continue to be unionized at higher rates than white workers. The reason is simple: Black union workers make far above and beyond what nonunion Black workers make, in salary and benefits. Black workers also tend to be concentrated in the sectors most under attack by the state—federal, state, and local government, including education and other municipal jobs."[227] That said, the relationship of the Black Lives Matter movement to white working-class and poor people remains unclear.[228]

For those on the left, there are signs of optimism. Throughout the United States, many of the protests condemning police violence witnessed significant working-class participation. Indeed, working-class members of all racial, gendered, and sexual subject positions rose up in solidarity with Black workers to protest against state-sanctioned violence. Throughout June 2020, more than six hundred strikes or work stoppages were carried out. For example, on June 9, the day of Floyd's funeral, Black dockworkers in Charleston, South Carolina, shut down the country's fourth busiest port in a show of camaraderie with the Black Lives Matter movement. This was part of a nationwide effort initiated by the International Longshore Association—a union that is 65 percent Black.[229] Impressive as these numbers are, they are perhaps just the tip of the iceberg, for the tally is likely an undercount of the full scale and scope of labor-led protests. According to Mike Elk, many workers, often in nonunionized workplaces, are organizing through social media wildcat strikes, work stoppages, and other nontraditional forms of resistance. In doing so, however, many white labor leaders fail to understand this new form of labor movement; these actions, in addition, are often unreported in the media, thereby contributing to an underestimation of their significance.

One event that did garner more attention was the momentous Strike for Black Lives held on July 20, 2020. Composed of workers representing dozens of unions and social justice organizations, a series of coordinated protests were staged in more than twenty-five cities across the United States. Standing alongside members of the Service Employees International Union (SEIU), the International Brotherhood of Teamsters, and the American Federation of Teachers, were members of the Fight for 15, United Farm Workers, the National Domestic Workers Alliance, the Movement for Black Lives, and the Poor People's Campaign. Collectively, participants protested not only police violence and racial injustice but also the Trump administration's mishandling of the Covid-19 pandemic.[230] As Mary Kay Henry, president of the SEIU, explains, "Across the country, people are gaining a new understanding that it is impossible to win economic justice without racial justice. That health care for all, fair immigration policies, and bold action on climate change all require racial justice."[231]

The Strike for Black Lives and countless other strikes, stoppages, and demonstrations reflect the actually existing conditions of labor across the United States and challenge the myth of the white working class promoted by so many pundits, politicians, academics, and journalists. And these workers are making the connections. Mary Kay Henry, for example, explains: "This is a unique and hopeful moment in our movement's history, because in organizing this strike with our partners, we found broad acceptance and acclamation that now is the time to take large-scale action to demand that corporations and government do more to dismantle structural racism and protect Black lives. We are all clear that until Black communities can thrive, none of us can win."[232] This is a common refrain; and one that resonates with Marx's premise that the proletariat in solidarity can form an effective adversary to capitalism. This requires, though, recognition of the heterogeneity of labor and the intersectionality of alienation, exploitation, and oppression. Unfortunately, for many whites accustomed to a privileged position within the labor movement, this does not always sit well.

White-dominated union leadership mostly ignored the wave of strikes that pulsed across the country over the summer of 2020.[233] Mike Duff, a sixty-year-old Black and longtime labor activist, worries about the lack of support from many traditional and well-established unions, many of which fail to take seriously the heterogeneity both of the protesters and the methods employed. He explains that the lack of support from white labor leaders "reinforces the idea that some white labor activists see issues solely in terms of class and underemphasize the impact of race in labor conflict." He continues: "Some people who feel the white labor establishment is overly focused on class to the exclusion of race and this quibbling in an academic way over the definition of work stoppages when Black, working-class people feel they are engaging in work stoppages feed into their [class reductionist] narrative."[234] In short, the contributions of Black members of the working class are discounted and seen not as viable, effective, or proper forms of labor activism.

Indeed, the overall response of the establishment form of labor has been lukewarm at best. In the aftermath of Floyd's death, for example, the AFL-CIO and many national labor unions issued statements in support of the protests and in opposition to systemic racism. Beyond these platitudes, little material support was forthcoming. As Alexia Fernández Campbell finds, leaders of the country's labor unions mostly "tiptoed" around the subject, and for reasons not wholly unexpected.[235] Markedly, the leadership of the AFL-CIO was hesitant to critique law enforcement agencies, for the fact that police unions routinely negotiate collective bargaining agreements that make it nearly impossible to discipline law enforcement officers who maim or kill Blacks and other persons of color.[236] Complicating the issue, also, is the reality that the livelihood of some workers, notably prison guards, depends on the carceral state.[237]

Still, Garza speaks to the optimism of the present moment, noting that young people especially "are making the connection between racism, poverty, and police and state violence." She elaborates that ongoing protests and demonstrations highlight "an opportunity for us to make sure we're addressing issues of racism in our communities and connecting racism to poverty and exploitation." Indeed, as Garza reaffirms, in many respects the Black Lives Matter movement is "really the face of the new labor movement."[238] To this end, "Although African American workers have launched multiple movements for living wages, reparations, and an end to economic exploitation, the lack of support from the labor movement has restricted access to the benefits of democracy."[239]

Indeed, around the world, as detailed earlier, those committed to social justice and the building of antiracist and antisexist societies make these connections and express solidarity through an ethos of care. In their statement of support, for example, the KJK concludes: "It is time to declare a meaningful war on this oppressive system in its entirety. This means that we have to understand and lead the fight against White Supremacy, nationalism, sexism and capitalism as one. We have to stand-up for an alternative system which values differences as the richness of society working towards a mosaic-like cohesion of diversity to unite our struggles. Simply, people should not be regarded as inferior just because of their skin color, gender, ethnic and religious identity. Let's build our free life beyond the state, power and hierarchy through democratic structures of self-organization and self-determination."[240]

But many white Americans did not—and still do not—make the connection. Indeed, many white Americans continue to take these killings in stride. Conditioned to accept the disposability of Black lives, the lack of direct action on the part of many whites revealed the pervasive indifference to Black people's heightened vulnerability to premature death—and not just at the hands of the police. Indeed, decades of strategically deployed color-blind ideology conditioned white Americans to remain apathetic at best to the plight of Blacks and other persons of color. As Tony Brown and colleagues explain, racial apathy "taps white indifference and nonchalance. Racial apathy represents whites covering their eyes when asked to view their privilege."[241] To this end, to be indifferent, that is, to express racial apathy, to the Black Lives Matter movement is to be indifferent to the underlying conditions that gave rise to the movement, notably racial inequalities, widespread police brutality, and a criminal justice system geared toward the profitable incarceration of (predominantly) persons of color and of working-class whites.

For many white people, therefore, the killing of Brown, Floyd, and so many other persons of color illustrates not systemic racism but—at most—the actions of a few bad apples. Accordingly, the demands among the Black Lives Matter protestors are misguided and misplaced, for all that is required is better training programs among law enforcement agencies. Anything beyond these individual-level reforms would constitute preferential treatment and thus go against their cherished myth of color-blind meritocracy. Consequently, the failings of Blacks and other persons of color—even their failure to avoid premature death at the hands of the police—is the result of their own bad decisions and behavior. George Floyd would be alive if he had obeyed Derek Chauvin's warnings; Michael Brown would be alive if he hadn't stolen cigarillos; Travyon Martin would be alive if he hadn't attacked George Zimmerman; and so on and so on.

The Black Lives Matter movement challenges these assumptions and, in doing so, troubled many white people and forced them out of their emotional comfort zone. With the ongoing and national coverage of the Black Lives Matter movement, inaction and indifference became more problematic. Certainly, many white people expressed outrage at racial injustice and joined in solidarity with the protesters; others, however, expressed intolerance and hatred toward the protesters. For these whites, the visibility of protests was discomforting to the point of anger. On this point, Robin DiAngelo introduces the concept of "white fragility," that is, an emotional state in which even a minimum amount of racial stress becomes intolerable and potentially triggers a range of defense behaviors, including the capacity to hurt.[242] Accustomed, for example, "to the false notion that we live in a color-blind society, whites are protected from feeling discomfort, shame, or personal responsibility for the realities of racism."[243] The Black Lives Matter movement made this all but impossible. As such, many white people read into the affirmation that Black Lives Matter is a threat to the value of white lives, that is, they interpreted a Black-affirming statement as being antiwhite.[244] To this end, the very phrase "Black Lives Matter" elicits tremendous anger and scorn among many whites, most notably among conservative whites.[245] Social media platforms, for example, Facebook, were (and remain) awash with vitriolic messages and conspiracy theories denouncing the Black Lives Matter movement as violently antiwhite. Members of these online communities have used profane slurs to refer to Black people and protestors, calling them "animals," "thugs," and worse; some have argued that protestors were paid to go to demonstrations; and still others have suggested that even the death of Floyd was staged.[246]

Drawing on a deep well of negative images of Black people, demonstrations by Black Lives Matter activists were (and are) portrayed by right-wing pundits and politicians as criminal, that is, as lawless, violent gatherings.[247] At a rally in support of the police in Philadelphia, for example, the police union president described Black Lives Matter activists as "a pack of rabid animals." Such dehumanizing language not only denies the constitutional right afforded to African Americans to make claims on the state but also minimalizes the human and civil rights abuses directed against African Americans.[248] And this response is not unique. Despite substantial data indicating that the vast majority of Black Lives Matter demonstrations are peaceful, a substantial number of people, but especially white people, believe that "most protesters are trying to incite violence or destroy property."[249] In June 2020, several surveys indicated disapproval with the demonstrations. According to one poll, for example, only 17 percent of respondents believed the actions of the protesters were fully justified, 37 percent felt the actions were partially justified, and 38 percent said they weren't justified at all; and in a separate poll, fully 55 percent of respondents supported the use of the U.S. military to quell the demonstrations.[250] By September 2020, a near-majority, 47 percent, of whites polled registered their opposition to the Black Lives Matter movement.[251]

That such a white backlash materialized in light of the Black Lives Matter movement is hardly surprising. On the one hand, as Barbara Applebaum explains, white privilege "insulates white people in a protected cocoon of comfort that creates an expectation of comfort."[252] In other words, white privilege provides not only meaning in life but also offers emotional stability. Confronted with the demand that Black Lives Matter, white people's complacency toward and complicity in the perpetuation of structures and institutions that fostered unequal vulnerabilities to premature death among persons of color became untenable. However, on the other hand, white supremacists and members of other far-right hate groups launched an insidious disinformation campaign to smear both the protesters and the overall Black Lives Matter movement. The Anti-Defamation League (ADL), for example, documented several organized disinformation campaigns aimed at spreading a "deliberate mischaracterization of groups or movements [involved in the protests], such as portraying activists who support Black Lives Matter as violent extremists or claiming that antifa [protesters who are antifascist] is a terrorist organization coordinated or manipulated by nebulous external forces."[253] As the ADL finds, these false claims were promoted with the clear intention to sow fear and division, while also undermining protesters' efforts to build coalitions and bring about lasting structural change.[254] In addition, in many instances where protests became violent, documented evidence revealed that much violence was initiated by agents provocateurs, that is, white supremacists and law enforcement officers posed as Black Lives Matter protesters and engaged in acts of physical violence and property destruction.[255] These actions, in turn, were disseminated via social media to supposedly prove the violent extremism of the Black Lives Matter movement.

No longer able to remain indifferent to racism, many white people registered their intolerance toward Black Lives Matter protests through a reframing of the narrative, notably, through the counterclaim that All Lives Matter. Superficially, the slogan "All Lives Matter" appears to share the recognition of humanity's shared mortality. This aligns readily with the belief in a color-blind ideology and a postracial society, whereby all people in society—as liberal subjects—are afforded equal opportunities. That some succeed (like Trump) and others fail (like Floyd) is conditioned not by racial hierarchies and structural and social relations of oppression but through hard work and diligence. However, as Garza explains, to adopt the counternarrative of All Lives Matter is to "perpetuate a level of White supremacist domination by reproducing a tired trope that we are all the same, rather than acknowledging that non-Black oppressed people in this country are both impacted by racism and domination, and simultaneously, BENEFIT from anti-Black racism."[256] To do so, Garza continues, is to "lose the ways in which the state apparatus has built a program of genocide and repression mostly on the backs of Black people—beginning with the theft of millions of people for free labor—and then adapted it to control, murder, and profit off of other communities of color and immigrant communities."[257] In the end, the counterclaim that All Lives Matter is far from a universal appeal to human rights or shared mortality; rather, it is a racist attempt to usurp solidarity centered around the challenge to confront a rampant anti-Blackness that conditions institutions such as law enforcement and the carceral state.

For those who profess that All Lives Matter, the financial precarity of African American workers is conveniently downplayed, in that the concerns expressed by supporters of the Black Lives Matter movement are prefigured as anything *but* economic. Thus, dismissing the realities of institutional and structural racism that severely circumscribes the economic opportunities of Blacks, critics portray unemployed and underemployed Blacks as lazy and irresponsible. Indeed, the undeserving poor Black remains juxtaposed against the deserving white alienated subject, a strategic move made possible by the decades-long promotion of the white alienated subject as the epitome of neoliberal ideology. Accordingly, as Cowie and Boehm explain, "as class was reified as a white, male construct, the problems of women and minorities tended to be isolated outside of the economics of class, limited to issues specific to relatively classless understandings of race and gender."[258] Thus, arguments that underscore the increased precarity of Black and Brown members of the working class are rejected in favor of arguments that place economic hardships squarely on the backs of poor people of color. That the response to a movement created to bring attention to the disproportionate violence and premature death faced by Black people should be the slogan "All Lives Matter" reveals how white grievance is in many ways constituted in response to symbolic losses.[259] If one's meaning in life is tied to white privilege, any attempt to challenge that hegemony will potentially be met with intolerance and likely violent opposition. As demonstrated in myriad surveys, whites tend not to understand their group's position in a purely relative manner and, consequently, fail to infer their group's under advantages arising from Blacks' unfair disadvantages.[260] This, ultimately, plays into the notion of zero-sum game, for in the twisted logic of white supremacy, the demand to protect Black lives can only come at the expense of saving white lives. On this point, the meaning of All Lives Matter operates in a different register than Black Lives Matter. As Daniel Shore explains, the slogan "All Lives Matter" "recasts the demand for equal treatment as a demand for special treatment, the demand for full inclusion in the law's protections as a violation of the law's universality."[261] In so doing, of course, the All Lives Matter countermovement belies its racist intent, that is, to deploy coded language in an effort to dismiss challenges to the preservation both of white privilege and white supremacy.

Thus, for those seeking to contest or to subvert the emancipatory aims of Black Lives Matter, the ambiguity of All Lives Matter is key to its political appeal. Unlike more overt racist dog whistles, All Lives Matter speaks openly to the existence of an ostensibly race-neutral liberal subject and thus offers its supporters plausible deniability when confronted with allegations of racism.[262] Appeals that All Lives Matter are framed also as recognition that people *regardless* of skin color are vulnerable to possible premature death via physical or structural violence. To this end, the subject position of All Lives Matter is the liberal subject in that all humans are ostensibly the same. The liberal subject, we recall, is an abstract figure premised on a denial of difference. Indeed, as Berg reminds us, "to even raise the specter of 'racial difference' is itself read as an act of racism."[263] In this way, the liberal subject—and especially its neoliberal counterpart—is blamed for its own failings. Poor people, for example, are poor because they have not responsibly participated in the "land of opportunity." However, just as the (neo-)liberal subject is racially coded, so too the lives in All Lives Matter. For underlying the criticism of Black Lives Matter is a deflection of responsibility away from structural and institutional forms of oppression and toward the lives of Black people. In a color-blind society, maimed and murdered Blacks are responsible for their being shot. If Floyd was shot by the police, so supporters of All Lives Matter maintain, he must have been doing something illegal. Alternatively, he should have obeyed the orders of the police. Either way, victims are blamed for their own premature deaths.

Garza and other members of the Black Lives Movement were well aware of a potential white backlash.[264] Writing in 2014, Garza explained: "We completely expect those who benefit directly and improperly from White supremacy to try and erase our existence."[265] Garza expounds: "Unfortunately, when something becomes a signifier for a movement, it can also become a brand and that gets commercialized and has its content stripped from it. So while we know what people are talking about, others who are still learning about the Black Lives Matter movement might not understand what's problematic about it."[266] On this point, Garza stresses that "We're not saying Black lives are more important than other lives, or that other lives are not criminalized and oppressed in various ways. We remain in active solidarity with all oppressed people who are fighting for their liberation and we know that our destinies are intertwined."[267] She continues: "Centering Black lives is not an act of violence or hatred against whites. This is about acknowledging that the system already treats white lives as far more valuable and more worthy of protection, safety and a higher quality of life than we are."[268] Garza, in fact, captures Eddie Glaude's concept of the "value gap."[269] For Glaude, the value gap refers to the idea that "no matter our stated principles or how much progress we think we've made, white people are valued more than others in this country, and that fact continues to shape the life chances of millions of Americans."[270] Notably, Glaude underscores the fact that it isn't just about equality or fairness; instead, it is the unyielding truth that white supremacy increases the vulnerability of Black people and other minorities in the United States to premature death.

Conclusions

The term *working class* is a shifting signifier and acquires considerable purchase in popular and political discourse.[271] When the working class is portrayed as comprising white people, alienation, as a concept and a condition of the working class, becomes whitened. And when alienation is understood as class struggle, it is a struggle among and between *white* workers. In other words, appeals to the unstated whiteness of the working class simultaneously masks four centuries of white supremacy while championing the heroics of the white worker. As such, white people (but especially white men) become the star players of America's fabled history as they heroically struggle against all odds in the face of growing adversity personified by nonwhite outsiders. This is why an intersectional approach toward alienation is required. In concrete terms, the alienated subject can be racist or the subject of racist attacks; the alienated subject can be misogynist or the subject of misogynist attacks; and the alienated subject can be the perpetrator or recipient of homophobic, xenophobic, Islamophobic attacks. There is no homogenized alienated subject beyond the abstract, for alienation is necessarily embodied and experienced spatially in a plurality of forms, mediated by one's subject position. And from this vantage point, the alienated subject, in the abstract, embodies both a capacity to hurt and to be hurt.

My argument is not to downplay the importance of class analyses and of the practice of the proletariat. The working class retains a pivotal role in the abolition of exploitation and oppression; indeed, were this not the case, there would be no need to suppress labor through antiunion legislation or the elimination of workers' rights. No, capitalists are well aware of the centrality of labor, of the need to appropriate surplus value through the exploitation of workers, but also of the ever-present threat of labor unrest. For these reasons, it is not coincidental that from Reagan onward, a generation of neoliberalists have co-opted and conned the working-class subject, offering it adulations with one hand while picking its pockets with the other. And here, racism, patriarchy, and other forms of oppression are used to divide the working class—to great effect. Casting the white alienated subject (in the abstract) as the embodiment of patriotism and nationalism, neoliberalists simultaneously portray other working-class members as perpetual outsiders, because of their ancestry, gender, sexuality, or citizenship status. To this end, the maintenance of white supremacy (and patriarchy) is a necessary condition for the reproduction of capitalism just as much as the reproduction of capitalism necessitates the continuance of white supremacy. The problem of our present moment is an inability or unwillingness of people conditioned to accept the predominance of whiteness to see people like George Floyd as an alienated subject, a precarious worker living within intersecting structures of oppression.

In the United States, a society founded upon settler colonialism and racial capitalism, ideologies of white supremacy have historically prevented, and continue to prevent, the establishment of a class-conscious revolutionary movement.[272] Indeed, as Inwood explains, "Whenever African Americans and other minority groups have achieved civil rights progress or when whites perceive their position in society as vulnerable, there has been an upsurge in white supremacist violence and opposition to the legal progress of people seen as socially suspect or material threats to the United States' racial and gendered hierarchy." In this fashion, the white alienated subject serves as a touchstone, an abstract ideal of American traditional values. Championed especially but not exclusively by Nixon, Reagan, and Trump, the white alienated subject provides symbolic sanctuary for a white working class seemingly embattled by external forces.[273] As Cowie and Boehm explain, politicians and pundits "tapped into the material, social, and moral concerns of the white, male working class, but actively and strategically reformulated what it meant to be working class by seeking to move the ground of resentments away from the economics of class and onto social issues."[274]

Within racial capitalism, there is little incentive for the white (and male) alienated subject to demand progressive change, for the privileges of its whiteness (and maleness) surpass, both materially and meaningfully, any economic exploitation that it might experience. From Reconstruction to the right-wing populisms of today, white wage laborers have always, in the end, sought not to topple but to be favored and accommodated by a capitalist class that nonetheless exploits them.[275] To be sure, the white alienated subject may want higher wages or even better working conditions, but the struggle to achieve these improvements often comes at the expense of nonwhites. Consequently, the white alienated subject is alternatively indifferent to (that is, professing a belief in a color-blind society) race problems or intolerant of racial Others and corresponding race-based policies and programs. In part, the reaction depends on the particular group formation in which the alienated subject finds itself. At a sporting event, for example, the white alienated subject can easily cheer for its favorite team alongside persons of color; in so doing, the white alienated subject can declare an indifference to race. Indeed, the white alienated subject may trot out the weary—but often effective—claim that it has many Black friends, as evidenced by the shared participation at the event. However, in other domains—perhaps when talking with other like-minded subjects—the white alienated subject will express feelings of intolerance of, for example, undocumented (and nonwhite) migrants or of the stereotypical (and Black) welfare queen who is taking advantage of the system and is effectively preventing whites from advancing economically.

The Black Lives Matter movement captures, I believe, the spirit, power, and optimism of spontaneous participatory democracy envisioned by Marx and other socialists; of the strength of grassroots mobilization able to challenge the hegemony of racial capitalism and white supremacy. Indeed, the vehemence directed against Black Lives Matter by conservative politicians and pundits demonstrates both the potency of collective action and the fragility of white supremacy. Throughout the 1980s, as Rod Bush explains, the epicenter of Black activism passed from the radicals (for example Malcolm X, Mumia Abu-Jamal, Kathleen Cleaver, Huey Newton) to elected officials.[276] A movement that served as a "wellspring of radical ideologies among the Black working class and its organic intellectuals" gradually gave way to a more sedate movement, one that appealed to, and was more tolerable for, white people.[277] Indeed, for Bush, "The repression of the radical wing of the Black Power movement was accompanied by the co-optation of its more moderate elements, who were opposed to the system's racism but thought the system could be reformed if Blacks were admitted to the system commensurate with their qualifications."[278] From Ferguson onward, however, the pendulum is perhaps swinging back. Keeanga-Yamahtta Taylor, for example, finds that "the young people of Ferguson had great reverence and respect for the memory of the civil rights movement, but the reality is that its legacy meant little in their everyday lives."[279] She explains, on the one hand, that this new generation of activists "bring new ideas, new perspectives, and often, new vitality to the patterns and rhythms of activism" while, on the other hand, "the tactical and strategic flexibility of the youth activists flowed from a developing politics that could not be constrained by a narrow agenda of voter registration or a simple electoral strategy."[280] Arguably more important, however, is the recognition, as Taylor writes, that the emerging politics are "embodied by the emergence of young Black women as a central organizing force."[281]

The centrality of the Black Lives Matter movement to the current political movement cannot be ignored by the revolutionary Left. That said, there remain many ardent socialists who fear the political power of movements such as Black Lives Matter, for these appear as diversionary to the task at hand, namely, the transformation of the alienated subject through class struggle. Cedric Johnson, for example, worries that an overemphasis of the centrality of racism obscures the class relations at the root of economic inequality.[282] However, if self-emancipation through collective self-determination of the working class is foundational to the struggle against capitalism, then it is indispensable for progressives to acknowledge the shifting demographic composition of class and class relations. As Benjamin Balthaser and Bill Mullen explain, this requires comprehension of the upsurge in wildcat strikes, teacher walkouts, organizing in the informal sector, the superexploitation of Black, immigrant, and women workers in the care economy; in short, virtually, everything.[283] In the end, it is likely the face of the proletarian struggle of the twenty-first century is not that of the white alienated subject but instead the face of a working-class queer Black woman.

5

The Emancipated Subject

"In the social production of their existence," Marx writes, people "inevitably enter into definite relations, which are independent of their will, namely relations of production appropriate to a given stage in the development of their material forces of production."[1] In this well-known passage, Marx affirms that people's choices are circumscribed by structural and social relations that precede them, that is, antecedent forms of social organization. This does not mean that our lives are determined but instead that our everyday lives are conditioned historically and geographically. Erich Fromm expands upon this point, noting that "the mode of life, as it is determined for the individual by the peculiarity of an economic system, becomes the primary factor in determining his whole character structure, because the imperative need for self-preservation forces him to accept the conditions under which he has to live."[2] Here, Fromm underscores the materiality of everyday life, notably that one's awareness of premature death *that might occur in the absence of the basic necessities that make life possible* impel people to conform to, or subject themselves to, those structural and social relations in existence. Under the capitalist mode of production, if one is precluded access to the means of production the only *legal* recourse is to obtain waged employment. That said, Fromm quickly qualifies his statement, clarifying, "This does not mean that [an individual] cannot try, together with others, to effect certain economic and political changes."[3] In other words, resistance is possible; and this resistance happens in solidarity with other, like-minded individuals.

In this concluding chapter I consider the emancipatory promise and potential of the alienated subject. Drawing insight and inspiration from ongoing efforts to promote an ethics of care, I reconsider Fromm's radical conception of productive love. Redolent of the spirit of the Black Lives Matter movement, an ethics of care centered on productive love provides a way forward, a path toward the emancipatory aspirations of a society that enables all to live meaningful, flourishing lives. This requires, however, an attentiveness to the siren's call of immature love, that is, a sadomasochistic relationship among people mediated by the false promises of capitalism. I begin, therefore, with a brief recapitulation of the meaninglessness of life in capitalism, followed by a repositioning of the alienated subject as sadomasochist. I then proceed to a reevaluation of freedom, necessity, and living as a framework for my forwarding of a loving, emancipated subject.

The Meaninglessness of Capitalism

As Todd May explains, meaningfulness is a human product but also a social product; our values, our morals, our sense of justice, are constrained, not necessarily by the material world but instead by the social relations in which we interact. To this end, the practices that emanate from particular social and spatial relations mediate what—and how—we value in, or give meaning to, society. Of these practices and relations, Fromm introduces the concept of "social character." Itself an expansion of Marx's notion of social formation, the concept of social character refers to those traits of a social group which have developed as the result of the basic experiences and mode of life common to that group.[4] Fromm in fact believed that Marx's focus on the process of production in shaping needs had unearthed the fundamental basis of a dynamic social psychology that would interpret material human needs and motivations as mediated by the social structure of a society.[5]

Stated differently, the concept of social character provides insight into how shared ideologies that reflect particular modes of production are produced and reproduced. Indeed, as Jason Read reminds us, every mode of production necessarily presupposes and reproduces particular forms of sociality and subjectivity.[6] Differences in the social character of societies, to this end, are fundamentally the result of adaptions to different modes of production, that is, how people live throughout their day-to-day interactions within different structural and social relations of production, distribution, and consumption. In chapter 2, for example, we saw how the shaping of the human being under capitalism, that is, the real subsumption of society, is mediated by the market-logics of capitalism. In other words, whereas capitalism is a social and economic system based on a combination of private ownership of property, self-interested pursuit of such property, the exchange of goods and services, and the market as means of determining prices of goods and services, capitalism *also* encourages endless consumption, entrenches inequalities, discourages community-mindedness, and privileges individual rather than social freedom.[7] The neoliberal subject, on this point, embodies economic rationalism, competition, entrepreneurialism, individualism, and independence; these values, in turn, are represented as the antithesis of governmental responsibilities for equitable and meaningful living conditions and care of the individual, the household, or social groups.[8] In turn, these values which are *mediated by one's position in society* inform both materially and symbolically everyday social interactions, often with grave consequences.

Capitalism, to this end, is inherently alienating and *sadomasochistic.* As Lynn Chancer writes, "The relationship between worker and capitalist is inclined in a highly symbiotic direction, creating a literally life-and-death situation: the worker requires the job for his or her subsistence or the subsistence of his or her family; the capitalist requires the worker's labor and acquiescence to the relations of production in order to be able to subsist qua capitalist."[9] Both worker and capitalist, in their unique ways, are alienated, subject to the mastery of dead labor over living labor. On the one hand, the capitalist worships the commodity and becomes dependent upon its continual exchange for his or her biological and class reproduction, while, on the other hand, the worker likewise remains dependent on the commodity for his or her own survival. Chancer elaborates: "Because capitalism makes the worker's ability to survive contingent not only upon his or her labor but on agreement to workplace conditions imposed from above without equal participation or consent, a worker's worth is never accepted and taken for granted simply because he or she exists and is a human being. Rather, value, worth, and legitimacy of self must constantly be earned, proved, sought, deserved. They are, as it were, conditional upon the approval of [someone or something else], in this case, the capitalist."[10]

The struggle between capital and labor, Fromm cautions, "is much more than the conflict between two classes, more than their fight for a greater share of the social product. It is the conflict between two principles of value: that between the world of things, and their amassment, and the world of life and its productivity."[11] Effectively, all social relations that comprise the capitalist mode of production are mediated by the vulnerability of premature death, that is, life itself is conditional upon the workings of capitalism. However, ideologies of individualism and competition work against the forwarding of solidarity and cooperation. In the United States, especially, the discourse of "rugged individualism" instills values that go against the fact that humans are social beings, conditioned to lead communal lives. The alienated subject in the abstract loses sight of this condition, believing instead that the ability to lead a flourishing life is a solitary activity or, at most, an activity circumscribed by members of one's own (and selective) subject position. Simply put, as Rainer Funk concludes, "The fact that we do not experience the emptying and devaluation of the subject, as well as the dependency on the market as something abnormal anymore is a central indication of what Fromm . . . calls 'the pathology of normalcy.'"[12] Capitalism appears as a source of comfort: it provides employment, and with this, wages to purchase goods and services we want. And capitalism provides consumers with a seemingly endless choice of wants. In actuality, capitalism deceives and distorts; commodities control us.

Capitalism is stultifying and deadens the possibilities and potentialities of living a flourishing, meaningful life. The negative freedom offered by capitalism, Fromm posits, has brought a false sense of independence and rationality and, in the process, conditioned people to find meaning in isolation. This isolation does not necessarily translate as physical isolation; it refers, rather, to an emotional estrangement that affects one's everyday life.[13] Consequently, Fromm maintains that the social character of capitalism is that of "marketing," that is, a character orientation grounded in the "experience of oneself as a commodity and of one's value as exchange value."[14] For Fromm,

> The modern market is no longer a meeting place but a mechanism characterized by abstract and impersonal demand. One produces for this market, not for a known circle of customers; its verdict is based on laws of supply and demand; and it determines whether the commodity can be sold and at what price. No matter what the use value of a pair of shoes may be, for instance, if the supply is greater than the demand, some shoes will be sentenced to economic death; they might as well not have been produced at all. The market day is the "day of judgement" as far as the exchange value of the commodities is concerned.[15]

Fromm's assertion has ominous implications for the alienated subject who has nothing to sell but its own labor-power. Given that one's sense of worth is conditioned under capitalism by market forces seemingly beyond one's control, Fromm argues that "one's self esteem is bound to be shaky and in constant need of confirmation by others."[16] Effectively, the alienated subject seeks an escape from its mundane, practico-inert life, that is, a search for meaning in *places beyond the work site.* However, meaning remains mediated by those attitudes and beliefs that emanate from capitalism. Fromm continues: "One is driven to strive relentlessly for success, and any setback is a severe threat to one's self-esteem; helplessness, insecurity, and inferiority feelings are the result. If the vicissitudes of the market are the judges of one's values, the sense of dignity and pride is destroyed."[17] Meaningful life under capitalism, as such, is fetishized and experienced in accordance to the market logic of exchange-value. Indeed, Fromm highlights the "burden of being unemployed," whereby "to have a job—regardless of what kind of a job it is—seems to many all they could want of life and something they should be grateful for." Such is the mindset of the alienated subject under neoliberalism who—aware of its vulnerability to premature death for fear of being unemployed—willingly submits to the precarity of an economic system oriented not to its own survival but instead toward the survival of the system.

In describing the rise of Nazism in Germany, for example, Fromm explains that millions of ordinary Germans were simply indifferent; they were not supporters of the Nazi ideology—but neither were they outspoken critics or resisters. Largely unaffected by the rising tide of intolerance and hatred, many Germans chose to look away. The Holocaust, as Elie Wiesel affirms, was made possible by indifference. Speaking before the United States Senate, Wiesel explains that "indifference can be tempting—more than that, seductive. It is so much easier to look away from victims. It is so much easier to avoid such rude interruptions to our work, our dreams, our hopes. It is, after all, awkward, troublesome, to be involved in another person's pain and despair. Yet, for the person who is indifferent, his or her neighbors are of no consequence. And, therefore, their lives are meaningless. Their hidden or even visible anguish is of no interest. Indifference reduces the other to an abstraction."[18]

For many people in the United States, ongoing police violence, pandemics, the devastation of climate change and of environmental degradation are interruptions in their comfortable, consuming lives; the victims are mere abstractions, faceless and nameless. It is easier to do nothing, to say nothing, to feel nothing. And in doing nothing, the status quo remains and the misery and suffering and premature death of those rendered more vulnerable by unjust structural and social relations continues. As Wiesel concludes, "to be indifferent to that suffering is what makes the human being inhuman."[19]

For Fromm, pervasive feelings of indifference contribute to a "pathology of normalcy." More precisely, Fromm argues that an "insane society" produces alienated subjects, and that capitalism is insanity par excellence.[20] How else are we to explain the cruelty and callousness of the Trump administration's response to both the global pandemic and rampant police violence? A sane society, conversely, is that which corresponds to the needs of humanity, that is, a society conditioned by concern, empathy, and a respect for humanity's mutual dependency with each other and the Earth we inhabit. A sane society is one that fosters a flourishing life for all. For alienated subjects, however, such a society appears utopian, the stuff of unrealistic dreams of idealists or "social justice wingnuts." Worse yet, a sane society appears to the alienated subject as weak, its members irresponsible and indolent. And for this alienated subject, indifference may readily transform into intolerance and, subsequently, the need to foster meaning in life elsewhere. Here, Fromm underscores the fact that the need to defend oneself against the loneliness and meaningless of society can take the form of submission to a powerful being (masochism) or of exerting controls over a relatively powerless party (sadism).[21] In other words, meaning in life is sought through the simultaneous "longing for submission and lust for power."[22] This has grim implications, however, for as Fromm warns, a principal avenue of escape for the sadomasochist is the gravitation toward authoritarianism. This is a key insight, as I develop in the following section, whereby I reposition the alienated subject as sadomasochist, that is, as one who is not indifferent to but instead intolerant of others and, as such, is readily capable of, and willing to, hurt others.

The Alienated Subject as Sadomasochist

The alienated subject, in the abstract, is one who is completely estranged from its own desires, from other humans, and from humanity itself; the alienated subject inhabits a material, social world in which everyday, normal functioning is incompatible with the capacity to live a meaningful, flourishing life.[23] Accordingly, Fromm postulates, the alienated subject, the "insane" subject, is "one who has completely failed to establish any kind of union, and is imprisoned, even if he is not behind barred windows."[24] To this end, the alienated subject yearns for fulfillment, for a sense of belonging, to participate in meaningful social relations. That it does so within the social character of capitalism, however, mediates the outcome of its attempt to overcome its sense of estrangement. In societies marked and marred by racial capitalism, for example, this mediation appears in the form of white supremacy.

In this penultimate section, following Fromm, Chancer, Sandra Lee Bartky, and others, I elaborate a political philosophy of sadomasochism and, more precisely, reposition the alienated subject as sadomasochist, a subject position prone to authoritarianism. We have seen, for example, that members of the working class feel not only dependent but extremely dubious about their sense of worth, forever hoping to find recognition or meaning that has seemingly been denied.[25] This follows, Chancer explains, because "the social psychological ramifications under capitalism of an omnipotent orientation toward exchange value is that we evaluate everything, including ourselves, with greater regard to meaning for them than for us. How can we best sell ourselves, we wonder, best package ourselves in order to obtain a particular job."[26] Even the capitalist is subject to these demands, compelled as he or she is to out-compete or out-consume other capitalists. To this end, workers and capitalists both seek external confirmation and so sacrifice even more their sense of autonomy. In other words, the alienated subject *regardless of personal wealth* exhibits a tendency to give up the independence of its own individual self and to fuse its self with somebody or something else in order to acquire the strength which it feels is lacking.[27] In Sartrean terms, we may surmise that the alienated subject pledges itself, for example, to a group and its leader in an attempt to derive meaning in life. As Fromm explains, "the sadomasochist person is always characterized by his attitude toward authority. He admires authority and tends to submit to it, but at the same time he wants to be an authority himself and have others submit to him."[28]

Sadism and masochism are not exclusive subject positions but instead two sides of the same coin. In other words, the alienated subject as sadomasochist demonstrates the intersectionality of multiple subject positions and the contingency of myriad and interlocking structures and social relations of oppression. On the one hand, the alienated subject attempts to transcend its sense of estrangement by becoming part of somebody or something larger than itself, that is, by its submission to a person, a group, or an institution.[29] Feelings of loss, inferiority, powerlessness, insignificance, of being under attack, or of being left behind all contribute to the desire to be part of something larger, that is, to submit oneself to a person, a movement, or an ideology, such as Trump and Trumpism. As Cheryl Matias and Ricky Allen explain, "Masochists doubt their capabilities. They give up freedom to decide for themselves, be responsible for their own fate, and contribute creatively to the betterment of humanity, all in the name of their compulsion not to be alone."[30] Under conditions of racial capitalism, for example, white privilege affords for many white people emotional comfort, clarity, stability, and meaning in an otherwise meaningless, precarious, and chaotic society. In doing so, however, the white alienated subject as masochist invariably exchanges class solidarity for racial privilege, for as the white alienated subject willingly submits to the privileges of being white, it does so at its own class expense. That is, the white alienated subject implicitly submits to the desires of the more powerful capitalist and, subsequently, deepens its own estrangement, for, as Fromm concludes, "every act of submissive worship is an act of alienation and idolatry."[31]

On the other hand, the alienated subject can try to find meaning through the domination of another, by having power over another. As sadist, the alienated subject "needs the person over whom he rules, he needs him very badly, since his own feeling of strength is rooted in the fact that he is the master over someone."[32] Trump, through his narcissism, embodies the need to attain meaning in life through sadism. His incessant rallies; his demeaning of women, African Americans, Hispanics, and the differently abled; and his greed all testify to his need to dominate. However, although extreme in his sadism, Trump is not that exceptional. Thus, the white alienated worker, while submitting to, pledging to, an authority figure such as Trump who embodies and channels white supremacy, also seeks meaning through its domination of other people seen as racially inferior and threatening. Insecure in its own precarious class position, the exploited white member of the working class is able to cash in the psychological wages of whiteness and thus (attempt to) exert racial dominance over Blacks and other people of color. So too the misogynist seeks to find meaning in an uncertain existence through the control over women. In so doing, the racist or misogynist alienated subject finds security in association with other like-minded individuals. As Fromm concludes, the attempt to overcome feelings of isolation and powerlessness are matched with an attempt to become part of something bigger and more powerful; and this subjugation can assume the form of a person, an institution, the nation, and so on. Regardless of the focus of subjugation, "one surrenders one's own self and renounces all strength and pride connected with it, one loses one's integrity as an individual and surrenders freedom; but one gains a new security and a new price in the participation in the power in which one submerges."[33] The alienated subject as sadomasochist is thus saved from the doubts and insecurities of an uncertain world; its submission to a power greater than itself allows it to simultaneously dominate others seen as weak or threatening.

This configuration of the sadomasochist effectively captures the authoritarian tendency of alienated subjects. Authoritarianism, Matthew MacWilliams explains, "is best understood not as a policy preference, the way we talk about lower taxes or strong defense, but rather as a world view that can be 'activated' in the right historical moment by anyone with a big enough megaphone who is willing to play on voters' fears and insecurities."[34] This is extremely salient, for authoritarian leaders cut across both the political spectrum and socioeconomic divisions, such as education, income, age, and even ethnicity.[35] In the broadest sense of the term, authoritarians are described as rigid thinkers who perceive the world in black-and-white terms.[36] MacWilliams continues: "Uniformity and order are authoritarian watch words. Authoritarians obey. They seek order. They follow authoritarian leaders. They eschew diversity, fear 'the other,' act aggressively toward others, and, once they have identified friend from foe, hold tight to their decision." In short, authoritarians are, in Sartre's terminology, members of sworn groups and thus are intolerant of those perceived as outside their own narrowly circumscribed group of like-minded individuals. Alienated subjects are emotive subjects. It is precisely for this reason that Fromm warns of "the readiness [of the alienated subject] to accept any ideology and any leader, if only he promises excitement and offers a political structure and symbols which allegedly give meaning and order to an individual's life."[37] In other words, authoritarian leaders capitalize on the alienation of their subjects in pursuit of their own agendas.

Trump, as such, is a prototypical authoritarian figure. Throughout his presidential election campaign and subsequent administration, Trump's incessant rhetoric and behavior electrified many Americans predisposed to authoritarianism and activated by feelings of alienation. They rallied to his banner—literally—and obediently followed his lead.[38] Of Trump's rise to the presidency, Daniel Burston writes that "millions of Americans elected a candidate who rose to fame as the host of a 'reality TV' show in which he dominated, controlled, and humiliated prospective employees;

who promoted 'law and order' while quoting Mussolini; a candidate whose policy pronouncements frequently ignored (or negated) the US Constitution; who thrives on tabloid style conspiracy theories; who lies and fabricates freely, without inhibition or remorse; whose sexist, racist and anti-Semitic attitudes are plain to see; who retweets posts from white supremacist websites, and openly praises dictators like Vladimir Putin."[39] As Matt Karamazov sums up, "Modern propaganda is all about making people love their servitude. You can give them stock options, a white picket fence, fast food, and some trash TV, and most people will forget that they have never been free."[40]

That so many conservative voters flocked to an authoritarian figure such as Trump is really no surprise. For although authoritarianism is not limited to any one party, it is highly correlated with conservatism. Indeed, surveys demonstrate repeatedly the preponderance of authoritarian attitudes among conservatives in general, and white conservatives specifically. One study, for example, found that 44 percent of white respondents nationwide scored as "high" or "very high" authoritarians. And while there were authoritarian voters in both political parties, more than 65 percent of people who scored highest on the authoritarianism questions were Republican voters.[41]

American authoritarians, MacWilliams finds, overwhelmingly fear diversity, that is, they are most fearful of internal threats that they viewed as undermining the stability of the social hierarchy that gives them meaning in life—a patriarchal, heterosexual, white America. As such, "they are more likely to agree that increasing racial, religious and ethnic diversity is a clear and present threat to national security. They are more fearful of people of other races, and agree with the statement that 'sometimes other groups must be kept in their place.'"[42] To this end, authoritarian voters want a strong leader who promises to eliminate the threats, if necessary by violence, in order to preserve the status quo. As Jennifer Mercieca concludes, if there was a choice to be made between democracy and the stability of the social hierarchy, authoritarian voters were likely to choose stability over democracy.[43] For example, only 49 percent of Trump supporters agreed that the freedom of the press to criticize political leaders is essential to maintaining a strong democracy; and only 69 percent of Trump supporters thought it was very important that people have a right to nonviolent protest.[44] Conservative politicians, likewise, express authoritarian views, providing emotional ammunition to their supporters. Just weeks before the 2020 presidential election, for example, Senator Mike Lee posted on Twitter that "Democracy isn't the objective; liberty, peace, and [prosperity] are. We want the human condition to flourish. Rank democracy can thwart that."[45] Here, Lee tapped into the emotional vulnerabilities of an alienated populace and promised a meaningful life not through the democratic process but rather through blind devotion to authoritarianism.

The rise of Trumpism effectively illustrates how generations of white people internalized the hyperpatriotism of American exceptionalism and took to heart the idolatry of the (white) working class. Trump routinely pledged his love and devotion to this group and promised he would protect them from dangerous nonwhite Others. And although Trump was disingenuous, often blatantly so, it mattered little to his followers who, in turn, pledged their loyalty and support to the president. What truly mattered was the restoration of an emotional void created by a perceived loss of whiteness, patriarchy, and heteronormativity.

Crucially, as Amanda Taub explains, authoritarians frequently support forceful, decisive action against people or ideas they perceive as threats to their elevated positions. This often includes the threat or actual use of physical violence, whether enacted by law enforcement agencies, private militias, or vigilantes. Indeed, authoritarians are exceptionally capable and willing to commit harm, that is, they embody the Sartrean notion of the terror-fraternity. On October 8, 2020, for example, six white militia members were arrested for conspiring to kidnap Michigan's Democratic governor Gretchen Whitmer. Over a period of months, militia members discussed the violent overthrow of local governments and talked about "murdering . . . tyrants" or "taking" a sitting governor, in this case, Whitmer, and placing her on trial for "treason." Indeed, one militia member said of Whitmer, she "has no checks and balances at all. She has uncontrolled power right now. All good things must come to an end." In addition, two of the alleged conspirators "agreed to unite others in their cause and take violent action against multiple state governments that they believe are violating the U.S. Constitution." The targeting of Whitmer was not random. Over a period of several months, Whitmer was called out repeatedly by Trump for her approach to the pandemic, specifically her promotion of mask-wearing regulations, social distancing, and sheltering in place. More precisely, Trump goaded his supporters to "liberate Michigan."[46]

The authoritarian Trump supporter effectively captures the sadomasochistic tendencies postulated by Fromm, namely, the masochistic devotion to an authoritarian figure and the capacity to commit sadistic violence against people deemed dangerous, inferior, or weak. To this end, Trump was well aware of this power he held over his supporters, as demonstrated by his infamous remark, "I could stand in the middle of Fifth Avenue and shoot somebody. And I wouldn't lose any voters, OK. It's like incredible." This is why Trump's rhetoric and style proved so intoxicating to his supporters. As Taub explains, Trump's willingness to flout all the conventions of civilized discourse when it came to the minority groups that alienated white people feared proved a benefit rather than a liability; hence, when Trump decried Mexicans as rapists and criminals or spoke of massacring Muslims with pig-blood-tainted bullets, he sent a message to his supporters that he would not let "political correctness" hold him back in attacking those people they feared.[47]

Freedom, Necessity, and Living

Throughout his writings Marx is circumspect on the topic of unalienated life. In part, this results from his dialectic epistemology. For Marx it was improper to specify with any degree of certainty how a future postcapitalist society might appear or function. Nevertheless, scattered among his writings are various clues that shed insight into his thinking. To this end, much attention has focused on Marx's forwarding of the "realms of freedom" and "realms of necessity."[48] Together, these concepts have generated substantial debate among historians and philosophers; they are also of considerable importance toward our understanding of the emancipation of the alienated subject.

Briefly stated, the realm of necessity refers to work, while the realm of freedom refers to time outside the working day.[49] Beyond this simple explanation, however, lies a more nuanced journey into the ideas and ideals of freedom, democracy, and labor. At issue is not merely how humans spend their time, whether at work or at play, but instead how the temporal and spatial allocations of productive and reproductive tasks impinge on political participation and, equally importantly, on how individuals (and society) may promote and lead an unalienated life. As Hägglund writes, "Because we are living beings, we must work to maintain ourselves. Yet, all the time we have is not necessarily required to ensure our biological survival and it is an open question for us what we should do with the surplus of time."[50]

Depending on the context, Marx uses the terms *work* and *labor* in precise ways. In reference to the realm of necessity, Marx refers to labor as that directed toward satisfying the basic needs of society.[51] This aligns with historical materialism and Marx's first premise: the production of food, water, shelter, and clothing are necessary requirements for the biological, material, and ideological reproduction of society. The realm of freedom would thus *appear* to be in opposition to the realm of necessity. Indeed, one reading would suggest that the realm of freedom equates with leisure, or time away from the drudgery of work. As Jan Kandiyali explains, the "natural temptation is to see the 'realm of freedom' and the 'realm of necessity' as being opposed to one another, so that the contrast is between a 'realm of freedom,' that comprises all that is free, and a 'realm of necessity,' comprising its opposite, namely, alienation, unfreedom and such like."[52] This is not Marx's intention. Kandiyali suggests that Marx is actually positing two realms of freedom: on the one hand, there is freedom as *self-determination,* understood as collectively determining one's activity instead of being ruled by external forces, and, on the other hand, freedom as *self-realization,* understood as the development of one's distinctly human capacities and potentialities.[53]

A materialist understanding of history holds that societies at a basic level are concerned first and foremost with satisfying the conditions necessary for life itself. In so-called primitive societies, notably those characterized as "hunting and gathering," labor is performed by humans, but it is labor marked by necessity. Ollman explains, "Such labor is mere energy expended to satisfy immediate physical needs and has little in common with human productive activity."[54] In this context, human labor is largely indistinguishable from that of animals; all species by necessity need to acquire food and water and to seek shelter. In such a society, the human condition is one of unfreedom, as everyday life is characterized by the perennial struggle to satisfy the most basic physical needs.[55] Humans, however, have the capability of performing something else, namely, genuinely creative work.[56]

Throughout human history the productive means of satisfying biological needs have been transformed. Technological innovations, reconfigured divisions of labor, and complex systems of barter and trade all steadily distance humans from the realm of necessity. In other words, humans gradually, almost inexorably, become free from the physical constraints of nature. Indeed, the dialectic relationship between humans and nature is transformed. Eventually, under capitalism, the industrialization and automation of the labor process initiated unprecedented levels of productive power. Paradoxically though, these transformations brought about a fundamental societal contradiction. Production under capitalism, it promises, can provide the means to humanize labor, to reduce the working day, and to lead to greater leisure time.[57] The accumulation of greater wealth, likewise, promises a better quality of life, one where children will no longer go to bed hungry and paupers no longer die in the streets for lack of housing. And yet, Marx observed, under capitalism, societal inequalities became *more* pronounced as humans became alienated from their productive, creative, and meaningful activities. Humanity's conscious activity in a capitalist factory, Ollman writes, "can mean little more than being awake and knowing that one is pulling a lever rather than turning a handle."[58] Hägglund echoes these remarks, noting, "Insofar as we spend our time working a job that is not fulfilling but merely serves as a means for our survival, our labor time is unfree, since we cannot affirm that what we do is an expression of who we are. Instead of being free to engage the question of what makes our life worth living—the question of what we ought to do with our time—our lives are mortgaged to a form of labor that is required for our survival."[59]

Socialism, for Marx, transcends the stultifying condition of alienation and provides the necessary freedom for the development of human creativity and personal fulfillment. In a postcapitalist society, the absence of exploitative and oppressive relations will provide the opportunity to fully cultivate one's life activities and aesthetic endeavors.[60] As Kandiyali concludes, while the realm of necessity may be understood as a realm of self-determination, where men and women exercise control over their economic activity, the realm of freedom is the realm of self-realization, the sphere of life where individuals develop their distinctly human powers and capacities.[61] With the transcendence of capitalism, according to Marx, both self-determination and self-realization become possible. Men and women, while engaging in labor necessary for the production and reproduction of society, exhibit self-determination; they are no longer subject to structures of domination imposed by a ruling class. Work is voluntary, communal, unalienated, and personally fulfilling. Moreover, men and women are able to develop and express their creative capabilities and potentialities.

Missing from this account, however, is an understanding that the alienated subject embodies multiple subject positions, that the alienated subject is simultaneously a member of a particular class and also a member of myriad other groups, some ephemeral, others more permanent. Both white supremacy and patriarchy, for example, are enduring features of many societies and, as such, continue to provide meaning for many people in an otherwise meaningless world. For this reason, it is necessary to expand upon Marx's lead and to reconsider the power and promise of productive activity of the emancipated subject

Love and the Emancipated Subject

Marx's understanding of revolutionary transformations is fundamentally that of *grassroots democracy.* On this point, Fromm argues for an expanded concept of revolution, of the need to address, in contemporary terminology, the intersectionality of sadomasochism embodied in the alienated subject, that is, sexism, racism, nationalism, and other forms of oppression that mediate the capacity to foster a meaningful life free from prejudice, hatred, and violence.

The alienated person is lacking a sense of self; this lack of self creates deep anxiety.[62] It is experienced in many ways: as a sense of loss, of isolation, of powerlessness, and of meaninglessness. Regardless, alienation appears much as the late arrival of a bus, as something disruptive that impels one to act, but often in harmful ways. The alienated subject, for example, might engage in maladaptive practices that effectively reproduce alienation. Consequently, "the realization of the submissive (masochistic) or the domineering (sadistic) passion never leads to satisfaction."[63] To that end, neither sadism nor masochism offers a path toward emancipation, either for one's self or for that of humanity. Consequently, for Fromm, the "art of loving" holds emancipatory promise for the alienated subject.

Fromm is far from alone in affirming the power of love. bell hooks, for example, contends, "Without love, our efforts to liberate ourselves and our world community from oppression and exploitation are doomed."[64] She elaborates, "As long as we refuse to address fully the place of love in struggles for liberation we will not be able to create a culture of conversion where there is a mass turning away from an ethic of domination."[65] In other words, the transformation of the alienated subject into an emancipated subject is doomed to failure without an explicit forwarding of an ethics of love. It is notable that the emancipatory promise of love figures prominently within the Black Lives Matter movement, as illustrated by Alicia Garza's affirmation that Black Lives Matter was addressed as "A Love Letter to Black People." Indeed, as Hebah Farrag and Ann Gleig observe of the Black Lives Matter movement, "Since its inception, BLM organizers have expressed their founding spirit of love through an emphasis on spiritual healing, principles, and practices in their racial justice work."[66]

It may be difficult to see how love offers emancipatory hope. So fully subsumed is society to the market logic of capital that even our attitudes toward love are increasingly commodified. And yet, bell hooks writes: "Though many folks recognize and critique the commercialization of love, they see no alternative. Not knowing how to love or even what love is, many people feel emotionally lost; others search for definitions, for ways to sustain a love ethic in a culture that negates human value and valorizes materialism."[67] In short, love is experienced as alienating and, as such, deepens feelings of aloneness and meaninglessness.

For this reason, Fromm differentiates between "immature" and "mature" forms of love.[68] The former refers to that love experienced by sadists and masochists; in other words, alienation is manifest as a form of immature love. The masochist, for example, escapes from unbearable feelings of isolation, powerlessness, and meaninglessness by making him- or herself part and parcel of another person or group. Finding no meaning in work, the alienated subject looks beyond the job site and submits to a domineering, authoritative figure for guidance and purpose. As Eduardo Bonilla-Silva explains, poor and working-class whites, among others, love Trump not just because of class concerns seemingly addressed by Trump's populism—bringing jobs back, draining the swamp, and dealing with coastal elites who do not represent "real" Americans. Instead, many white people loved Trump precisely because he validated and vowed to protect their white privilege.[69] Trump promised white people tangible ways—such as the building of a wall and the imposition of immigration bans—to uphold a particular way of life in which meaning is derived from their vaunted position in the racial hierarchy of the United States. For white alienated subjects, the persona of Trump and their love for him offered emotional salvation in an uncertain world.

Sadism is also a form of immature love. The sadist wants to escape from his or her aloneness and sense of imprisonment by making another person submit to their relative power; in the process, the sadist acquires meaning through his or her ability to command, exploit, hurt, and humiliate.[70] This is seen especially in the sadistic actions of the alienated capitalist class. As Bertell Ollman writes, "The outstanding qualities which Marx observes in capitalists are greed, cruelty and hypocrisy."[71] Ollman elaborates, "Greed is seen as the motive of most capitalist actions, cruelty as its all too willing handmaiden, and hypocrisy as the mask capitalists wear to hide their motives and means from others."[72] By way of illustration, consider the actions of the meatpacking industry during the Covid-19 pandemic. Meatpacking plants—despite being viral hotspots—were pressed to remain open by Trump and Republican politicians. On the one hand, this decision, coupled with efforts to deny workers' compensation for employees who became ill, laid bare the perverted greed of the employers. On the other hand, the political spectacle of forcing workers to choose between an avoidable risk and of losing a job revealed a sadism indifferent to employees' vulnerability to premature death. In his executive order, for example, Trump forwarded the argument that "it is important that processors of beef, pork, and poultry . . . in the food supply chain continue operating and fulfilling orders to ensure a continued supply of protein for Americans. . . . For example, closure of a single large beef processing facility can result in the loss of over 10 million individual servings of beef in a single day."[73] Notably, Trump failed to address the working conditions of the employees; nor did he frame his executive order as a response to the potential dismissal of workers during an economic downturn. Indeed, as Steven Greenhouse observes, what made Trump's order especially disdainful toward workers' well-being was that "it treats workers and worker health as an afterthought. It's all about production; the workers are forgotten, invisible cogs in Trump's political machinations."[74] In other words, workers—for Trump and his followers—were inconsequential beyond their productive functions to ensure a continual supply of commodities for abstract consumers.

In opposition to immature forms of love are those Fromm describes as mature. Mature love, in this sense, is an active power in humanity, that is, it is productive. However, we should quickly clarify that productivity in this context should not be confused with productive labor in a capitalist sense. Fromm postulates that the active character of productive love implies certain basic elements: *care, responsibility, respect,* and *knowledge.*[75]

Admittedly, on a superficial read, these elements are suggestive of neoliberalism, notably responsibility, which can be understood as being a responsible, productive worker, and respect, implying a deference to authority. However, Fromm clarifies how these elements provide the scaffolding for a radical ethics of love that transcends the market-oriented relations of capitalism and offers a path toward emancipation. Care, to begin, indicates an active concern for the life and well-being of another. As Lydia Wood and colleagues write, "Care is essential to the creation and maintenance of nurturing relations that support well-being and are fundamental to a socially just society."[76] Responsibility, following Fromm, refers to one's ability to be able and ready to *respond* to, that is, to care for, the needs of another. Far from a self-centered quality—of being responsible for one's self—responsibility in this account is entirely selfless and underscores our capacity to help others. Respect entails also a selfless quality, here referring to the ability to see a person as they are, that is, to be aware and accepting of their unique individuality. Respect, simply put, implies the absence of prejudice and bigotry. To respect a person is to *know* a person, that is, to have an empathetic knowledge of the other. As Fromm explains, "Care and responsibility would be blind if they were not guided by [empathetic] knowledge."[77]

Thus conceived, mature love, or what Fromm describes also as "genuine love," becomes an "expression of productiveness"; love is an active striving for the well-being and flourishing of the loved person, grounded in one's own capacity to love. Matias and Allen echo these sentiments and call for "a *humanizing love,* one where those involved in personal or collective relationships give love so as to foster the mutual growth and healing of one another depending on their respective relational needs within traumatizing systems of oppression."[78] As a mode of life, productive, or humanizing, love is premised on the act of giving.[79] Here, also, language matters. Indeed, the act of giving as productive love has a meaning quite specific in the context of emancipatory possibilities. For Fromm, *giving* does not equate with the act of sacrificing something, or letting go. It is not the same as *giving up* when one faces defeat; nor is it the same as *giving away* something and thus being deprived. Rather, "giving is the highest expression of potency" for "in the act of giving lies the expression of my aliveness."[80] To this end, the productive and loving act of giving *provides meaning in life* in solidarity. This stands in contrast to the deadening form of commodified love inherent to capitalism.

Self-emancipation of the alienated subject is a necessary condition for the transformation and eventual overcoming of capitalism. However, as the human species-being is inherently a social and spatial being, this means that self-emancipation is simultaneously mediated by the concrete social and spatial relations in which the alienated subject inhabits. In other words, we need to direct attention toward the mutual co-constitution of emancipation, that is, to always bear in mind that revolutions are social and spatial phenomena. Self-emancipation can only appear through communal action grounded in place. An exclusive focus on individuality, for example, as expressed by neoliberalist ideology, mitigates against the transformation of capitalism.

To this end, scholars have advanced the notion of an "ethics of care"—a guiding principle premised on the notion that all relational practices should be done in a more care-full way, with an emphasis on interdependence and the values of caring.[81] Notably, as Joan Tronto writes, to place care at the center of human life requires that we rethink many of the assumptions that we make about social and political theory.[82] Indeed, Tronto continues, "Care may be ubiquitous in human life, but it has remained hidden from the conceptual lenses of social and political thought."[83] On this point, let me be as clear as possible. If we posit the human condition in accordance with liberalism, that is, as composed of autonomous, rational actors pursuing their own goals and maximizing their interests, alienation appears as the negation of these self-interests. The path toward emancipation, subsequently, would appear to consist of bringing about a material reality that *restores* the pursuit and maximization of the liberal subject's self-interests. If, however, we begin with the supposition that humans are interdependent rather than independent, we begin from the standpoint that people are always and already enmeshed in relationships of care.[84] Alienation, therefore, is understood as the negation of caring relationships; the alienated subject is alienated *precisely* because its everyday life is removed from the ethical interdependency of being human. The path toward emancipation, consequently, entails the restoration of these relations, that is, an ethics of care.

As Victoria Lawson writes, "care ethics begin from the deeply social character of our existence and the ways that caring relations of dependency, frailty, grief and love all shape the ways we reason and act in the world."[85] For these reasons, an awareness of our shared but uneven vulnerability to premature death must figure prominently toward the emancipation of the alienated subject. To be aware of one's possible death is to be aware of the possible death of others; a shared mortality is accompanied by the realization that our lives are dependent on the actions and inactions of ourselves and others; that is, conditions that make possible for the provisioning of food and water, and the avoidance of violent conditions, both structural and physical, that threaten our well-being. Framed in the positive, the manner in which we choose to produce our lives may either complement or hinder the reproduction of others' lives. From this, meaningful life can be fostered through those care-full practices that advance and do not inhibit the flourishing of others. The alienated subject as sadomasochist, for example, is unable to love on equal human terms but instead expresses a love conditional upon its relative position within hierarchical systems of oppression.[86]

A similar ethics of care guided Fromm throughout his life and informed much of his work. Heavily influenced by Rabbi Nehemiah Nobel, himself a student of the socialist and neo-Kantian Herman Cohen, Fromm advocated a humanism built around three basic elements.[87] First, it is imperative for those who stand for ideals of progressive change to practice these in their daily lives; second, one has to take seriously the questions and needs of others and to provide help and guidance; and third, that no ideal can be reached through raw power.[88] Instead, love, humility, and the embrace of justice through solidarity mark the proper path.[89] Notably, Fromm underscores the need to see love as the *capacity to love,* rather than merely being *in* love.[90] Taking this as our cue, we need to think through the transformation of the alienated subject's *capacity to hurt* into a *capacity to love.* For unlike sadomasochistic relations, as Matias and Allen explain, those in a humanizing relation give love to nurture and strengthen the other depending on their situated and relative needs.[91] This raises, in turn, crucial questions of practice, for as Lawson explains, care ethics cannot be practiced in the abstract because they focus on specific sites and social relations. On this point, we return to—and elaborate upon—Marx's distinction between realms of necessity and realms of freedom.

Strangely, the Covid-19 pandemic in the United States generated heated debate over something seemingly as benign (yet life saving) as wearing a mask and, in doing so, underscored the contestation surrounding the very idea of freedom. Coronaviruses, such as Covid-19, are respiratory pathogens, and the use of masks helps prevent the spread of the disease. However, despite repeated calls by scientists, medical doctors, and public health specialists to wear masks (coupled with a suite of other precautionary measures), Trump and many other (mostly) Republican and conservative politicians and pundits refused to wear masks or impose compulsory regulations that would require the wearing of masks. Consequently, many people throughout the United States—but predominantly conservatives—equated the wearing of masks as a forfeiture of their freedoms.[92] Indeed, not only were people intolerant toward the use of masks, many resorted to physical violence in an effort to "protect their freedom" to not wear a mask. Across the country, people were verbally and physically assaulted as they enforced mask-wearing guidelines. In Michigan, for example, a security guard at a Family Dollar store was shot to death by three family members who refused to wear masks.[93]

As Robert Kane explains, *freedom* is a word with many meanings, and there are many different notions of freedom.[94] For our immediate task, three usages are especially helpful, all of which can be promoted or discouraged within Marx's realms of freedom and necessity. First, we can consider the *freedom of self-realization,* that is, "the power or ability to do what we want or will to do, which entails an absence of external constraints or impediments preventing us from realizing our wants and purposes in action."[95] This form of freedom aligns with our commonsense understanding and is manifest in the guarantee of surface freedoms, such as being free to go where we please and live as we choose. Protests against the wearing of masks or of sheltering-in-place were directed toward surface freedoms associated with personal gratification and pleasure, for example, going to bars or restaurants or public beaches. However, the freedom of self-realization has a deeper connotation, one that informs also our understanding of productive activities, both at work and beyond. Here, freedom of self-realization refers to our ability to "see ourselves both in the purpose of our occupation and in the social conditions of the labor that sustains our lives; to recognize our own commitment to freedom in the institutions on which we depend and to which we contribute."[96]

A second form of freedom is the *freedom of reflective self-control.* Kane defines this as "the power to understand and reflectively evaluate the reasons and motives one wants to act upon, or should act upon, and to control one's behavior in accordance with such reflectively considered reasons."[97] This conception of freedom, central to Marx's realm of freedom, calls to question the sadomasochist. For example, the masochist who surrenders his or her freedom to an authoritarian figure exhibits an absence of critical self-reflection. Religion, for example, limit's one's behavior to the extent that one acts in accordance with the dictates of one's God or place of worship. To this end, feelings of alienation, manifest in the realm of necessity, inhibit one's freedom of reflective self-control in the realm of freedom, such that the actions of the alienated subject as sadomasochist are mediated by its acquiescence to some other object or idol. In this way, the alienated subject, lacking a freedom of reflective self-control, finds immature love through an escape from freedom.

The freedom of reflective self-control provides an ethical context for subsequent decisions on how or how not to act. In turn, the morality of concrete freedoms provides a basis for our third and final form of freedom, the *freedom of self-perfection*. For Kane, this is "the power to understand and appreciate the right reasons for action and to guide one's behavior in accordance with the right reasons."[98] In other words, the freedom of self-perfection is a normative freedom—it is emancipatory—and informs our interactions with others. Following Susan Wolf, we realize that freedoms of self-perfection both are relational and provide meaning in life. She explains, "By living in a way that is partly occupied by and directed toward the preservation or promotion or creation of value that has its source outside of oneself, one does something that can be understood, admired or appreciated from others' point of view."[99] To this end, one's awareness of death mediates that which is important and, in doing so, conditions also our wanting to preserve life. This follows from the realization that our lives are dependent on the actions or inactions of others; for the provisioning of food and water, for example, and the avoidance of or response to vulnerabilities to our well-being, such as illness or physical violence. As Hägglund affirms, "Acting on behalf of the one you love is not an alien purpose but the expression of a commitment in which you can recognize yourself, since caring for the interests and the well-being of the other is part of your own understanding of who you are."[100] Likewise, we realize that certain actions (freedoms of reflective self-control) we may take, or fail to take, could lead to the harm of others. Framed in the positive, the manner in which we choose (freedoms of self-perfection) to produce our own lives may either compliment or hinder, constrain or impede, the reproduction of others' lives. From this, we understand that meaning in life is cultivated through those freedoms, those actions and inactions that advance and do not inhibit the life and flourishing of others. Hence, the reproduction of *meaningful life*—not just biological life—is understood as a social good.

So what about regulations to wear masks? Most people would probably agree that public orders to wear masks manifest as *potential* constraints on one's superficial freedoms. Such regulations are understood as coercive measures and, consequently, are perceived as constraints on the exercise of free will. But what precisely is being limited? Simply wearing a mask does not prevent one from enjoying a meal with friends at the local Applebee's, nor does wearing a mask prevent one from getting a haircut. However, exposing *other people* to a potentially life-ending or life-harming disease does negatively constrain or impede *their* well-being and ability to not die a premature death. In short, the selfish (and sadistic) exercise of one's freedom of self-realization, without the associated exercise of one's freedom of reflective self-control and freedom of self-perfection, contributes to a pervasive attitude of indifference to or intolerance of others and, often, is manifest in the capacity to hurt others. Simply put, freedom in capitalism is understood by alienated subjects largely through the fetishized lens of the commodity. Lacking the freedom of reflective self-control, the alienated subject believes that freedom of consumption stands for a deeper, more meaningful freedom of self-perfection. Hence, the alienated subject is willing (impelled) to freely sacrifice civil liberties and thus risk premature death or, as corollary, cause the premature death of others for the sake of momentary pleasures. As Fromm concludes, "In an alienated society the mode in which people express their will is not very different from that of their choice in buying commodities. They are listening to the drums of propaganda and facts mean little in comparison with the suggestive noise which hammers at them."[101] It is ironic—and tragic—that alienated subjects as sadomasochists, such as many Trump supporters, adopt a fatalistic attitude toward Covid-19, that is, an attitude that whatever happens, happens. Indeed, as Trump infamously remarked in response to the rising death toll of the pandemic, "They are dying, that's true. And you have—it is what it is."[102]

In the end, how we lead our lives in the realm of freedom is inseparable from how we live our lives in the realm of necessity.[103] If, for example, we lovingly cooperate within the realm of necessity with each other in a nonexploitative and nonoppressive way, we may likewise cultivate a communal sense of love that extends to the realm of freedom. Likewise, the cultivation of our capacity to love within the realm of freedom, that is, in our everyday activities and aesthetic endeavors, helps us revalue our understanding of productive activity within the realm of necessity. Here, the ongoing efforts of the Black Lives Matter movement underscore the praxis of social organizing, that is, grounded actions—rallies, protests, social media campaigns—coupled with theory. For the multiple Black Lives Matter campaigns, both in the United States and those inspired around the world, initiate particular *historically* and *geographically* specific actions as informed by concrete knowledges of intersecting oppressions.

Conclusions

On the eve of the 2020 presidential election, chaos reigned in the United States. The Covid-19 pandemic, ignored, downplayed, or simply mismanaged from the beginning, continued to spike throughout the country. Over 7.5 million persons were infected, with a death toll in excess of 200,000. The Trump administration had, by this point, washed its hand of the whole affair, thereby consigning millions more to the possibility of premature death. The economy, apart from a widely vacillating stock market, remained in shambles. Nearly 30 million people were receiving unemployment benefits, including over 14 million receiving so-called Pandemic Unemployment Assistance. These numbers do not include an additional 12 million workers who were still waiting to receive any assistance of any type because they fell through the cracks of a mismanaged and, simply put, uncaring government. In July, a program that authorized an additional $600 weekly for the unemployed expired and neither the Republican-dominated Senate nor the Trump administration were motivated to provide any further assistance. Republican politicians overwhelmingly favored a "skinny" stimulus package, at most, that would provide a one-time $1,200 payment for all Americans making $75,000 or less in adjusted gross income. The Democrat-led House of Representatives had passed the HEROES Act in May. This $3 trillion package included $500 billion for states, $365 billion for local governments, $20 billion for tribal communities, and $20 billion for Puerto Rico, Guam, and the U.S. Virgin Islands; an additional $755 million was allocated for coronavirus aid. Provisions also called for additional funds for the Supplemental Nutrition Assistance Program in an effort to reduce food insecurity. It died in the Senate.

And while the working class, collectively, suffered and struggled, the wealthy prospered and flourished at their expense. Indeed, the deliberate responses of the Trump administration and Republican-controlled Senate to the Covid-19 pandemic obscenely exacerbated inequality in the United

States. Throughout the first half of 2020, the top 1 percent of Americans tallied a combined net worth of $34.2 trillion, with the 50 richest people in the country accounting for almost $2 trillion. Conversely, the poorest 50 percent held just $2.08 trillion, that is, just 1.9 percent of all household wealth.[104] Stated more bluntly, just 50 people in the United States controlled more wealth than more than 165 million people *in total.* Moreover, the struggles were experienced differently within the working-class population. Minorities continued to suffer disproportionately, both from the ravages of the pandemic and the precarity of the economy. In August 2020, the white unemployment rate had fallen to 7.3 percent. The unemployment rate for persons of color, however, remained stubbornly high: Black unemployment rate was at 13 percent, the Hispanic rate at 10.5 percent, and Asian Americans at 10.7 percent. Overall, white Americans held 83.9 percent of the country's wealth, compared, for example, with 4.1 percent for Black households.[105] These disparities underscored the bifurcated economic recovery during the pandemic, wherein the wealthy did very well while the condition of the working poor worsened. As Matthew Yglesias explains, if you worked in an office and owned stock or a home, things were bouncing back after the initial financial jolt in March and April; for those who lacked assets, however, especially those persons of color deemed essential workers, vulnerability increased precipitously. The failure of government to respond to these people, Aaron Coleman concludes, left millions with no aid at all, abandoned to suffer the effects of high unemployment in an unprecedented recession, all the while faced with the mortal uncertainties of a deadly virus.[106]

And despite the inevitable onset of media fatigue, protests and demonstrations against police violence continued.[107] From California to Maine, Minnesota to Texas, thousands of people continued to rally in opposition to the oppression and impunity of law enforcement specifically, but also to the everyday vulnerability of people of color to exploitation and systemic racism, sexism, and xenophobia. As Oluchi Omeoga, cofounder of Black Visions Collective, explains, "We are in the biggest social movement this country has ever seen. When we say this is what will be written in the history books, it's not an exaggeration. The folks calling for change in this moment are the folks who are going to be on the right side of history."[108]

Omeoga is not alone in his optimism. Peter Hudis, for example, suggests that the United States is at a turning point—a crossroads. "These massive and ongoing protests," he writes, "are defined by the clash between two absolute opposites—the forces of death embodied in police murder, racism, misogyny, environmental destruction, and the domination of dead labor (or capital) over living labor—and the forces of life, embodied in those aspiring for human emancipation."[109] Accordingly, we are in a position to take stock of what truly *matters* in life, to reevaluate progressive efforts to promote a just, caring, and loving society. As Benjamin Balthaser and Bill Mullen conclude, "Conventional assessments of what constitutes socialism and socialism from below in the U.S. in this historical moment need to begin with participatory observation of how in fact socialism is being conceived of, thought of, debated, and most importantly practiced by a new, radicalized generation."[110] On this point, the Black Lives Matter protests in particular seem to embody the spirit of Marx's postulation of spontaneous, worker-led revolutionary movements. As Paul D'Amato explains, the form of social organization expressed by Marx and Engels, notably in the *Communist Manifesto,* sees the proletariat neither as mere participants in the struggle, nor as an elite that dictates to the masses; rather, the proletariat act as comrades in struggle.[111] D'Amato continues: Marx's notion of the "workers' party acts not only to disseminate socialist ideas, but is involved directly in every struggle. Moreover, it doesn't offer utopian descriptions of the socialist future, but rather gathers together and distills the most important historical lessons of past struggles, in order that those experiences can provide lessons for future struggles."[112] Perhaps no better description fits the deliberate approach of organizing undertaken by the various branches of the Black Lives Matter movement. Indeed, the Black Lives Matter movement, collectively, aligns with centuries of socialist movements that have long sought to build a society in which people could exercise choice over how to achieve human flourishing and utilize their talents in ways that brought meaningful cooperation but without exploiting others.[113]

The working class must remain central to any political left formation and the struggle to overcome the deadening effects of capitalism, if only because of their unique structural ability to impose economic costs on capitalists and to disrupt society at large by collectively withdrawing their labor.[114] That said, we should be mindful that Marx's own faith in the emancipatory promise and potential of the proletariat was always tendential, conditioned upon myriad determinations, not least of which were the noticeable social divisions within the working class itself. In other words, we must resist the idolatry of the mythical (white) alienated subject, especially as this figure remains co-opted by the capitalist class. Inheritors of the Marxist tradition—as well as its detractors—have long favored or feared the working class as agents of revolutionary change. And yet, in the end, emancipation from the structures and relations of oppression and exploitation, if it is to happen, may not in actuality be led by the iconic "mallet-wielding man" as Holly Lewis so memorably describes. Rather, it might appear through the actions of queer Black women.

Peter Lamb, on this point, explains that socialism remains a critical element in the struggle against alienation and exploitation; however, he cautions that "socialists should recognize the need to combine with other movements fighting oppression in contemporary capitalist society, without assuming that socialism should hold precedence."[115] For this reason, an intersectional approach is required that, in positioning the proletariat as revolutionary subject, is sensitive to the myriad and ambiguous subject positions of the alienated population *in total.* Simply put, as Karen Sacks concludes, one should not expect to find any generic worker or essential worker, or for that matter, working-class consciousness; for not only is class experienced in historically and geographically specific ways, but it is also experienced in race-specific and gender-specific ways, among many, many others.[116]

At a minimum, any progressive move forward demands a critical and self-reflective decentering and renouncement of the whiteness, the maleness, the heteronormativity, and the citizenship of the alienated subject both in theory and practice. As Brian Jones explains,

> If millions of working-class white people learn to see racism as a pervasive evil—if they learn to see it in their kids' curriculum, if they see it in the little jokes at work, if they see it in the president's policies, in the unfairness of hiring and firing happening right in front of them, in the zoning of their neighborhood, of their school, in the country's history, if they see a black athlete kneeling during the national anthem and think, "right on!," then we will have a chance at building a movement that takes seriously the idea that an injury to one really is an injury to all.[117]

Efforts to promote class emancipation that fail to address interlocking systems of oppression, including but not limited to racism, sexism, homophobia, transphobia, and xenophobia are inescapably incomplete and inadequate. If, as Marx argues, political emancipation is a necessary but insufficient path toward human emancipation, it holds also that human emancipation *without* political emancipation for the marginalized is not possible. It is therefore not a matter of privileging class over race, sex, or gender but rather of recognizing, as Kimberlé Crenshaw, Patricia Hill Collins, and others do, the intersectionality of these structures of oppression. It is a matter of recognizing the materiality of social and spatial struggle, of the need to place human needs above profits and property, that is, the necessity to allow for the sustenance of life free from want and harm. Fromm concludes: "If I love, I care—that is, I am actively concerned with the other person's growth and happiness; I am not a spectator. I am responsible, that is, I respond to his needs, to those he can express and more so to those he cannot or does not express. I respect him, that is, I look at him as he is, objectively and not distorted by my wishes and fears."[118] In the end, the *emancipated subject* is one who is neither indifferent to the suffering of others nor is intolerant of others; the emancipated subject is one who finds meaning in its generative, that is, life-fulfilling and loving, capacity to heal rather than hurt, and to care rather than cause harm.

Acknowledgments

Where do we find meaning in life? When I was much younger, home for me provided comfort; so too did spending my summer days playing baseball and riding bicycles with my friends. Travel was important, and I have fond memories of drinking hot chocolate with my parents as we sat around a campfire, with snow-capped peaks silhouetted by the fading evening light behind us. Now, looking back, I appreciate how fortunate I was. There were hardships and challenges, to be sure, although for the most part my parents kept these from me. I did not comprehend, then, the downside of academia, of entrenched sexism and of the precarious employment of being an adjunct instructor. Now, having survived many years as a professor, I understand better the difficult life choices my parents made, and how these shaped my own life. Now, when I think about finding meaning in life, and what it means to have a meaningful life, my thoughts turn to an uncertain future. This manuscript is, in large part, written in response to my concerns.

I am deeply appreciative of Jason Weidemann, for his support and guidance of this project, from our early conversations (conducted in person) to the final product (confirmed via Zoom). Heartfelt thanks are extended to Ana Bichanich, Zenyse Miller, Haley Bennett, and the entire staff at the University of Minnesota Press, to Kristine Hunt who copyedited the manuscript, and to those scholars who reviewed the initial prospectus and those who read the completed manuscript. At every stage, countless individuals—some known, many anonymous—provided critical feedback, constructive criticism, and invaluable support. Any remaining errors, of course, remain mine.

Throughout my tenure at Kent State University, I have been fortunate to work with, and learn from, countless students—friends—who have sharpened my thinking and honed my writing, including Gabriela Brindis Alvarez, Sutapa Chattopadhyay, Jaerin Chung, Alex Colucci, Gordon Cromley, Christabel Devadoss, Hanieh Hajj Molana, Sam Henkin, Donna Houston, Olaf Kulke, Josh Inwood, Sokvisal Kimsroy, Robert Kruse, Gabe Popescue,

Mark Rhodes, Stian Rice, Andy Shears, Dave Stasiuk, and Rachel Will. I have also benefited from conversations, both formal and informal, in person and virtual, from innumerable scholars over the years, including Stuart Aitken, Derek Alderman, Noel Castree, Thom Davies, Michael Dear, Stuart Elden, Salvatore Engel-Dimauro, Jim Glassman, Audrey Kobayashi, Don Mitchell, Heidi Nast, Chris Philo, Laura Pulido, Curt Roseman, Ian Shaw, and Simon Springer. None of this work would be possible without the generosity of these scholars who, over the years, offered their wisdom and tolerated my queries, which, retrospectively, must appear terribly pedantic.

I thank my family for their encouragement: first and foremost, my parents, Dr. Gerald Tyner and Dr. Judith Tyner, for their inspiration and encouragement over the years, for the sacrifices they made as I pursued my dreams. I thank also my daughters, Jessica and Anica Lyn, for their sense of humor, particularly when the days seemed cloudy; my wife and life partner, Belinda, who continues to provide emotional support and, if needed, a sharp kick to my shins, when books and papers begin to topple over on the dining room table—your love and care, to our family, is boundless, and I am forever in your debt; and of course, to Carter and Bubba, our five-year-old and two-year-old rescue dog and cat, respectively, who provide us all with meaning in life. My final thanks, however, extend beyond 3,000 miles away, to my sisters-in-law, Meredith, Benilda, and Janet. All three are front-line medical personnel, and throughout the pandemic, while I was privileged to shelter in place, they risked their lives to selflessly help others. I am truly in awe of them, for who they are and of the personal sacrifices they have made and continue to make. Collectively, they embody an ethos of care and an unyielding capacity to help and to heal. And so, to Meredith, Benilda, and Janet, I warmly dedicate this book.

Notes

Introduction

1. Initially health experts sought to link the illnesses to previous diseases, such as severe acute respiratory syndrome (SARS) and Middle East respiratory syndrome (MERS). In 2002 a SARS outbreak in China sickened over 8,000 people and resulted in nearly 800 deaths. Doctors, however, ruled out both SARS and MERS as possible causes. See Yan-Rong Guo, Qing-Dong Cao, Zhong-Si Hong, Yuan-Yang Tan, Shou-Deng Chen, Hong-Jun Jin, Kai-sen Tan, De-Yun Wang, and Yan Yan, "The Origin, Transmission and Clinical Therapies on Coronavirus Disease 2019 (Covid-19) Outbreak—An Update on the Status," *Military Medical Research* 7, no. 11 (2020): 1–10; Erin Schumaker, "Mysterious Pneumonia Outbreak Sickens Dozens in China," *ABC News,* January 6, 2020, https://abcnews.go.com/Health/mystery-pneumonia-outbreak-sickens-dozens-china/story?id=68094861.

2. Erin Schumaker, "Timeline: How Coronavirus Got Started," *ABC News,* April 23, 2020, https://abcnews.go.com/Health/timeline-coronavirus-started/story?id=69435165.

3. Schumaker, "Timeline."

4. Yasmeen Abutaleb, Josh Dawsey, Ellen Nakashima, and Greg Miller, "The U.S. Was Beset by Denial and Dysfunction as the Coronavirus Raged," *Washington Post,* April 4, 2020, https://www.washingtonpost.com/national-security/2020/04/04/coronavirus-government-dysfunction/?arc404=true.

5. In December 2019 Trump was impeached by the Democrat-controlled House of Representatives, although the Republican-controlled Senate acquitted Trump in the first week of January. Trump framed Covid-19—when he acknowledged it at all—as simply another weapon in the arsenal of his political opponents. This would prove a dangerous narrative in the coming months.

6. Other Republican politicians—although publicly supporting Trump's dismissal of the virus—in private also took the warnings seriously. That is, seriously enough to recognize an opportunity for quick and easy riches. Having been briefed on the threat posed by Covid-19 in a closed door meeting, Senators Richard Burr (R-NC) and Kelly Loeffler (R-GA), among others, benefited from stock trades worth millions of dollars, selling off shares of stock that would be adversely affected by a virus-induced slowdown of the economy. See Robert Faturechi and

Derek Willis, "On the Same Day Sen. Richard Burr Dumped Stock, So Did His Brother-in-Law. Then the Market Crashed," *ProPublica,* May 6, 2020, https://www.propublica.org/article/burr-family-stock; Rebecca Shabad, "Woodward: 'The President of the United States Possessed the Specific Knowledge That Could Have Saved Lives,'" *NBC News,* September 14, 2020, https://www.nbcnews.com/politics/2020-election/woodward-president-u-s-possessed-specific-knowledge-could-have-saved-n1240006; Peter Wade, "New Audio: While Trump Defended Sharing 'Fire Fauci' Tweet, He Told Woodward Virus 'Is the Plague,'" *Rolling Stone,* September 15, 2020, https://www.rollingstone.com/politics/politics-news/new-audio-while-trump-shared-fire-fauci-tweet-he-told-woodward-virus-is-plague-1059787/; and Susan B. Glasser, "'It Was All About the Election': The Ex-White House Aide Olivia Troye on Trump's Narcissistic Mishandling of Covid-19," *New Yorker,* September 18, 2020, https://www.newyorker.com/news/letter-from-trumps-washington/it-was-all-about-the-election-the-ex-white-house-aide-olivia-troye-on-trumps-narcissistic-mishandling-of-covid-19.

7. Quoted in Jonathan Chait, "Trump: I Was Right, Coronavirus Cases 'Will Go Down to Zero, Ultimately,'" *New York Magazine,* April 28, 2020, https://nymag.com/intelligencer/2020/04/trump-coronavirus-cases-will-go-down-to-zero-ultimately.html.

8. Libby Cathey and Ben Gittleson, "Pence to Lead US Response to Coronavirus as Trump Urges Americans to Prepare," *ABC News,* February 26, 2020, https://abcnews.go.com/Politics/trump-announces-news-conference-coronavirus-cdc-days-mixed/story?id=69228747.

9. Katherine Eban, "'That's Their Problem': How Jared Kushner Let the Markets Decide America's COVID-19 Fate," *Vanity Fair,* September 17, 2020, https://www.vanityfair.com/news/2020/09/jared-kushner-let-the-markets-decide-covid-19-fate.

10. Toluse Olorunnipa, Josh Dawsey, Chelsea Janes, and Isaac Stanley-Becker, "Governors Plead for Medical Equipment from Federal Stockpile Plagued by Shortages and Confusion," *Washington Post,* March 31, 2020, https://www.washingtonpost.com/politics/governors-plead-for-medical-equipment-from-federal-stockpile-plagued-by-shortages-and-confusion/2020/03/31/18aadda0-728d-11ea-87da-77a8136c1a6d_story.html.

11. Olorunnipa, Dawsey, Janes, and Stanley-Becker, "Governors Plead."

12. Upwards of 19 percent of Latinx workers and 17 percent of Black workers were unemployed compared with whites, of whom about 14 percent were unemployed. These job losses, moreover, occurred as Latinx households, especially, were still recovering from a devastating recession in 2007–2008. During that calamity, the Latinx community lost 66 percent of its household wealth; the pandemic, however, quickly decimated most gains achieved over the past decade. See Suzanne Gamboa, "Latinos Hardest Hit by Coronavirus Job Losses, with a

Staggering 18.9% Unemployed," *NBC News,* May 8, 2020, https://www.nbcnews.com/news/latino/latinos-hardest-hit-coronavirus-job-losses-staggering-18-9-unemployed-n1202881; Suzanne Gamboa, "Latinos Still Have Highest Unemployment Rate, as Joblessness Drops Slightly," *NBC News,* June 5, 2020, https://www.nbcnews.com/news/latino/unemployment-still-highest-among-latinos-joblessness-drops-slightly-n1225861; Alexia Fernández Campbell, "Even with Positive Jobs Report, Latinas Still Hardest Hit by Covid-19 Slowdown. Here's Why," *Public Integrity,* June 5, 2020, https://publicintegrity.org/health/coronavirus-and-inequality/even-with-positive-jobs-report-latinas-still-hardest-hit-by-covid-slowdown-heres-why/.

13. APM Research Lab Staff, "The Color of Coronavirus: Covid-19 Deaths by Race and Ethnicity in the U.S.," *APM Research Lab,* September 16, 2020, https://www.apmresearchlab.org/covid/deaths-by-race.

14. Kevin B. Anderson, "On the Battle of Ideas: Responding to the New World of COVID-19, Economic Crisis, and Anti-Racist Uprisings," *International Marxist-Humanist,* July 22, 2020, https://imhojournal.org/articles/on-the-battle-of-ideas-responding-to-the-new-world-of-covid-19-economic-crisis-and-anti-racist-uprisings.

15. Heather Brown, "Covid-19 Lays Bare Capitalism's Deference to Profits Over Lives," *International Marxist-Humanist,* March 25, 2020, https://imhojournal.org/articles/covid-19-lays-bare-capitalisms-deference-to-profits-over-lives.

16. Vicky Ward, "How the Very Rich are Different in the Covid-19 Fight," *CNN,* April 5, 2020, https://www.cnn.com/2020/04/05/opinions/coronavirus-wealthy-false-security-vicky-ward-opinion/index.html.

17. James A. Tyner, *Violence in Capitalism: Devaluing Life in an Age of Responsibility* (Lincoln: University of Nebraska Press, 2016); James A. Tyner, *Dead Labor: Toward a Political Economy of Premature Death* (Minneapolis: University of Minnesota Press, 2019).

18. Adam Jeffery, "Scenes of Protests Across the Country Demanding States Reopen the Economy amid Coronavirus Pandemic," *CNBC,* April 18, 2020, https://www.cnbc.com/2020/04/18/coronavirus-scenes-of-protests-across-the-country-demanding-states-reopen-the-economy.html.

19. Matthew Valasik, "Why Are White Supremacists Protesting to 'Reopen' the U.S. Economy?," *Salon,* April 30, 2020, https://www.salon.com/2020/04/30/why-are-white-supremacists-protesting-to-reopen-the-us-economy_partner/. See also Marcie Bianco, "Michigan Coronavirus Protestors Shout 'Liberty!'—as Right-Wing Rhetoric Weaponizes Freedom," *NBC News,* May 14, 2020, https://www.nbcnews.com/think/opinion/michigan-coronavirus-protesters-shout-liberty-right-wing-rhetoric-weaponizes-freedom-ncna1206596.

20. Stephen Sorace, "Protestors Rally Against Washington's Coronavirus Stay-at-Home Order: 'Give Me Liberty or Give Me Covid 19,'" *Fox News,* April 20,

2020, https://www.foxnews.com/us/washington-coronavirus-protest-inslee-stay-at-home.

21. Steve Benen, "Texas' Dan Patrick: 'There are More Important Things than Living," *MSNBC,* April 22, 2020, https://www.msnbc.com/rachel-maddow-show/texas-dan-patrick-there-are-more-important-things-living-n1189811).

22. Zygmunt Bauman, *Mortality, Immortality and Other Life Strategies* (Stanford, Calif.: Stanford University Press, 1992), 50.

23. Frank I. Michelman, "The Subject of Liberalism," *Stanford Law Review* 46, no. 6 (1994): 1807–33; at 1813.

24. Daniel Rueda Garrido, "Deaths of the Subject and Negated Subjectivity in the Era of Neoliberal Capitalism," *tripleC* 17, no. 1 (2019): 159–84.

25. Greta Bird, "The White Subject as Liberal Subject," *ACRAWSA E-Journal* 4, no. 2 (2008): 1–14.

26. Lisa Lowe, "History Hesitant," *Social Text* 33, no. 4 (2015): 85–107; at 90.

27. Lowe, "History Hesitant," 90.

28. Lowe, "History Hesitant," 91.

29. Eduardo Bonilla-Silva, "Feeling Race: Theorizing the Racial Economy of Emotions," *American Sociological Review* 84, no. 1 (2019): 1–25; at 14.

30. Sean Sayers, *Marx and Alienation: Essays on Hegelian Themes* (New York: Palgrave Macmillan, 2011), x.

31. Christian Fuchs, "Donald Trump: A Critical Theory-Perspective on Authoritarian Capitalism," *tripleC* 15, no. 1 (2017): 1–72; Paul Bleakley, "Situationism and the Recuperation of an Ideology in the Era of Trump, Fake News and Post-Truth Politics," *Capital & Class* 42, no. 3 (2018): 419–34; David Norman Smith and Eric Hanley, "The Anger Games: Who Voted for Donald Trump in the 2016 Election, and Why?," *Critical Sociology* 44, no. 2 (2018): 195–212; Robert J. Antonio, "Reactionary Tribalism Redux: Right-Wing Populism and De-Democratization," *Sociological Quarterly* 60, no. 2 (2019): 201–9. For a critique of this position, see Eduardo Bonilla-Silva, *Racism without Racists: Color-Blind Racism and the Persistence of Racial Inequality in America*, 5th ed. (Lanham, Md.: Rowman & Littlefield, 2018).

32. Bonny Wells, "Whose Land are We Fighting For? A Critique of Leftist Attempts to Engage the 'White Working Class,'" *Tubman Brown Organization,* January 12, 2018, https://tubmanbrownorganization.wordpress.com/2018/01/12/whose-land-are-we-fighting-for-a-critique-of-leftist-attempts-to-engage-the-white-working-class/).

33. Katherine J. Cramer, *The Politics of Resentment: Rural Consciousness in Wisconsin and the Rise of Scott Walker* (Chicago: University of Chicago Press, 2016); Justin Gest, *The New Minority: White Working Class Politics in an Age of Immigration and Inequality* (New York: Oxford University Press, 2016); Arlie R. Hochschild, *Strangers in Their Own Land: Anger and Mourning on the American*

Right (New York: New Press, 2016); James D. Vance, *Hillbilly Elegy: A Memoir of a Family and Culture in Crisis* (New York: HarperCollins, 2016).

34. Diana C. Mutz, "Status Threat, Not Economic Hardship, Explains the 2016 Presidential Vote," *PNAS* 115, no. 19: E4330–E4339. See also Christine J. Walley, "Trump's Election and the 'White Working Class': What We Missed," *American Ethnologist* 44, no. 2 (2017): 231–36.

35. Nate Silver, "The Mythology of Trump's 'Working Class' Support," *FiveThirtyEight,* May 3, 2016, https://fivethirtyeight.com/features/the-mythology-of-trumps-working-class-support/.

36. Gurminder K. Bhambra, "Brexit, Trump, and 'Methodological Whiteness': On the Misrecognition of Race and Class," *British Journal of Sociology* 68, no. S1 (2017): S214–S232; at S226.

37. Eduardo Bonilla-Silva, "'Racists,' 'Class Anxieties,' Hegemonic Racism, and Democracy in Trump's America," *Social Currents* 6, no. 1 (2019): 14–31; at 20.

38. Bhambra, "Brexit, Trump," S226.

39. See for example Audrey Kobayashi and Linda Peake, "Racism Out of Place: Thoughts on Whiteness and an Antiracist Geography in the New Millennium," *Annals of the Association of American Geographers* 90, no. 2 (2000): 392–403; Patricia Daley, "Lives Lived Differently: Geography and the Study of Black Women," *Area* 52 (2020): 794–800; and Azeezat Johnson, "Throwing Our Bodies Against the White Background of Academia," *Area* 52 (2020): 89–96.

40. Eduardo Bonilla-Silva, "Toward a New Political Praxis for Trumpamerica: New Directions in Critical Race Theory," *American Behavioral Scientist* 63, no. 13 (2019): 1776–88; at 1781.

41. Peter Goodwin, "Where's the Working Class?" *tripleC* 16, no. 2 (2018): 535–45, at 535.

42. David W. Lovell, *Marx's Proletariat: The Making of a Myth* (New York: Routledge, 1988), 13.

43. Lovell, *Marx's Proletariat,* 11.

44. Georg Lukács, *History and Class Consciousness,* trans. Rodney Livingston (London: Merlin, 1971).

45. Rashad Shabazz, *Spatializing Blackness: Architectures of Confinement and Black Masculinity in Chicago* (Urbana: University of Illinois Press, 2015); LaToya E. Eaves, "Black Geographic Possibilities: On a Queer Black South," *Southeastern Geographer* 57, no. 1 (2017): 80–95; Peter Hopkins, "Social Geography I: Intersectionality," *Progress in Human Geography* 43, no. 5 (2019): 937–47.

46. Garrido, "Deaths of the Subject," 160.

47. Douglas Burnham and Peter Lamb, *The First Marx: A Philosophical Introduction* (London: Bloomsbury Academic, 2018), 116.

48. W. E. B. Du Bois, *Black Reconstruction in America, 1860–1880* (New York: Free Press, 1998 [1935]).

49. John Fischer, *Death, Immortality, and Meaning in Life* (Oxford: Oxford University Press, 2020), 5.

50. Erik Olin Wright, "The Continuing Relevance of the Marxist Tradition for Transcending Capitalism," *tripleC* 16, no. 2 (2018): 490–500; at 491.

51. Wright, "The Continuing Relevance," 492.

52. Joshua Inwood, "White Supremacy, White Counter-Revolutionary Politics, and the Rise of Donald Trump," *Environment and Planning C: Politics and Space* 37, no. 4 (2019): 579–96; at 589.

53. Brown, "Covid-19 Lays Bare Capitalism's Deference."

54. Marx, *Capital,* Volume I, 799.

55. Anderson, "On the Battle of Ideas."

56. Martin Hägglund, *This Life: Why Mortality Makes Us Free* (London: Profile Books, 2019), 13.

57. Karl Marx, "Alienation in the Productive Process," in *Karl Marx: Selected Writings,* 2nd ed., ed. David McLellan (New York: Oxford University, 2000), 547–50; at 548.

58. Ellen Meiksins Wood, *Empire of Capital* (London: Verso, 2003), 9. There is of course no monolithic "capitalist" mode of production. As Geoff Mann succinctly writes, "capitalism does not look the same everywhere you go." See Geoff Mann, *Disassembly Required: A Field Guide to Actually Existing Capitalism* (Baltimore, Md.: AK Press, 2013), 12.

59. Michael Heinrich, *An Introduction to the Three Volumes of Karl Marx's* Capital (New York: Monthly Review Press, 2012), 181.

60. Hartley Dean, "Eudaimonia and 'Species Being': A Marxist Perspective," in *Handbook of Eudaimonic Well-Being,* ed. Joar Vittersø (Cham, Switzerland: Springer International, 2016), 507–20; at 512.

61. Karl Marx, *Economic and Philosophic Manuscripts of 1844,* trans. Martin Milligan (Amherst, N.Y.: Prometheus Books, 1988). See also Bertell Ollman, *Alienation: Marx's Conception of Man in Capitalist Society,* 2nd ed. (New York: Cambridge University Press, 1976), 136.

62. Gajo Petrović, "Alienation," in *A Dictionary of Marxist Thought,* 2nd ed., ed. Tom Bottomore (Malden, Mass.: Blackwell, 1991), 11–16; at 14.

63. Epifanio San Juan Jr., "Problems in the Marxist Project of Theorizing Race," *Rethinking Marxism* 2, no. 2 (1989): 58–80; Kobayashi and Peake, "Racism Out of Place"; David Camfield, "Elements of a Historical-Materialist Theory of Racism," *Historical Materialism* 24, no. 1 (2016): 31–70; Caroline Faria and Sharlene Mollett, "Critical Feminist Reflectivity and the Politics of Whiteness in the 'Field,'" *Gender, Place & Culture* 23, no. 1 (2016): 79–93; Ashley Bohrer, "Intersectionality and Marxism: A Critical Historiography," *Historical Materialism* 26, no. 2 (2018): 46–74; Sharlene Mollett and Caroline Faria, "The Spatialities of Intersectional Thinking: Fashioning Feminist Geographic Futures," *Gender,*

Place & Culture 25, no. 4 (2018): 565–77; Caroline Faria and Sharlene Mollett, "'We Didn't Have Time to Sit Still and be Scared': A Postcolonial Feminist Reading of 'An Other Geography,'" *Dialogues in Human Geography* 10, no. 1 (2020): 23–29; Sean Walton, "Why the Critical Race Theory Should Not be Dismissed by Neo-Marxists: Lessons from Contemporary Black Radicalism," *Power and Education* 12, no. 1 (2020): 78–94.

64. Keeanga-Yamahtta Taylor, *From #BlackLivesMatter to Black Liberation* (Chicago: Haymarket Books, 2016); Barbara Ransby, *Making All Black Lives Matter: Reimagining Freedom in the 21st Century* (Berkeley: University of California Press, 2018).

65. Willie Jamaal Wright, "As Above, So Below: Anti-Black Violence as Environmental Racism," *Antipode* 53, no. 3 (2021): 791–809.

66. Katherine McKittrick, *Demonic Grounds: Black Women and the Cartographies of Struggle* (Minneapolis: University of Minnesota Press, 2006), xiv.

67. McKittrick, *Demonic Grounds,* xiv.

68. McKittrick, *Demonic Grounds,* xv.

69. An engagement with Fromm is not without its challenges. For more in-depth discussions on the benefits and limitations of Fromm, see Mauricio Cortina, "The Greatness and Limitations of Erich Fromm's Humanism," *Contemporary Psychoanalysis* 51, no. 3 (2015): 388–422; at 389; and Lynn S. Chancer, "Feminism, Humanism, and Erich Fromm," in *Erich Fromm's Critical Theory: Hope, Humanism, and the Future,* ed. Kieran Durkin and Joan Braune (London: Bloomsbury Academic, 2020), 101–14.

70. Lynn S. Chancer, *Sadomasochism in Everyday Life: The Dynamics of Power and Powerlessness* (New Brunswick, N.J.: Rutgers University Press, 1992), 10.

71. Chancer, *Sadomasochism,* 16.

72. Carl Ratner, "Pathological Normalcy: A Construct for Comprehending and Overcoming Psychological Aspects of Alienation," *Humanistic Psychologist* 42 (2014): 298–303; at 298.

73. Eric Fromm, *The Sane Society* (New York: Henry Holt, 1990 [1955]), 6.

74. Neal Harris, "Reconstructing Erich Fromm's 'Pathology of Normalcy': Transcending the Recognition-Cognitive Paradigm in the Diagnosis of Social Pathologies," *Social Science Information* 58, no. 4 (2019): 714–33; at 719.

75. Eric Fromm, *Beyond the Chains of Illusion: My Encounter with Marx and Freud* (London: Abacus, 1983 [1962]), 15.

76. See for example David Conradson, "Geographies of Care: Spaces, Practices, Experiences," *Social & Cultural Geography* 4, no. 4 (2003): 451–54; Victoria Lawson, "Geographies of Care and Responsibility," *Annals of the Association of American Geographers* 97, no. 1 (2007): 1–11; Joshua F. J. Inwood, "Searching for the Promised Land: Examining Dr. Martin Luther King's Concept of the Beloved Community," *Antipode* 41, no. 3 (2009): 487–508; Victoria Lawson, "Instead of

Radical Geography, How About Caring Geography?" *Antipode* 41, no. 1 (2009): 210–13; Carey-Ann Morrison, Lynda Johnston, and Robyn Longhurst, "Critical Geographies of Love as Spatial, Relational and Political," *Progress in Human Geography* 37, no. 4 (2012): 505–21; Joshua F. J. Inwood, "Love and the Other: A Response to Morrison et al. (2012)," *Progress in Human Geography* 37, no. 5 (2013): 721–23; Carey-Ann Morrison, Lynda Johnston, and Robyn Longhurst, "'It's Complicated': Love, Selves and Others—A Response to Inwood," *Progress in Human Geography* 37, no. 5 (2013): 724–26; Andrew Power and Edward Hall, "Placing Care in Times of Austerity," *Social & Cultural Geography* 19, no. 3 (2018): 303–13; and Lydia Wood, Kate Swanson, and Donald E. Colley III, "Tenets for a Radical Care Ethics in Geography," *ACME: An International Journal for Critical Geographies* 19, no. 2 (2020): 424–47.

1. A Flourishing, but Mortal Life

1. Bertell Ollman, *Alienation: Marx's Conception of Man in Capitalist Society*, 2nd ed. (New York: Cambridge University Press, 1976), 151.

2. Ollman, *Alienation*, 134.

3. James C. Klagge, "Marx's Realms of 'Freedom' and 'Necessity,'" *Canadian Journal of Philosophy* 16, no. 4 (1986): 769–78; at 769. See also Aaron Jaffe, "From Aristotle to Marx: A Critical Philosophical Anthropology," *Science & Society* 80, no. 1 (2016): 56–77; at 58. See also Norman Geras, *Marx and Human Nature: Refutation of a Legend* (London: Verso Books, 1983); John G. Fox, *Marx, the Body, and Human Nature* (New York: Palgrave Macmillan, 2015); Chris Byron, "Essence and Alienation: Marx's Theory of Human Nature," *Science & Society* 80, no. 3 (2016): 375–94; Hartley Dean, "Eudaimonia and 'Species Being': A Marxist Perspective," in *Handbook of Eudaimonic Well-Being*, ed. Joar Vittersø (Cham, Switzerland: Springer International, 2016), 507–20; Karsten J. Struhl, "Marx and Human Nature: The Historical, the Trans-Historical, and Human Flourishing," *Science & Society* 80, no. 1 (2016): 78–104; Jamie Morgan, "Species Being in the Twenty-First Century," *Review of Political Economy* 30, no. 3 (2018): 377–95; and Nguyen Anh Quoc, "Karl Marx's Theory of Human Nature," *European Journal of Social Sciences Studies* 4, no. 4 (2019): 200–209.

4. Martin Hägglund, *This Life: Why Mortality Makes Us Free* (London: Profile Books, 2019), 20.

5. Karl Marx, *Economic and Philosophic Manuscripts of 1844*, trans. Martin Milligan (Amherst, N.Y.: Prometheus Books, 1988), 19.

6. See, for example, Sven-Eric Liedman, *A World to Win: The Life and Works of Karl Marx*, trans. Jeffrey N. Skinner (London: Verso, 2018), 15.

7. Egidijus Mardosas, "Marxist and Aristotelian Ethics," *Filosofija Sociologija* 27, no. 3 (2016): 214–21; at 215.

8. Karl Marx, *Capital*, trans. Ben Fowkes (New York: Penguin, 1990), Volume 1, 811.

9. Hägglund, *This Life*, 22.

10. Mardosas, "Marxism and Aristotelian Ethics," 216.

11. Morgan, "Species Being," 386.

12. Peter Goodwin, "Where's the Working Class? *tripleC* 16, no. 2 (2018): 535–45; at 535.

13. Leslie Stevenson, David L. Haberman, Peter M. Wright, and Charlotte Witt, *Thirteen Theories of Human Nature* (New York: Oxford University Press, 2018), 3.

14. Stevenson et al., *Thirteen Theories*, 97.

15. Stevenson et al., *Thirteen Theories*, 91.

16. Stevenson et al., *Thirteen Theories*, 105.

17. Cornelius Castoriadis, "From Marx to Aristotle, from Aristotle to Us," *Social Research* 45, no. 4 (1978): 667–738; George E. McCarthy, "German Social Ethics and the Return to Greek Philosophy: Marx and Aristotle," *Studies in Soviet Thought* 31, no. 1 (1986): 1–24; George E. McCarthy, ed., *Marx and Aristotle: Nineteenth-Century German Social Theory and Classical Antiquity* (Lanham, Md.: Rowman & Littlefield, 1992); Nathaniel Cline, William McColloch, and Kirsten Ford, "An Aristotelian View of Marx's Method," *Working Paper, No. 2011–08,* University of Utah, Department of Economics; Sabeen Ahmed, "Communism as *Eudaimonia*: An Aristotelian Reading of Human Emancipation," *International Journal of Philosophy & Social Values* 1, no. 2 (2018): 31–48; Jonathan E. Pike, *From Aristotle to Marx: Aristotelianism in Marxist Social Ontology* (New York: Routledge, 2019).

18. Ahmed, "Communism as *Eudaimonia,*" 31.

19. Mardosas, "Marxism and Aristotelian Ethics," 215.

20. See, for example, Timothy D. Roche, "Ergon and Eudaimonia in Nicomachean Ethics I: Reconsidering the Intellectualist Interpretation," *Journal of the History of Philosophy* 26, no. 2 (1988): 175–94; Deborah Achtenberg, "On the Metaphysical Presuppositions of Aristotle's *Nicomachean Ethics,*" *Journal of Value Inquiry* 26 (1992): 217–340; and Rachel Barney, "Aristotle's Argument for a Human Function," *Oxford Studies in Ancient Philosophy* 34 (2008): 293–322.

21. Thomas Nagel, "Aristotle on Eudaimonia," *Phronesis* 17, no. 3 (1972): 252–59; at 253.

22. Roche, "Ergon and Eudaimonia," 178; Achtenberg, "On the Metaphysical Presuppositions," 330.

23. Roche, "Ergon and Eudaimonia," 183.

24. Mardosas, "Marxism and Aristotelian Ethics," 215.

25. Karl Marx and Friedrich Engels, *The German Ideology, including Theses on Feuerbach* (Amherst, N.Y.: Prometheus, 1998), 37.

26. Marx, *Economic and Philosophic Manuscripts,* 76–77.

27. Thomas E. Wartenberg, "'Species-Being' and 'Human Nature' in Marx" *Human Studies* 5, no. 1 (1982): 77–95; at 79.

28. Marx and Engels, *The German Ideology,* 37.

29. Ian G. R. Shaw and Marv Waterstone, *Wageless Life: A Manifesto for a Future Beyond Capitalism* (Minneapolis: University of Minnesota Press, 2019), 7.

30. Wartenberg, "'Species-Being,'" 80.

31. Marx, *Economic and Philosophic Manuscripts,* 77.

32. Struhl, "Marx and Human Nature," 84.

33. Marx, *Economic and Philosophic Manuscripts,* 77.

34. Marx, *Capital,* Volume I, 284.

35. Marx and Engels, *The German Ideology,* 49.

36. Morgan, "Species Being," 387.

37. Isidor Wallimann, *Estrangement: Marx's Conception of Human Nature and the Division of Labor* (Westport, Conn.: Greenwood, 1981), 12.

38. Nagel, "Aristotle on Eudaimonia," 257.

39. Wartenberg, "'Species-Being,'" 94.

40. Ted Benton, "Humanism = Speciesism: Marx on Humans and Animals," *Radical Philosophy* 50 (1988): 4–18; David Sztybel, "Marxism and Animal Rights," *Ethics and the Environment* 2, no. 2 (1997): 169–85; Katherine Perlo, "Marxism and the Underdog," *Society & Animals* 10, no. 3 (2002): 303–18; Ted Benton, "Marxism and the Moral Status of Animals," *Society & Animals* 11, no. 1 (2003): 73–79; Renzo Llorente, "Reflections on the Prospects for a Non-Speciesist Marxism," in *Critical Theory and Animal Liberation,* ed. John Sanbonmatsu (Lanham, Md.: Rowman and Littlefield, 2011), 121–35. For counterarguments, see Ryan Gunderson, "Marx's Comments on Animal Welfare," *Rethinking Marxism* 23, no. 4 (2011): 543–48 and John Bellamy Foster and Brett Clark, "Marx and Alienated Speciesism," *Monthly Review* 70, no. 7 (2018): 1–20.

41. Todd May, *Death* (Durham, UK: Acumen, 2009), 25.

42. Marx, *Economic and Philosophic Manuscripts,* 165; Foster and Clark, "Marx and Alienated Speciesism," 4.

43. Foster and Clark, "Marx and Alienated Speciesism," 4.

44. Marx, *Economic and Philosophic Manuscripts,* 76.

45. Foster and Clark, "Marx and Alienated Speciesism," 4–5.

46. Paul Burkett, "Ecology and Marx's Vision of Communism," *Socialism and Democracy* 17, no. 2 (2003): 41–72; Paresh Chattopadhyay, "Worlds Apart: Socialism in Marx and in Early Bolshevism," *Economic and Political Weekly* 40, no. 53 (2005): 5629–34; Paresh Chattopadhyay, "Passage to Socialism: The Dialectic of Progress in Marx," *Historical Materialism* 14, no. 3 (2006): 45–84; Paresh Chattopadhyay, "The Myth of Twentieth-Century Socialism and the Continuing Relevance of Karl Marx," *Socialism and Democracy* 24, no. 3 (2010): 23–45; and

Michael D. Yates, "Nothing to Lose but Their Chains," *Monthly Review* 70, no. 5 (2018): 15–29.

47. Brett Clark and John Bellamy Foster, "The Dialectic of Social and Ecological Metabolism: Marx, Mészáros, and the Absolute Limits of Capital," *Socialism and Democracy* 24, no. 2 (2010): 124–38; at 125.

48. John Bellamy Foster, "Marx and the Rift in the Universal Metabolism of Nature," *Monthly Review* 65, no. 7 (2013): 1–19; at 5.

49. John Bellamy Foster and Brett Clark, "Marxism and the Dialectics of Ecology," *Monthly Review* 68, no. 5 (2016): 1–17; at 11; Brett Clark and John Bellamy Foster, "Ecological Imperialism and the Global Metabolic Rift: Unequal Exchange and the Guano/Nitrates Trade," *International Journal of Comparative Sociology* 50, nos. 3–4 (2009): 311–34; at 314.

50. Brett Clark and Richard York, "Rifts and Shifts," *Monthly Review* 60, no. 6 (2008): 13–24; at 14–15.

51. John Bellamy Foster and Brett Clark, "The Expropriation of Nature," *Monthly Review* 69, no. 10 (2018): 1–27; at 1.

52. John Bellamy Foster, "Marx's Theory of Metabolic Rift: Classical Foundations for Environmental Sociology," *American Journal of Sociology* 105, no. 2 (1999): 366–405; at 383.

53. Marx, *Capital,* Volume III, 949.

54. Clark and Foster, "The Dialectic of Social and Ecological Metabolism," 129.

55. Marx and Engels, *The German Ideology,* 43.

56. Marx and Engels, *The German Ideology,* 570.

57. Karl Marx, *A Contribution to the Critique of Political Economy* (New York: International, 1970), 20.

58. Marx and Engels, *The German Ideology,* 37.

59. Struhl, "Marx and Human Nature," 83.

60. Marx and Engels, *The German Ideology,* 37.

61. Marx and Engels, *The German Ideology,* 42.

62. Struhl, "Marx and Human Nature," 84.

63. Karl Marx, "The Eighteenth Brumaire of Louis Bonaparte," in *Karl Marx: Selected Writings*, 2nd ed., ed. David McLellan (New York: Oxford University Press, 2000), 329–55; at 329.

64. Struhl, "Marx and Human Nature," 81.

65. Struhl, "Marx and Human Nature," 86.

66. Sébastien Rioux, "Embodied Contradictions: Capitalism, Social Reproduction and Body Formation," *Women's Studies International Forum* 48 (2015): 194–202; at 195. See also Reecia Orzeck, "What Does Not Kill You: Historical Materialism and the Body," *Environment and Planning D: Society and Space* 25 (2007): 496–514.

67. Rioux, "Embodied Contradictions," 195.

68. John M. Fischer, *Death, Immortality, and Meaning in Life* (New York: Oxford University Press, 2020), 2.

69. There is a vast literature on meaningful life; the following accounts have been helpful in shaping my understanding: Viktor E. Frankl, *Man's Search for Meaning* (Boston: Beacon, 2006); Susan Wolf, *Meaning in Life and Why it Matters* (Princeton, N.J.: Princeton University Press, 2010); and Thaddeus Metz, *Meaning in Life* (Oxford: Oxford University Press, 2013).

70. Dean, "Eudaimonia and 'Species Being,'" 50; see also Struhl, "Marx and Human Nature," 90.

71. James Daly, *Marx: Justice and Dialectic* (London: Greenwich Exchange, 1996), 117; Mardosas, "Marxism and Aristotelian Ethics," 220.

72. Patrick O. Nyabul and Joseph W. Situma, "The Meaning of Eudemonia in Aristotle's Ethics," *International Journal of Philosophy and Theology* 2, no. 3 (2014): 65–74; Joar Vittersø (ed.), *Handbook of Eudaimonic Well-Being* (Cham, Switzerland: Springer International, 2016); Richard Kim, "Well-Being, Eudaimonia, and Nature-Fulfillment," in *Aristotelian Naturalism,* ed. Martin Hähnel (Cham, Switzerland: Springer International, 2020), 371–85.

73. Todd May, *A Significant Life: Human Meaning in a Silent Universe* (Chicago: University of Chicago Press, 2015), 4; Dean, "Eudaimonia and 'Species Being,'" 508.

74. Kim, "Well-Being, Eudaimonia," 372.

75. Richard M. Ryan and Frank Martela, "Eudaimonia as a Way of Living: Connecting Aristotle with Self-Determination Theory," in *Handbook of Eudaimonic Well-Being,* ed. Joar Vittersø (Cham, Switzerland: Springer International, 2016), 109–22; at 110.

76. Dean, "Eudaimonia and 'Species Being,'" 508. As Dean notes, Aristotle further distinguished between free men, on the one hand, and women and slaves on the other.

77. Dean, "Eudaimonia and 'Species Being,'" 508.

78. Kim, "Well-Being, Eudaimonia," 376.

79. Ryan and Martela, "Eudaimonia as a Way of Living," 110.

80. Ryan and Martela, "Eudaimonia as a Way of Living," 110.

81. Kim, "Well-Being, Eudaimonia," 376.

82. Ryan and Martela, "Eudaimonia as a Way of Living," 110.

83. Marx and Engels, *The German Ideology,* 42.

84. Liedman, *A World to Win,* 457.

85. Dean, "Eudaimonia and 'Species Being,'" 512.

86. May, *A Significant Life,* 5.

87. Jaffe, "From Aristotle to Marx," 59.

88. Walliman, *Estrangement,* xx.

89. Walliman, *Estrangement,* xx.

90. Dean, "Eudaimonia and 'Species Being,'" 509.

91. Sandro Mezzadra, *In the Marxian Workshops: Producing Subjects,* trans. Yari Lanci (London: Rowman & Littlefield International, 2018), xv.

92. Fischer, *Death,* 105.

93. Todd May, *Death* (Durham, UK: Acumen, 2009), 7.

94. May, *Death,* 7. There is speculation as to the awareness of death in nonhuman animals. Certainly, many nonhuman animals are aware of danger and also mourn their dead. This is not the same as having an awareness of the certainty, and finitude, of death itself. Regardless, whether nonhuman animals are aware of death is beside the point. If we learn that dogs or whales are aware of death, this does not change the fact that human awareness of death greatly informs human societal organization.

95. Zygmunt Bauman, *Mortality, Immortality, and Other Life Strategies* (Stanford, Calif.: Stanford University Press, 1992), 9.

96. Olivia Stevenson, Charlotte Kenten, and Avril Maddrell, "And Now the End Is Near: Enlivening and Politizising the Geographies of Dying, Death and Mourning," *Social & Cultural Geography* 17, no. 2 (2016): 153–65; at 157. See also Philippe Ariès, *Western Attitudes Toward Death: From the Middle Ages to the Present* (Baltimore, Md.: Johns Hopkins University Press, 1975); Philippe Ariès, *The Hour of Our Death* (New York: Vintage, 1981); Allan Kellehear, *A Social History of Dying* (New York: Cambridge University Press, 2007); James D. E. Watson, "The Harm of Premature Death: Immortality—the Transhumanist Challenge," *Ethical Perspectives* 16, no. 4 (2009): 435–58; Hans Ruin, *Being with the Dead: Burial, Ancestral Politics, and the Roots of Historical Consciousness* (Stanford, Calif.: Stanford University Press, 2018).

97. Bauman, *Mortality,* 4.

98. Timothy C. Baker, *Writing Animals: Language, Suffering, and Animality in Twenty-First Century Fiction* (Cham, Switzerland: Palgrave Macmillan, 2019), 109.

99. Judith Butler, *Frames of War: When Is Life Grievable?* (London: Verso Books, 2009); Avril Maddrell and James D. Sidaway (eds.), *Deathscapes: Spaces for Death, Dying, Mourning and Remembrance.* (Aldershot, UK: Ashgate, 2012).

100. Martha C. Nussbaum, *The Therapy of Desire: Theory and Practice in Hellenistic Ethics* (Princeton, N.J.: Princeton University Press, 2013), 229.

101. Alan Segal, *Life After Death: A History of the Afterlife in Western Religion* (New York: Doubleday, 2010).

102. Colleen McDannell and Bernhard Lang, *Heaven: A History* (New Haven, Conn.: Yale University Press, 2001).

103. Samuel Scheffler, *Death and the Afterlife* (New York: Oxford University Press, 2016), 68.

104. May, *Death,* 36.

105. Watson, "The Harm of Premature Death," 438.

106. Marx and Engels, *The German Ideology,* 47; Joseph Fracchia, "Beyond the Human-Nature Debate: Human Corporeal Organization as the 'First Fact' of Historical Materialism," *Historical Materialism* 13, no. 1 (2005): 33–62; at 48.

107. Bauman, *Mortality,* 5.

108. Marx and Engels, *The German Ideology,* 47.

109. Fracchia, "Beyond the Human-Nature Debate," 48.

110. May, *Death,* 11.

111. Karl Marx, *Grundrisse,* trans. Martin Nicolaus (New York: Penguin Books, 1973), 604.

112. Marx, *Grundrisse,* 609.

113. Bauman, *Mortality,* 4.

114. Bauman, *Mortality,* 4.

115. Marx, *Economic and Philosophic Manuscripts,* 21.

116. Fischer, *Death,* 81.

117. May, *Death,* 28.

118. Fischer, *Death,* 40; Thomas Nagel, *Mortal Questions* (Cambridge: Cambridge University Press, 1979), 9.

119. Brooke A. Trisel, "What Is Premature Death?" *Minerva—An Internet Journal of Philosophy* 11 (2007): 54–82; Zohreh Bayatrizi, *Life Sentences: The Modern Ordering of Mortality* (Toronto, ON: University of Toronto Press, 2008); and Stephen Hetherington, "Where Is the Harm in Dying Prematurely? An Epicurean Answer," *Journal of Ethics* 17 (2013): 79–97.

120. Watson, "The Harm of Premature Death," 443.

121. Watson, "The Harm of Premature Death," 443.

122. Bayatrizi, *Life Sentences,* 53; Zohreh Bayatrizi, "Erasing Death: The Science That Is Rewriting the Boundaries between Life and Death," *Canadian Studies in Population* 42, nos. 3–4 (2015): 111.

123. Bayatrizi, *Life Sentences,* 54.

124. Trisel, "What Is Premature Death?," 61.

125. Ruth Wilson Gilmore, "Fatal Couplings of Power and Difference: Notes on Racism and Geography," *Professional Geographer* 54, no. 1 (2002): 15–24; at 16.

126. James A. Tyner and Joshua Inwood, "Violence as Fetish: Geography, Marxism, and Dialectics," *Progress in Human Geography* 38, no. 6 (2014): 771–84; at 774.

127. James A. Tyner, *Dead Labor: Toward a Political Economy of Premature Death* (Minneapolis: University of Minnesota Press, 2019), 10.

128. Emma W. Laurie and Ian G. R. Shaw, "Violent Conditions: The Injustices of Being," *Political Geography* 65 (2018): 8–16; at 15.

129. Butler, *Frames of War,* 25. See also Judith Butler, *Precarious Life: The Powers of Mourning and Violence* (London: Verso, 2004).

130. Christopher Harker, "Precariousness, Precarity, and Family: Notes from Palestine," *Environment and Planning A* 44 (2012): 849–65; at 859.

131. Sean Hill II, "Precarity in the Era of #BlackLivesMatter," *Women's Studies Quarterly* 45, nos. 3–4 (2017): 94–109; at 100.

132. Kimberlé Crenshaw, "Mapping the Margins: Intersectionality, Identity, and Violence against Women of Color," *Stanford Law Review* 43, no. 6 (1991): 1241–300.

133. Crenshaw, "Mapping the Margins," 1245.

134. Sharlene Mollett and Caroline Faria, "The Spatialities of Intersectional Thinking: Fashioning Feminist Geographic Futures," *Gender, Place & Culture: A Journal of Feminist Geography* 25, n. 4 (2018): 565–577; at 567.

135. Martha A. Fineman, "The Vulnerable Subject: Anchoring Equality in the Human Condition," *Yale Journal of Law and Feminism* 20, no. 1 (2008): article 2 (22 pp.), at 10.

136. Fineman, "The Vulnerable Subject," 2.

137. Fineman, "The Vulnerable Subject," 2–3.

138. Fineman, "The Vulnerable Subject," 10.

139. Kathryn A. Gillespie and Patricia J. Lopez, "Introducing Economies of Death," in *Economies of Death: Economic Logics of Killable Life and Grievable Death,* edited by Patricia J. Lopez and Kathryn A. Gillespie (New York: Routledge, 2015), 1–13; at 8. See also Sharon D. Jones-Eversley, Johnny Rice II, A. Christson Adedoyin, and Lori James-Townes, "Premature Death of Young Black Males in the United States," *Journal of Black Studies* 51, no. 3 (2020): 251–72.

140. Wartenberg, "'Species-Being,'" 95.

141. Marx, *Economic and Philosophic Manuscripts,* 73.

142. Morgan, "Species Being," 391.

143. Marx and Engels, *The German Ideology,* 37.

144. Wartenberg, "'Species-Being,'" 88.

145. Wartenberg, "'Species-Being,'" 88.

146. Morgan, "Species Being," 386.

2. The Alienated Subject

1. Zygmunt Bauman, *Consuming Life* (Malden, Mass.: Polity, 2007).

2. Nolen Gertz, *Nihilism* (Cambridge, Mass.: MIT Press, 2019), 132–33.

3. Gertz, *Nihilism,* 135.

4. John Holloway, "Read *Capital*: The First Sentence or, *Capital* Starts with Wealth, Not with the Commodity," *Historical Materialism* 23, no. 3 (2015): 3–26; at 5.

5. Chris Byron, "Essence and Alienation: Marx's Theory of Human Nature," *Science & Society* 80, no. 3 (2016): 375–94; at 385.

6. Karl Marx, *Grundrisse,* trans. Martin Nicolaus (New York: Penguin Books, 1973), 488.

7. Marx, *Grundrisse,* 488.

8. Holloway, "Read *Capital,*" 6.

9. Holloway, "Read *Capital,*" 7.

10. Holloway, "Read *Capital,*" 7.

11. Bauman, *Consuming Life,* 87.

12. Douglas Burnham and Peter Lamb, *The First Marx: A Philosophical Introduction* (London: Bloomsbury Academic, 2019), 21.

13. Burnham and Lamb, *The First Marx,* 68.

14. István Mészáros, *Marx's Theory of Alienation* (London: Merlin, 1970); Richard Schacht, *Alienation* (London: George Allen & Unwin, 1970); Bertell Ollman, *Alienation: Marx's Conception of Man in Capitalist Society*, 2nd ed. (New York: Cambridge University Press, 1976); Isidor Wallimann, *Estrangement: Marx's Conception of Human Nature and the Division of Labor* (Westport, Conn.: Greenwood, 1981); and Sean Sayers, *Marx and Alienation: Essays on Hegelian Themes* (New York: Palgrave Macmillan, 2011).

15. Sandra Lee Bartky, *Femininity and Domination: Studies in the Phenomenology of Oppression* (New York: Routledge, 1990), 34.

16. Gajo Petrović, "Marx's Theory of Alienation," *Philosophy and Phenomenological Research* 23, no. 3 (1963): 419–26; at 426.

17. Bartky, *Femininity and Domination,* 32.

18. Ian G. R. Shaw and Marv Waterstone, *Wageless Life: A Manifesto for a Future beyond Capitalism* (Minneapolis: University of Minnesota Press, 2019), 49.

19. Karl Marx, *Capital: A Critique of Political Economy, Volume I,* trans. Ben Fowkes (New York: Penguin Books), 875.

20. Marx, *Capital,* Volume I, 915.

21. Epifanio San Juan Jr., "From Race to Class Struggle: Marxism and Critical Race Theory," *Nature, Society, and Thought* 18, no. 3 (2005): 333–53; at 341.

22. San Juan Jr., "From Race to Class," 343 and 350.

23. Mészáros, *Marx's Theory of Alienation,* 63–64.

24. Karl Marx, *A Contribution to the Critique of Political Economy* (New York: International, 1970), 20.

25. John Haldon, "Mode of Production, Social Action, and Historical Change: Some Questions and Issues," in *Studies on Pre-Capitalist Modes of Production*, ed. Laura da Graca and Andrea Zingarelli (Boston: Brill, 2015), 204–36; at 209; A Haroon Akram-Lodhi and Cristobal Kay, "Back to the Future? Marx, Modes of Production and the Agrarian Question," in *Critical Perspectives on the Agrarian Transition*, ed. B. B. Mohanty (London: Routledge, 2016): 71–94; at 46.

26. Marx, *A Contribution,* 20.

27. Edgar Illas, "Base and Superstructure," in *The Bloomsbury Companion to Marx,* ed. Jeff Diamanti, Andrew Pendakis, and Imre Szeman (London: Bloomsbury Academic, 2019), 267–72; at 268.

28. Illas, "Base and Superstructure," 268.
29. Haldon, "Mode of Production," 208.
30. Haldon, "Mode of Production," 210.
31. Haldon, "Mode of Production," 210.
32. Illas, "Base and Superstructure," 268.
33. Marx, *A Contribution,* 21.
34. Marx, *A Contribution,* 21.
35. Akram-Lodhi and Kay, "Back to the Future," 46.
36. Marx and Engels, *German Ideology,* 38.
37. Marx, *Capital,* Volume I, 125.
38. Marx, *Capital,* Volume I, 163.
39. Michael Heinrich, *An Introduction to the Three Volumes of Karl Marx's* Capital (New York: Monthly Review, 2004), 72.
40. Marx, *Capital,* Volume I, 164–65.
41. Marx, *Capital,* Volume I, 126.
42. Marx, *Capital,* Volume I, 140.
43. Heinrich, *An Introduction*, 58.
44. Joseph Choonara, *A Reader's Guide to Marx's Capital* (London: Bookmarks, 2017), 21.
45. Choonara, *A Reader's Guide,* 22.
46. Choonara, *A Reader's Guide,* 25.
47. Marx, *Capital,* Volume I, 247.
48. Marx, *Capital,* Volume I, 247.
49. Marx, *Capital,* Volume I, 203.
50. Bobby Wilson, "Race in Commodity Exchange and Consumption: Separate but Equal," *Annals of the Association of American Geographers* 95, no. 3 (2005): 587–606; at 589.
51. Marx, *Capital,* Volume I, 248.
52. Marx, *Capital,* Volume I, 248.
53. Lange, "Capital," 274.
54. Marx, *Capital,* Volume I, 248.
55. Marx, *Capital,* Volume I, 250.
56. Marx, *Capital,* Volume I, 251.
57. Marx, *Capital,* Volume I, 251.
58. David Harvey, *A Companion to Marx's* Capital (New York: Verso, 2010), 85.
59. Marx, *Capital,* Volume I, 254.
60. Lange, "Capital," 275.
61. Marx, *Capital,* Volume I, 1038.
62. Murray E. G. Smith, "Productivity, Valorization and Crisis: Socially Necessary Unproductive Labor in Contemporary Capitalism," *Science & Society* 57, no. 3 (1993): 262–93; at 265.

63. Marx, *Capital,* Volume I, 1039.

64. Smith, "Productivity, Valorization," 265–66.

65. Smith, "Productivity, Valorization," 266.

66. Immanuel Wallerstein, "Ecology and Capitalist Costs of Production: No Exit," in *Ecology and the World System,* ed. Walter L. Goldfrank, David Goodman, and Andrew Szasz (Westport, Conn.: Greenwood, 1999): 3–12. See also Gerard Strange, "Capitalism, Valorization and the Political Economy of Ecological Crisis," *Capital & Class* 24, no. 2 (2000): 55–80.

67. Michael Hardt and Toni Negri, "The Multiplicities within Capitalist Rule and the Articulation of Struggles," *tripleC* 16, no. 2 (2018): 440–48; at 441.

68. Hardt and Negri, "The Multiplicities within Capitalist Rule," 441.

69. Hardt and Negri, "The Multiplicities within Capitalist Rule," 441.

70. Hardt and Negri, "The Multiplicities within Capitalist Rule," 441.

71. Burnham and Lamb, *The First Marx,* 29

72. Fracchia, "The Capitalist Labour-Process," 43.

73. Fracchia, "The Capitalist Labour-Process," 43.

74. Marx, *Capital,* Volume I, 300.

75. Paul D'Amato, *The Meaning of Marxism* (Chicago: Haymarket Books, 2006), 56.

76. Ernest Mandel, *An Introduction to Marxist Economic Theory* (New York: Pathfinder, 1969), 17.

77. Mandel, *Introduction to Marxist Economic Theory,* 17.

78. Karl Marx and Friedrich Engels, *The Communist Manifesto* (London: Verso, 2012), 42.

79. Marx, *Capital,* Volume I, 376.

80. Marx, *Capital,* Volume I, 377.

81. Prabhat Patnaik, "Contemporary Imperialism and the World's Labor Reserves," *Social Scientist* 35, no. 5–6 (2007): 3–18; at 3.

82. Michael McIntyre, "Race, Surplus Population and the Marxist Theory of Imperialism," *Antipode* 43, no. 5 (2011): 1489–515.

83. Marx, *Capital,* Volume I, 380.

84. See for example James A. Tyner, *Dead Labor: Toward a Political Economy of Premature Death* (Minneapolis: University of Minnesota Press, 2019), 54.

85. Shaw and Waterstone, *Wageless Life,* 24.

86. John Bellamy Foster, Robert W. McChesney, and R. Jamil Jonna, "The Global Reserve Army of Labor and the New Imperialism," *Monthly Review* 63, no. 6 (2011): 1–31; at 9.

87. Marx, *Capital,* Volume I, 795.

88. Marx, *Capital,* Volume I, 796.

89. Foster et al., "Global Reserve Army," 10.

90. As Denning (2010: 87) writes, Marx was no sympathizer of the *lumpenpro-*

letariat. Indeed, in his support of the proletariat, the "legitimate" *moral* working class, Marx viewed the *lumpenproletariat* as an unproductive, parasitic layer of society.

91. Marx, *Capital,* Volume I, 797.

92. Marx, *Capital,* Volume I, 797.

93. Tony C. Brown, "The Time of Globalization: Rethinking Primitive Accumulation," *Rethinking Marxism* 21, no. 4 (2009): 571–84; at 574.

94. Marx, *Capital,* Volume I, 784.

95. Mandel, *Introduction to Marxist Economic Theory,* 30.

96. Marx, *Capital,* Volume I, 129.

97. Moishe Postone, *Time, Labor, and Social Domination: A Reinterpretation of Marx's Critical Theory* (New York: Cambridge University Press, 1993), 193.

98. Alex Callinicos, *The Revolutionary Ideas of Karl Marx* (Chicago: Haymarket Books, 2011), 137.

99. Marx, *Capital,* Volume I, 1024.

100. Choonara, *A Reader's Guide,* 64.

101. Marx, *Capital,* Volume I, 275.

102. Choonara, *A Reader's Guide,* 64.

103. Marx, *Capital,* Volume I, 275.

104. Marx, *Capital,* Volume I, 275.

105. Karl Marx, *Economic and Philosophic Manuscripts of 1844,* trans. Martin Milligan (Amherst, NY: Prometheus, 1988), 86.

106. Marx, *Economic and Philosophic Manuscripts,* 20.

107. Marx, *Capital,* Volume I, 436–37.

108. Marx, *Capital,* Volume I, 1034–35.

109. Marx, *Capital,* Volume I, 1035.

110. Burnham and Lamb, *The First Marx,* 53.

111. Burnham and Lamb, *The First Marx,* 115.

112. Lynn S. Chancer, *Sadomasochism in Everyday Life: The Dynamics of Power and Powerlessness* (New Brunswick, N.J.: Rutgers University Press, 1992), 33.

113. Jake Sherman, Meridith McGraw, and Quint Forgey, "Schumer Urges Trump to Invoke Defense Production Act to Rush Medical Equipment to Providers," *Politico,* March 20, 2020. https://www.politico.com/states/new-york/albany/story/2020/03/20/schumer-urges-trump-to-invoke-defense-production-act-to-rush-medical-equipment-to-providers-1268366; Eric Schlosser, "America's Slaughterhouses Aren't Just Killing Animals," *The Atlantic,* May 12, 2020, https://www.theatlantic.com/ideas/archive/2020/05/essentials-meatpacking-coronavirus/611437; Michael Grabell, Claire Perlman, and Bernice Yeung, "Emails Reveal Chaos as Meatpacking Companies Fought Health Agencies over Covid-19 Outbreaks in Their Plants," *ProPublica,* June 12, 2020, https://www.propublica.org/article/emails-reveal-chaos-as-meatpacking-companies-fought

-health-agencies-over-covid-19-outbreaks-in-their-plants; Kimberly Kindy, "More than 200 Meat Plant Workers in the U.S. Have Died of Covid-19. Federal Regulators Just Issued Two Modest Fines," *Washington Post,* September 13, 2020, https://www.msn.com/en-us/news/us/more-than-200-meat-plant-workers-in-the-u-s-have-died-of-covid-19-federal-regulators-just-issued-two-modest-fines/ar-BB18ZqQK.

114. Kindy, "More than 200 Meat Plant Workers."

115. Schlosser, "America's Slaughterhouses."

116. Karl Marx and Friedrich Engels, *The Communist Manifesto* (London: Verso, 2012), 42.

117. Schlosser, "America's Slaughterhouses."

118. Ollman, *Alienation,* 131.

119. Brett Clark and John Bellamy Foster, "Ecological Imperialism and the Global Metabolic Rift: Unequal Exchange and the Guano-Nitrates Trade," *International Journal of Comparative Sociology* 50, nos. 3–4 (2009): 311–34; at 313.

120. Marx, *Capital,* Volume I, 548.

121. Clark and Foster, "Ecological Imperialism," 314.

122. Marx, *Grundrisse,* 88.

123. John Bellamy Foster and Brett Clark, "The Expropriation of Nature," *Monthly Review* 69, no. 10 (2018): 1–27; at 3.

124. Paul Burkett, "Nature's 'Free Gifts' and the Ecological Significance of Value," *Capital & Class* 68 (1999): 89–110; at 95.

125. Marx, *Grundrisse,* 471.

126. Marx, *Grundrisse,* 489.

127. Ollman, *Alienation,* 134.

128. Ollman, *Alienation,* 136; Marx, *Economic and Philosophic Manuscripts.*

129. Shaw and Waterstone, *Wageless Life,* 45.

130. Shaw and Waterstone, *Wageless Life,* 45.

131. Wallimann, *Estrangement,* 12.

132. Ollman, *Alienation,* 136.

133. Shaw and Waterstone, *Wageless Life,* 45.

134. Marx, *Capital,* Volume 1, 271.

135. Marx, *Capital,* Volume 1, 272.

136. Marx, *Economic and Philosophic Manuscripts,* 74; italics in the original.

137. Ollman, *Alienation,* 136.

138. Karl Marx and Friedrich Engels, *The Communist Manifesto* (New York: Verso, 2012), 43–44.

139. Karl Marx, *Capital: A Critique of Political Economy,* Volume I, trans. Ben Fowkes (New York: Penguin, 1990), 548.

140. Ben Highmore, *Everyday Life and Cultural Theory: An Introduction* (New York: Routledge, 2002), 7.

141. Marx, *Capital,* Volume I, 548.

142. Ben Hamper, *Rivethead: Tales from the Assembly Line* (London: Fourth Estate, 1992), 95.

143. Lisa Marie Cacho, *Social Death: Racialized Rightlessness and the Criminalization of the Unprotected* (New York: New York University Press, 2012), 33.

144. Ben Highmore, *Everyday Life and Cultural Theory: An Introduction* (New York: Routledge, 2002), 8.

145. Marx, *Economic and Philosophic Manuscripts,* 77.

146. Marx, *Economic and Philosophic Manuscripts,* 72.

147. Marx, *Economic and Philosophic Manuscripts,* 73

148. Marx, *Economic and Philosophic Manuscripts,* 79.

149. Marx, *Economic and Philosophic Manuscripts,* 79–80.

150. Chancer, *Sadomasochism,* 33–34.

151. Wallimann, *Estrangement,* 33.

152. Martin Hägglund, *This Life: Why Mortality Makes Us Free* (London: Profile Books, 2019), 23.

153. Shaw and Waterstone, *Wageless Life,* 48.

154. Joel Kovel, *The Enemy of Nature: The End of Capitalism or the End of the World?* (London: Zed Books, 2007), 69.

155. Ollman, *Alienation,* chapter 23; Bradley Harris, "Alienation of the Capitalist Class: Toward a More Careful Reading of Marx," *Social Praxis* 7, nos. 1–2 (1980): 77–90.

156. Karl Marx, "The Holy Family," in *Karl Marx: Selected Writings,* 2nd ed., ed. David McLellan (New York: Oxford University Press, 2000), 146–70; at 148.

157. Sandra Lee Bartky, *Femininity and Domination: Studies in the Phenomenology of Oppression* (New York: Routledge, 1990), 23.

158. Tyner, *Dead Labor,* 33 *passim.*

159. Harcourt, *Illusion of Free Markets,* 34.

160. Bauman, *Consuming Life,* 123.

161. Martha A. Fineman, "The Vulnerable Subject: Anchoring Equality in the Human Condition," *Yale Journal of Law and Feminism* 20, no. 1 (2008): article 2 (23 pp.), at 10.

162. Zygmunt Bauman and Leonidas Donskis, *Moral Blindness: The Loss of Sensitivity in Liquid Modernity* (Malden, Mass.: Polity, 2013), 7.

163. Hardt and Negri, "The Multiplicities within Capitalist Rule," 441–442; see also Toni Negri, *Marx Beyond Marx: Lessons on the* Grundrisse (New York: Autonomedia, 1991).

164. Hardt and Negri, "The Multiplicities within Capitalist Rule," 442.

165. Hardt and Negri, "The Multiplicities within Capitalist Rule," 442.

166. Herbert Marcuse, *One-Dimensional Man: Studies in the Ideology of Advanced Industrial Society* (Boston: Beacon, 1964).

167. David Harvey, "Universal Alienation," *tripleC* 16, no. 2 (2018): 424–39; at 426.

168. Harvey, "Universal Alienation," 427.

169. Harvey, "Universal Alienation," 429.

170. Harvey, "Universal Alienation," 429.

171. Chancer, *Sadomasochism in Everyday Life,* 94.

172. Hardt and Negri, "The Multiplicities within Capitalist Rule," 443.

173. Eric Williams, *Capitalism & Slavery* (Chapel Hill: University of North Carolina Press, 1944); Manning Marable, *How Capitalism Underdeveloped Black America* (Boston: South End, 1983); John Ashworth, *Slavery, Capitalism, and Politics in the Antebellum Republic: Volume 1: Commerce and Compromise, 1820–1850* (Cambridge: Cambridge University Press, 1995); and Edward E. Baptist, *The Half Has Never Been Told: Slavery and the Making of American Capitalism* (New York: Basic Books, 2014).

174. Nathan McClintock, "Urban Agriculture, Racial Capitalism, and Resistance in the Settler-Colonial City," *Geography Compass* 12, no. 6 (2018): e12373. See Cedric Robinson, *Black Marxism: The Making of the Black Radical Tradition* (Chapel Hill: University of North Carolina Press, 1983).

175. McClintock, "Urban Agriculture."

176. Laura Pulido, "Geographies of Race and Ethnicity II: Environmental Racism, Racial Capitalism and State-Sanctioned Violence," *Progress in Human Geography* 41, no. 4 (2017): 524–33; at 526–27.

177. Pulido, "Geographies of Race," 527.

178. Robinson, *Black Marxism,* 9.

179. Hardt and Negri, "The Multiplicities within Capitalist Rule," 443.

180. Robin D. G. Kelley, "What Did Cedric Robinson Mean by Racial Capitalism?" *Boston Review,* January 12, 2017, https:bostonreview.net/race/robin-d-g-kelley-what-did-cedric-robinson-mean-racial-capitalism.

181. Hardt and Negri, "The Multiplicities within Capitalist Rule," 443.

182. See for example Heidi Hartmann, "The Unhappy Marriage of Marxism and Feminism: Towards a More Progressive Union," *Capital & Class* 3, no. 2 (1979): 1–33; Valeria Bryson, "Marxism and Feminism: Can the 'Unhappy Marriage' be Saved?" *Journal of Political Ideologies* 9, no. 1 (2004): 13–30.

183. Hardt and Negri, "The Multiplicities within Capitalist Rule," 444.

184. Marx and Engels, *The German Ideology,* 67.

185. Anne Bonds and Joshua Inwood, "Beyond White Privilege: Geographies of White Supremacy and Settler Colonialism," *Progress in Human Geography* 40, no. 6 (2016): 715–33; at 720.

186. Bonds and Inwood, "Beyond White Privilege," 720.

187. Marx and Engels, *The German Ideology,* 67.

188. Erik Olin Wright, "The Continuing Relevance of the Marxist Tradition for Transcending Capitalism," *tripleC* 16, no. 2 (2018): 490–500; at 491.

189. Members of the capitalist class also understood this and so countered these possibilities with the threat of unemployment or state-sanctioned police repression.

190. Burnham and Lamb, *The First Marx,* 99.

191. David W. Lovell, *Marx's Proletariat: The Making of a Myth* (New York: Routledge, 1988), 216.

192. Lovell, *Marx's Proletariat,* 216.

193. Marx, *Economic and Philosophic Manuscripts,* 19.

194. Michael D. Yates, "COVID-19, Economic Depression, and the Black Lives Matter Protests," *Monthly Review,* September 1, 2020, https://www.monthlyreview.org/2020/09/01/covid-19-economic-depression-and-the-black-lives-matter-protests.

195. APM Research Lab Staff, "The Color of Coronavirus: Covid-19 Deaths by Race and Ethnicity in the U.S.," September 16, 2020, https://www.apmresearchlab.org/covid/deaths-by-race.

196. Heather Brown, "Covid-19 Lays Bare Capitalism's Deference to Profits Over Lives," *The International Marxist-Humanist,* March 25, 2020, https://imhojournal.org/articles/covid-19-lays-bare-capitalisms-deference-to-profits-over-lives.

197. Mike Ludwig, "Essential Sanitary Workers Strike for Hazard Pay and PPE in New Orleans," *Truthout,* May 15, 2020, https://truthout.org/articles/essential-sanitary-workers-strike-for-hazard-pay-and-ppe-in-new-orleans/.

198. Michael Sainato, "Strikes Erupt as US Essential Workers Demand Protection Amid Pandemic," *The Guardian,* May 19, 2020, https://www.theguardian.com/world/2020/may/19/strikes-erupt-us-essential-workers-demand-better-protection-amid-pandemic.

199. Roland Simon, "Self-Organization is the First Act of the Revolution; It then Becomes an Obstacle Which the Revolution Has to Overcome," *Libcom.Org,* April 30, 2017, https://libcom.org/library/self-organisation-is-the-first-act-of-the-revolution-it-then-becomes-an-obstacle-which-the-revolution-has-to-overcome.

200. Simon, "Self-Organization."

201. Hardt and Negri, "The Multiplicities within Capitalist Rule," 445.

3. The Intersectionality of Alienation

1. Ebony Bowden, "Trump Blasts Biden, Appeals to Working-Class Voters at Ohio Rallies," *New York Post,* September 21, 2020, https://nypost.com/2020/09/21/trump-blasts-biden-while-appealing-to-working-class-voters-in-ohio/. Trump's phrase of being "stabbed in the back" is especially telling, as it evokes the Nazi

refrain that Jewish people stabbed the German nation-state in the back and betrayed them in the First World War.

2. And yet, many journalists, including those affiliated with more "reputable" presses, such as the *New York Times,* steadfastly refused to call out Trump's racism.

3. A. Mechele Dickerson, "America's Uneasy Relationship with the Working Poor," *Hastings Law Journal,* 51, no. 1 (1999): 17–72; at 17.

4. W. E. B. Du Bois, *Black Reconstruction in America* (New York: Free Press, 1998 [1935]), 700.

5. Du Bois, *Black Reconstruction,* 700.

6. Karl Marx, *A Contribution to the Critique of Political Economy,* ed. Maurice Dobb (New York: International, 1970), 21.

7. Charles A. Barone, *Radical Political Economy: A Concise Introduction* (New York: Routledge, 2015), 8. See also John Molyneux, "The Working Class," *Irish Marxist Review* 7, no. 20 (2018): 5–8.

8. Peter Knapp and Alan J. Spector, *Crisis and Change Today: Basic Questions of Marxist Sociology*, 2nd ed. (Lanham, Md.: Rowman & Littlefield, 2011), 110.

9. Henri Lefebvre, *Critique of Everyday Life, Volume II: Foundations for a Sociology of the Everyday,* trans. John Moore (New York: Verso, 2002), 209.

10. See, for example, David Harvey, *Seventeen Contradictions and the End of Capitalism* (New York: Oxford University Press, 2014).

11. Harvey, *Seventeen Contradictions,* 4.

12. Harvey, *Seventeen Contradictions,* 4.

13. Karl Marx, *Capital: A Critique of Political Economy,* Volume I, trans. Ben Fowkes (New York: Penguin, 1990), 723.

14. See, for example, Michael Löwy, *The Theory of Revolution in the Young Marx* (Chicago: Haymarket Books, 2005); Guido Starosta, *Marx's* Capital*: Method and Revolutionary Subjectivity* (Chicago: Haymarket Books, 2016); and Douglas Burnham and Peter Lamb, *The First Marx: A Philosophical Introduction* (London: Bloomsbury Academic, 2019).

15. Jan Kandiyali, "Freedom and Necessity in Marx's Account of Communism," *British Journal for the History of Philosophy* 22, no. 1 (2014): 104–23; at 109.

16. Lynn S. Chancer, *Sadomasochism in Everyday Life: The Dynamics of Power and Powerlessness* (New Brunswick, N.J.: Rutgers University Press, 1992), 33.

17. Karl Marx, "General Rules of the International Workingmen's Association, October 1864," https://www.marxists.org/history/international/iwma/documents/1864/rules.htm.

18. Karl Marx, *Early Writings* (New York: Penguin, 1970), 348.

19. Marx, "General Rules."

20. Ian Fraser and Lawrence Wilde, *The Marx Dictionary* (New York: Continuum, 2011), 166.

21. Andrew Bowie, *Introduction to German Philosophy: From Kant to Habermas* (Malden, Mass.: Polity, 2003), 118.

22. Alicja A. Gęścińska and Steven Lepez, "Freedom as Praxis: A Comparative Analysis of August Cieszkowski and Nikolaj Berdjaev," *Studies in East European Thought* 62, no. 1 (2010): 109–23; at 113. See also Lawrence S. Stepelevich, "August von Cieszkowski: From Theory to Praxis," *History and Theory* 13, no. 1 (1974): 39–52; and Daniel Kubat, "Marx and Cieszkowski," *American Slavic and East European Review* 20, no. 1 (1961): 114–17.

23. Gęścińska and Lepez, "Freedom as Praxis," 113.

24. Gęścińska and Lepez, "Freedom as Praxis," 115; Kubat, "Marx and Cieszkowski," 115.

25. Quoted in Gęścińska and Lepez, "Freedom as Praxis," 115.

26. Marx draws heavily on these philosophers, sometimes in agreement, often in dissent, and scholars continue to debate the degree of influence on Marx. Of this vast literature, see for example Zyi Rosen, "The Influence of Bruno Bauer on Marx's Concept of Alienation," *Social Theory and Practice* (1970): 50–68; D. A. Strickland and Kyriakos Kontopoulos, "Ideology and Praxis: Fichte to Marx," *Il Politico* (1973): 99–122; Tom Rockmore, "Activity in Fichte and Marx," *Idealistic Studies* 6, no. 2 (1976): 191–214; Lawrence S. Stepelevich, "Max Stirner and Ludwig Feuerbach," *Journal of the History of Ideas* (1978): 451–63; Hans-Martin Sass, "The 'Transition' from Feuerbach to Marx: A Re-interpretation," *Studies in Soviet Thought* 26, no. 2 (1983): 123–42; Widukind De Ridder, "Max Stirner, Hegel and the Young Hegelians: A Reassessment," *History of European Ideas* 34, no. 3 (2008): 285–97; Jacob M. Held, "Marx via Feuerbach: Species-Being Revisited," *Idealistic Studies* 39, no. 1/3 (2009): 137–48; and Jan Kandiyali, ed., *Reassessing Marx's Social and Political Philosophy: Freedom, Recognition, and Human Flourishing* (New York: Routledge, 2018).

27. Bowie, *Introduction to German Philosophy,* 122.

28. Bowie, *Introduction to German Philosophy,* 124.

29. Karl Marx, "Theses on Feuerbach," https://www.marxists.org/archive/marx/works/1845/theses/theses.htm.

30. Douglas Burnham and Peter Lamb, *The First Marx: A Philosophical Introduction* (London: Bloomsbury Academic, 2019), 187.

31. Marx, *Economic and Philosophic Manuscripts,* 74.

32. Erich Fromm, *The Sane Society* (New York: Henry Holt, 1955), 109–10.

33. Sandro Mezzadra, *In the Marxian Workshops: Producing Subjects,* trans. Yari Lanci (London: Rowman & Littlefield International, 2018), xv.

34. André Gorz, "Sartre and Marx," *New Left Review* 37, no. 5 (166): 33–52; George J. Stack, "Sartre's Dialectic of Social Relations," *Philosophy and Phenomenological Research* 31, no. 3 (1971): 394–408; Robert W. Connell, "Class, Patriarchy, and Sartre's Theory of Practice," *Theory and Society* 11, no. 3 (1982): 305–20;

Tony Stigliano, "Jean-Paul Sartre on Understanding Violence," *Crime and Social Justice* 19 (1983): 52–64; Iris Marion Young, "Gender as Seriality: Thinking about Women as a Social Collective," *Signs* 19, no. 3 (1994): 713–38; Kevin Boileau, "How Foucault Can Improve Sartre's Theory of Authentic Political Community," *Sartre Studies International* 10, no. 2 (2004): 77–91; Mark Boyle, "Sartre's Circular Dialectic and the Empires of Abstract Space: A History of Space and Place in Ballymun, Dublin," *Annals of the Association of American Geographers* 95, no. 1 (2005): 181–201; Mark Boyle and Audrey Kobayashi, "Metropolitan Anxieties: A Critical Appraisal of Sartre's Theory of Colonialism," *Transactions of the Institute of British Geographers* 36, no. 3 (2011): 408–24; Gavin Rae, "Sartre, Group Formations, and Practical Freedom: The Other in the *Critique of Dialectical Reason*," *Comparative and Continental Philosophy* 3, no. 2 (2011): 183–206; and Peter Caws, "Sartre's Theory of Groups," in *Jean-Paul Sartre: Key Concepts*, ed. Steven Churchill and Jack Reynolds (New York: Routledge, 2014), 184–194.

35. Jean-Paul Sartre, *Critique of Dialectical Reason*, trans. Alan Sheridan-Smith (New York: Verso, 1991 [1960]). It is important to clarify that Sartre, in his *Critique*, reinterprets Marx's account of alienation as a condition of material scarcity. I do not follow Sartre in this account.

36. Stack, "Sartre's Dialectic," 394.

37. Stack, "Sartre's Dialectic," 395.

38. Young, "Gender as Seriality," 718.

39. Young, "Gender as Seriality," 718.

40. Young, "Gender as Seriality," 724.

41. Ben Highmore, *Everyday Life and Cultural Theory: An Introduction* (New York: Routledge, 2002), 8.

42. Highmore, *Everyday Life*, 9.

43. Susan Stewart, *On Longing: Narratives of the Miniature, the Gigantic, the Souvenir, the Collection* (Durham, N.C.: Duke University Press, 1993), 14.

44. Highmore, *Everyday Life*, 8.

45. Alyson Cole and Estelle Ferrarese, "How Capitalism Forms Our Lives," *Journal for Cultural Research* 22, no. 2 (2018): 105–12; at 107.

46. Cole and Ferrarese, "How Capitalism Forms Our Lives," 107.

47. Karl Marx and Friedrich Engels, *The Communist Manifesto* (London: Verso, 2012), 38.

48. Zygmunt Bauman, *Liquid Modernity* (Cambridge, Mass.: Polity, 2000). See also Zygmunt Bauman and Mark Haugaard, "Liquid Modernity and Power: A Dialogue with Zygmunt Bauman," *Journal of Power* 1, no. 2 (2008): 111–30.

49. Raymond L. M. Lee, "Bauman, Liquid Modernity and Dilemmas of Development," *Thesis Eleven* 83 (2005): 61–77; at 65.

50. Peter Abrahamson, "Liquid Modernity: Bauman on Contemporary Welfare Society," *Act Sociologica* 47, no. 2 (2004): 171–79; at 171.

51. Raymond L.M. Lee, "Reinventing Modernity: Reflexive Modernization vs Liquid Modernity vs Multiple Modernities," *European Journal of Social Theory* 9, no. 3 (2006): 355–68; at 357.

52. Abrahamson, "Bauman, Liquid Modernity," 177.

53. Henri Lefebvre, *Everyday Life in the Modern World,* trans. Sacha Rabinovitch (New Brunswick, N.J.: Transaction, 1984), 21.

54. Caws, "Sartre's Theory of Groups," 185.

55. Gill Valentine, "The Geography of Women's Fear," *Area* 21, no. 4 (1989): 385–90; Rachel Pain, "Space, Sexual Violence and Social Control: Integrating Geographical and Feminist Analyses of Women's Fear of Crime," *Progress in Human Geography* 15, no. 4 (1991): 415–31; Clare Madge, "Public Parks and the Geography of Fear," *Tijdschrift voor Economische en Sociale Geografie* 88, no. 3 (1997): 237–50; Robin Law, "Beyond 'Women and Transport': Towards New Geographies of Gender and Daily Mobility," *Progress in Human Geography* 23, no. 4 (1999): 567–88; and Erica Wilson and Donna E. Little, "The Solo Female Travel Experience: Exploring the 'Geography of Women's Fear,'" *Current Issues in Tourism* 11, no. 2 (2008): 167–86.

56. Law, "Beyond 'Women and Transport,'" 570.

57. Stigliano, "Jean-Paul Sartre," 57.

58. Raewyn W. Connell, "Class, Patriarchy, and Sartre's Theory of Practice," *Theory and Society* 11, no. 3 (1982): 305–20; at 309.

59. Connell, "Class, Patriarchy," 309.

60. Sartre, *Critique of Dialectical Reason,* 67.

61. Caws, "Sartre's Theory of Groups," 187.

62. Caws, "Sartre's Theory of Groups," 187.

63. Caws, "Sartre's Theory of Groups," 188.

64. Caws, "Sartre's Theory of Groups," 188.

65. Stack, "Sartre's Dialectic," 400.

66. Caws, "Sartre's Theory of Groups," 188.

67. Connell, "Class, Patriarchy," 310.

68. Swathi Shanmugasundaram, "Trump Cites Hate Group at Conservative Political Action Conference," *Southern Poverty Law Center,* March 04, 2019, https://www.splcenter.org/hatewatch/2019/03/04/trump-cites-hate-group-conservative-political-action-conference.

69. Shanmugasundaram, "Trump Cites Hate Group."

70. Young, "Gender as Seriality," 735; Caws, "Sartre's Theory of Groups," 189.

71. Caws, "Sartre's Theory of Groups," 189.

72. Rae, "Sartre, Group Formations," 196.

73. Caws, "Sartre's Theory of Groups," 190.

74. Eduardo Bonilla-Silva, "Feeling Race: Theorizing the Racial Economy of Emotions," *American Sociological Review* 84, no. 1 (2019): 1–25; Eduardo

Bonilla-Silva, "Toward a New Political Praxis for Trumpamerica: New Directions in Critical Race Theory," *American Behavioral Scientist* 63, no. 13 (2019): 1776–88.

75. Bonilla-Silva, "Toward a New Political Praxis," 1779.

76. Bonilla-Silva, "Toward a New Political Praxis," 1779

77. Sartre, *Critique of Dialectical Reason,* 437–44. Here, Sartre uses the term "traitor"; I prefer the term "enemy."

78. Right-wing extremist violence has increased dramatically in the twenty-first century, but especially in the United States, which has seen a 1,450 percent increase in far-right attacks between 2007 and 2017. By far, white supremacists and other far-right groups commit the vast majority of extremist-related murders in the United States. See Kennett Werner, "White Supremacists Committed Most Extremist Killings in 2017, ADL Says," *NBC News*, January 18, 2018, https://www.nbcnews.com/news/us-news/white-supremacists-committed-most-extreme-killings-2017-adl-says-n838896.

79. Jesse J. Norris, "Why Dylann Roof Is a Terrorist under Federal Law, and Why It Matters," *Harvard Journal on Legislation* 54 (2017): 501–41; at 504.

80. Carla Herreria, "El Paso Shooting Suspect May Have Shared Anti-Immigrant Manifesto Before Attack," *Huffpost,* August 4, 2019, https://www.huffpost.com/entry/patrick-crusius-manifesto-el-paso-shooting_n_5d460ba5e4b0aca341lec308; Brett Barrouquere and Hatewatch Staff, "El Paso Shooting Suspect May Have Authored Manifesto Containing White Nationalist Talking Points," *Southern Poverty Law Center,* August 3, 2019, https://www.splcenter.org/hatewatch/2019/08/03/el-paso-shooting-suspect-may-have-authored-manifesto-containing-white-nationalist-talking.

81. Berrouquere and Hatewatch Staff, "El Paso Shooting."

82. Jacob Ware, "Siege: The Atomwaffen Division and the Rising Far-Right Terrorism in the United States," *ICCT Policy Brief* (The Hague, Netherlands: International Centre for Counter-Terrorism, 2019), 4.

83. Peter Baker and Michael D. Shear, "El Paso Shooting Suspect's Manifesto Echoes Trump's Language," *New York Times,* August 4, 2019, https://www.nytimes.com/2019/08/04/us/politics/trump-mass-shootings.html.

84. Raw, "Sartre, Group Formations," 201.

85. Sartre, *Critique of Dialectical Reason,* 443–44.

86. Caws, "Sartre's Theory of Groups," 190.

87. Mezzadra, *In the Marxian Workshops,* xvi.

88. Peter Goodwin, "Where's the Working Class?," *tripleC* 16, no. 2 (2018): 535–45; at 541.

89. Goodwin, "Where's the Working Class?," 543.

90. Marx, *Economic and Philosophic Manuscripts,* 19.

91. See, for example, Rogers Brubaker and Frederick Cooper, "Beyond

'Identity,'" *Theory and Society* 29, no. 1 (2000): 1–47; Jeff McMahan, *The Ethics of Killing: Problems at the Margins of Life* (New York: Oxford University Press, 2002); and Steven Luper, *The Philosophy of Death* (Cambridge: Cambridge University Press, 2009) for considered arguments on the relative merits of these terms.

92. Catherine Belsey, *Poststructuralism: A Very Short Introduction* (New York: Oxford University Press, 2002), 52.

93. Avtar Brah and Ann Phoenix, "Ain't I a Woman? Revisiting Intersectionality," *Journal of International Women's Studies* 5, no. 3 (2004): 75–86; at 76.

94. Frantz Fanon, *Black Skin, White Masks,* trans. Charles Lam Markmann (New York: Grove, 1967), 113–14.

95. For a more thorough analysis of this passage, see Sylvia Wynter, "Towards the Sociogenic Principle: Fanon, Identity, the Puzzle of Conscious Experience, and What It Is Like to Be 'Black,'" in *National Identities and Sociopolitical Changes in Latin America,* ed. M. F. Durán-Cogan and A. Gómez-Moriana (New York: Routledge, 2001), 30–66.

96. Michel Foucault, *Power/Knowledge: Selected Interviews and Other Writings, 1972–1977,* trans. Colin Gordon, Leo Marshall, John Mepham, and Kate Soper, ed. Colin Gordon (New York: Pantheon Books, 1980), 155.

97. Paola Rebughini, "Subject, Subjectivity, Subjectivation," *Sociopedia.Isa* (2014): 1–11; at 4.

98. Rebughini, "Subject," 4.

99. Sylvia Wynter, "Ethno or Socio Poetics," *Alcheringa* 2 (1976): 78–94; at 83.

100. Orisanmi Burton, "To Protect and Serve Whiteness," *North American Dialogue* 18, no. 2 (2015): 38–50; at 41.

101. Kimberlé Crenshaw, "Mapping the Margins: Intersectionality, Identity Politics, and Violence against Women of Color," *Stanford Law Review* 43, no. 6 (1991): 1241–99; at 1244.

102. Crenshaw, "Mapping the Margins," 1244.

103. Elena Ruíz, "Framing Intersectionality," in *The Routledge Companion to Philosophy of Race,* ed. Paul C. Taylor, Linda Martín Alcoff, and Luvell Anderson (New York: Routledge, 2017), 335–48; at 336.

104. Ruíz, "Framing Intersectionality," 336.

105. The Combahee River Collective Statement was written in 1977 primarily by Barbara Smith, Beverly Smith, and Demita Frazier; it was first published as "A Black Feminist Statement," in *Capitalist Patriarchy and the Case for Socialist Feminism,* ed. Zillah Eisenstein (New York: Monthly Review, 1978), 210–18. Quotations here appear from a 2014 reprint of the chapter. See Combahee River Collective, "A Black Feminist Statement," *Women's Studies Quarterly,* 42, nos. 3–4 (2014): 271–80.

106. Combahee River Collective, "A Black Feminist Statement," 273.
107. Combahee River Collective, "A Black Feminist Statement," 274.
108. Terrion L. Williamson, "Why Did They Die? On Combahee and the Serialization of Black Death," *Souls* 19, no. 3 (2017): 328–41; at 329.
109. Amartya Sen, *Identity and Violence: The Illusion of Destiny* (New York: W.W. Norton, 2006), 4–5.
110. Combahee River Collective, "A Black Feminist Statement," 274.
111. Combahee River Collective, "A Black Feminist Statement," 274.
112. Sumi Cho, Kimberlé Crenshaw, and Leslie McCall, "Toward a Field of Intersectionality Studies: Theory, Applications, and Praxis," *Signs* 38, no. 4 (2013): 785–810; at 788.
113. Combahee River Collective, "A Black Feminist Statement," 273.
114. Keeanga-Yamahtta Taylor, "Until Black Women Are Free, None of Us Will Be Free," *New Yorker*, July 20, 2020, https://www.newyorker.com/news/our-columnists/until-black-women-are-free-none-of-us-will-be-free.
115. Taylor, "Until Black Women Are Free."
116. Bohrer, "Intersectionality and Marxism," 69.
117. Combahee River Collective, "A Black Feminist Statement," 274.
118. Michael Löwy, *The Theory of Revolution in the Young Marx* (Chicago: Haymarket Books, 2005),
119. David W. Lovell, *Marx's Proletariat: The Making of a Myth* (New York: Routledge, 1988), 222.
120. Löwy, *The Theory of Revolution,* viii.
121. Epifanio San Juan Jr., "From Race to Class Struggle: Marxism and Critical Race Theory," *Nature, Society, and Thought* 18, no. 3 (2005): 333–53; at 340.
122. San Juan Jr., "From Race to Class Struggle," 340.
123. Zygmunt Bauman, *Work, Consumerism and the New Poor* (Buckingham, UK: Open University Press, 1998), 97.
124. Heather Brown, "Covid-19 Lays Bare Capitalism's Deference to Profits Over Lives," *International Marxist-Humanist,* March 25, 2020, https://imhojournal.org/articles/covid-19-lays-bare-capitalisms-deference-to-profits-over-lives.
125. Brown, "Covid-19 Lays Bare Capitalism's Deference."
126. Abdul El-Sayed, "Coronavirus Is Exploiting an Underlying Condition: Our Epidemic of Insecurity," *The Guardian,* March 19, 2020, https://www.theguardian.com/commentisfree/2020/mar/19/coronavirus-insecurity-anxiety-us-epidemic.
127. Whitney N. Laster Pirtle, "Racial Capitalism: A Fundamental Cause of Novel Coronavirus (COVID-19) Pandemic Inequities in the United States," *Health Education & Behavior* 47, no. 4 (August 2020): 504–8.
128. Michael D. Yates, "COVID-19, Economic Depression, and the Black Lives Matter Protests," *Monthly Review*, September 1, 2020, https://www.monthly

review.org/2020/09/01/covid-19-economic-depression-and-the-black-lives-matter-protests.

129. Abdul El-Sayed, "Communities Enduring Racism & Poverty Will Suffer Most Due to Covid-19," *Democracy Now!,* March 31, 2020, https://www.democracynow.org/2020/3/31/abul_el_sayed_epidemic_of_insecurity.

130. Yates, "COVID-19, Economic Depression."

4. Whose Lives Matter?

1. Manny Fernandez and Audra D. S. Burch, "George Floyd, From 'I Want to Touch the World' to 'I Can't Breathe,'" *New York Times,* July 29, 2020, https://www.nytimes.com/article/george-floyd-who-is.html; "George Floyd: What Happened in the Final Moments of His Life," *BBC News,* July 16, 2020, https://www.bbc.com/news/world-us-canada-52861726; Toluse Olorunnipa and Griff Witte, "Born with Two Strikes: How Systemic Racism Shaped Floyd's Life and Hobbled His Ambition," *Washington Post,* October 8, 2020. https://www.washingtonpost.com/graphics/2020/national/george-floyd-america/systemic-racism/.

2. Fernandez and Burch, "George Floyd."

3. Quoted in Olorunnipa and Witte, "Born with Two Strikes."

4. "George Floyd: What Happened"; Minyvonne Burke, "Owner of Minneapolis Grocery Store Says He Told Employee 'Call the Police on the Police' as She Witnessed George Floyd Death," *NBC News,* May 29, 2020, https://www.nbcnews.com/news/us-news/owner-minneapolis-grocery-store-says-he-told-employee-call-police-n1216461.

5. Burke, "Owner of Minneapolis Grocery Store"; "George Floyd: What Happened."

6. On April 20, 2021, Derek Chauvin was found guilty for the murder of George Floyd. Chauvin was convicted on three counts: second-degree murder, third-degree murder, and second-degree manslaughter.

7. ACLED, "Demonstrations & Political Violence in America: New Data for Summer 2020, https://acleddata.com/acleddatanew/wp-content/uploads/2020/09/ACLED_USDataReview_Sum2020_SeptWebPDF_HiRes.pdf. The protests, moreover, were overwhelmingly peaceful—despite the rhetoric of the Trump administration, spokespersons of which continually portrayed the protests as "Leftist" extremists, anarchists, thugs, and criminals. Indeed, in the few instances of violence reported, these more often than not followed an excessive police presence, including the deployment of Special Weapons and Tactics (SWAT) units of law enforcement and the National Guard. To take one incident, on May 31, 2020, in Las Vegas, Nevada, a peaceful protest was shattered when members of the Las Vegas Metro Police Department and SWAT unit

released tear gas and fired rubber bullets at both protestors and journalists. See for example "SWAT, Police Uses Tear Gas and Rubber Bullets on Las Vegas Strip Protesters," *MSNBC News,* June 1, 2020, https://www.msn.com/en-us/news/us/dozens-of-black-lives-matter-protesters-gather-on-las-vegas-strip-for-george-floyd/ar-BB14QQR3.

8. Nor should the fact be lost that the demonstrations surrounding the public lynching of Floyd occurred in the midst of a global pandemic. Many of those protesting were among the most vulnerable to Covid-related premature death.

9. Michael D. Yates, "COVID-19, Economic Depression, and the Black Lives Matter Protests," *Monthly Review,* September 1, 2020, https://www.monthlyreview.org/2020/09/01/covid-19-economic-depression-and-the-black-lives-matter-protests.

10. Yates, "COVID-19, Economic Depression."

11. Peter Hudis, "The Seeds of Revolution Have Sprouted: What Is to Be Done?" *New Politics,* August 6, 2020, https://newpol.org/the-seeds-of-revolution-have-sprouted-what-is-now-to-be-done/.

12. Martha Biondi, "From Hope to Disposability," *In These Times,* August 19, 2013, https://inthesetimes.com/article/from-hope-to-disposability-50-years-after-march-on-washington.

13. "International Solidarity with the Minneapolis Uprising," *CrimethInc.,* June 2, 2020, https://crimethinc.com/2020/06/02/international-solidarity-with-the-minneapolis-uprising-demonstrations-graffiti-hacking-and-riots-on-six-continents.

14. "From Chile to Minneapolis: An Open Letter," *CrimethInc.,* June 3, 2020, https://crimethinc.com/2020/06/03/from-chile-to-minneapolis-an-open-letter-global-solidarity-with-the-rebellion-against-police-and-white-supremacy. See also Syrine Attia, "Front-Line Activists 'Primera Linea' Protect Chile's Protestors, but Some Criticize Their Methods," *The Observers,* January 3, 2020, https://observers.france24.com/en/20200103-frontline-activists-primera-linea-protecting-protesters-chile-santiago-super-heroes.

15. "From Chile to Minneapolis."

16. "KJK: The Murder of George Floyd Is Not an Isolated Incident," *ANF News,* May 31, 2020, https://anfenglishmobile.com/news/kjk-the-murder-of-george-floyd-is-not-an-isolated-incident-44166.

17. "KJK: The Murder of George Floyd is Not an Isolated Incident."

18. David Gillborn, "The White Working Class, Racism and Respectability: Victims, Degenerates and Interest-Convergence," *British Journal of Educational Studies* 58, no. 1 (2010): 3–25; Gurminder K. Bhambra, "Brexit, Trump, and 'Methodological Whiteness': On the Misrecognition of Race and Class," *British Journal of Sociology* 68, no. S1 (2017): S214–S232; Hugh Gusterson, "From Brexit to Trump: Anthropology and the Rise of Nationalist Populism," *American Ethnol-*

ogist 44, no. 2 (2017): 209–14; Douglas Schrock, Benjamin Dowd-Arrow, Kristen Erichsen, Haley Gentile, and Pierce Dignam, "The Emotional Politics of Making America Great Again: Trump's Working Class Appeals," *Journal of Working-Class Studies* 2, no. 1 (2017): 5–22; Aurelien Mondon and Aaron Winter, "Whiteness, Populism and the Racialization of the Working Class in the United Kingdom and the United States," *Identities* 26, no. 5 (2019): 510–28.

19. David W. Lovell, *Marx's Proletariat: The Making of a Myth* (New York: Routledge, 1988), 4.

20. Anne Bonds and Joshua Inwood, "Beyond White Privilege: Geographies of White Supremacy and Settler Colonialism," *Progress in Human Geography* 40, no. 6 (2016): 715–33; at 717.

21. Minelle Mahtani, "Challenging the Ivory Tower: Proposing Anti-Racist Geographies within the Academy," *Gender, Place & Culture* 13, no. 1 (2006): 21–25; Lawrence D. Berg, "Geographies of Identity I: Geography—(Neo) Liberalism—White Supremacy," *Progress in Human Geography* 36, no. 4 (2012): 508–17; Minelle Mahtani, "Toxic Geographies: Absences in Critical Race Thought and Practice in Social and Cultural Geography," *Social & Cultural Geography* 15, no. 4 (2014): 359–67; and Caroline Faria and Sharlene Mollett, "Critical Feminist Reflexivity and the Politics of Whiteness in the 'Field,'" *Gender, Place & Culture* 23, no. 1 (2016): 79–93.

22. W. E. B. Du Bois, *Black Reconstruction in America* (New York: Free Press, 1998 [1935]), 700.

23. Russell Rickford, "Black Lives Matter: Toward a Modern Practice of Mass Struggle," *New Labor Forum* 25, no. 1 (2016): 35–42; Garrett Chase, "The Early History of the Black Lives Matter Movement, and the Implications Thereof," *Nevada Law Journal* 18, no. 3 (2018): 1091–112; Keeanga-Yamahtta Taylor, *From #BlackLivesMatter to Black Liberation* (Chicago: Haymarket Books, 2016); Barbara Ransby, *Making All Black Lives Matter: Reimagining Freedom in the Twenty-First Century* (Oakland: University of California Press, 2018).

24. Siddhant Issar, "Listening to Black Lives Matter: Racial Capitalism and the Critique of Neoliberalism," *Contemporary Political Theory* 20 (2021): 48–71. See also Gérard Duménil and Dominique Lévy, *Capital Resurgent: Roots of the Neoliberal Revolution* (Cambridge, Mass.: Harvard University Press, 2004); David Harvey, *A Brief History of Neoliberalism* (Oxford: Oxford University Press, 2005).

25. Harvey, *A Brief History*, 2.

26. David Harvey, *The New Imperialism* (Oxford: Oxford University Press, 2003), 63.

27. Nik Theodore, "Closed Borders, Open Markets: Day Laborers' Struggle for Economic Rights," in *Contesting Neoliberalism: Urban Frontiers*, ed. Helga Leitner, Jamie Peck, and Eric Sheppard (New York: Guilford, 2007), 250–65; at 252–53.

28. Katherine Schaeffer, "6 Facts About Economic Inequality in the

U.S.," *Pew Research Center,* February 7, 2020, https://www.pewresearch.org/fact-tank/2020/02/07/6-facts-about-economic-inequality-in-the-u-s/.

29. Tami Luhby, "US Black-White Inequality in 6 Stark Charts," *CNN,* June 3, 2020, https://www.cnn.com/2020/06/03/politics/black-white-us-financial-inequality/index.html. See also Howard Gold, "The Racial Wealth Gap Is at the Heart of America's Inequality," *Market Watch,* July 15, 2020, https://www.marketwatch.com/story/the-racial-wealth-gap-is-at-the-heart-of-americas-inequality-2020-07-15.

30. Issar, "Listening to Black Lives."

31. Nick Hanauer and David M. Rolf, "The Top 1% of Americans Have Taken $50 Trillion from the Bottom 90%—and That's Made the U.S. Less Secure," *Time,* September 14, 2020, https://time.com/58888024/50-trillion-income-inequality-america.

32. Joshua F. J. Inwood, "Neoliberal Racism: The 'Southern Strategy' and the Expanding Geographies of White Supremacy," *Social & Cultural Geography* 16, no. 4 (2015): 407–23; at 409–10. See also Jamie Peck and Adam Tickell, "Neoliberalizing Space," *Antipode* 34, no. 3 (2002): 380–404.

33. David J. Roberts and Minelle Mahtani, "Neoliberalizing Race, Racing Neoliberalism: Placing 'Race' in Neoliberal Discourses," *Antipode* 42, no. 2 (2010): 248–57; at 255.

34. Robert Albritton, *Let Them Eat Junk: How Capitalism Creates Hunger and Obesity* (New York: Pluto, 2009), 47.

35. Adam Shah, "The 1 Percent's Attack on Unemployment Benefits Is a Sign of Our Broken Democracy," *Inequality.Org,* July 21, 2020, https://inequality.org/research/crisis-unemployment-benefits/.

36. Shah, "The 1 Percent's Attack."

37. Joshua Simon, "A Conversation with Karl Marx (1818–1883) on Why There Is No Socialism in the United States," in *The Return of the Theorists: Dialogues with Great Thinkers in International Relations*, ed. Richard N. Lebow, Peer Schouten, and Hidemi Suganami (London: Palgrave Macmillan, 2016), 134–42.

38. Jeffrey Reiman and Paul Leighton, *The Rich Get Richer and the Poor Get Prison: Ideology, Class, and Criminal Justice,* 10th ed. (New York: Pearson, 2013), 198.

39. Laura Pulido, "Geographies of Race and Ethnicity I: White Supremacy vs White Privilege in Environmental Racism Research," *Progress in Human Geography* 39, no. 6 (2015): 809–17; Andrea Gibbons, "The Five Refusals of White Supremacy," *American Journal of Economics and Sociology* 77, nos. 3–4 (2018): 729–55.

40. Frances Lee Ansley, "White Supremacy (and What We Should Do About It)," in *Critical White Studies: Looking Behind the Mirror*, ed. Richard Delgado and Jean Stefancic (Philadelphia, Penn.: Temple University Press, 1997), 592–95; at 592.

41. Pulido, "Geographies of Race and Ethnicity I," 810.

42. Peggy McIntosh, "White Privilege and Male Privilege: A Personal Account of Coming to See Correspondences through Work in Women's Studies," in *Critical White Studies: Looking Behind the Mirror*, ed. Richard Delgado and Jean Stefancic (Philadelphia, Penn.: Temple University Press, 1997), 291–99; at 291.

43. Du Bois, *Black Reconstruction*, 700.

44. Du Bois, *Black Reconstruction*, 700.

45. Du Bois, *Black Reconstruction*, 30.

46. Martin Luther King Jr., "Remaining Awake through a Great Revolution," archived at the Martin Luther King, Jr. Research and Education Institute at Stanford University, at https://kinginstitute.stanford.edu/king-papers/publications/knock-midnight-inspiration-great-sermons-reverend-martin-luther-king-jr-10.

47. Bonds and Inwood, "Beyond White Privilege," 716.

48. Sean Walton, "Why the Critical Race Theory Concept of 'White Supremacy' Should Not Be Dismissed by Neo-Marxists: Lessons from Contemporary Black Radicalism," *Power and Education* 12, no. 1 (2020): 78–94; at 81.

49. Zeus Leonardo, "The Color of Supremacy: Beyond the Discourse of 'White Privilege,'" *Educational Philosophy and Theory* 36, no. 2 (2004): 137–52; at 137.

50. Bonds and Inwood, "Beyond White Privilege," 716.

51. Ruth Wilson Gilmore, *Golden Gulag: Prisons, Surplus, Crisis, and Opposition in Globalizing California* (Berkeley: University of California Press, 2007), 28.

52. Pulido, "Geographies of Race and Ethnicity I," 811.

53. Pulido, "Geographies of Race and Ethnicity I," 811.

54. Darrel Enck-Wanzer, "Barack Obama, the Tea Party, and the Threat of Race: On Racial Neoliberalism and Born Again Racism," *Communication, Culture & Critique* 4, no. 1 (2011): 23–30; at 24.

55. Enck-Wanzer, "Barack Obama," 25.

56. Harvey, *A Brief History*, 10.

57. Chris Harman, *Zombie Capitalism: Global Crisis and the Relevance of Marx* (Chicago: Haymarket Books, 2010), 161–62.

58. Harvey, *A Brief History*, 10–11.

59. Michael Roberts, *The Long Depression: How It Happened, Why It Happened, and What Happens Next* (Chicago: Haymarket Books, 2016), 59; Harvey, *A Brief History*, 11–12; Harman, *Zombie Capitalism*, 162.

60. Joshua Inwood, "Contextualizing the State Mode of Production in the United States: Race, Space, and Civil Rights," *Environment and Planning A* 45 (2013): 2120–34; at 2122.

61. Inwood, "Contextualizing the State," 2123.

62. Rod Bush, *We Are Not What We Seem: Black Nationalism and Class Struggle in the American Century* (New York: New York University Press, 2000), 156.

63. Kevern Verney, *Black Civil Rights in America* (New York: Routledge, 2000), 38.

64. Bruce H. Kalk, "Wormley's Hotel Revisited: Richard Nixon's Southern Strategy and the End of the Second Reconstruction," *North Carolina Historical Review* 71, no. 1 (1994): 85–105; at 87.

65. Michelle Alexander, "The New Jim Crow," *Ohio State Journal of Criminal Law* 9, no. 1 (2011): 7–26; at 15–16.

66. Alexander, "The New Jim Crow," 16. See also Terry Smith, "White Backlash in a Brown Country," *Valparaiso Law Review* 50, no. 1 (2015): 89–132.

67. Michael D. Forster and Tim Rehner, "The White Male Southern Democrat: Endangered Species or Already Extinct?," *Race, Gender & Class* 18, nos. 3–4 (2011): 230–37.

68. Cowie, "Nixon's Class Struggle," 260.

69. Michelle Alexander, *The New Jim Crow: Mass Incarceration in an Age of Colorblindness* (New York: New Press, 2010), 45.

70. Quoted in Forster and Rehner, "The White Male Southern Democrat," 233.

71. Quoted in Alexander, *The New Jim Crow,* 44.

72. This statement appears in an infamous 1981 interview conducted with Alexander Lamis, a political scientist at Case Western Reserve University. A full audio recording is available at http://www.thenation.com/article/170841/exclusive-lee-atwaters-infamous-1981-interview-southern-strategy#

73. Jefferson Cowie, "Nixon's Class Struggle: Romancing the New Right Worker, 1969–1973," *Labor History* 43, no. 3 (2002): 257–83; at 264.

74. Cowie, "Nixon's Class Struggle," 282.

75. Cowie, "Nixon's Class Struggle," 282.

76. Cowie, "Nixon's Class Struggle," 258.

77. Cowie, "Nixon's Class Struggle," 258.

78. Cowie, "Nixon's Class Struggle," 269.

79. Murray Edelman, *Political Language: Words that Succeed and Policies that Fail* (New York: Academic, 1977), 4.

80. Cowie, "Nixon's Class Struggle," 260.

81. Cowie, "Nixon's Class Struggle," 264.

82. Alexander, *The New Jim Crow,* 44–45.

83. Harvey, *A Brief History,* 12.

84. Roberts, *The Long Depression,* 61.

85. Jefferson Cowie and Lauren Boehm, "Dead Man's Town: 'Born in the U.S.A.,' Social History, and Working-Class Identity," *American Quarterly* 58, no. 2 (2006): 353–78; at 371.

86. Inwood, "Neoliberal Racism," 410.

87. Harvey, *A Brief History,* 19.

88. Ann Cammett, "Deadbeat Dads & Welfare Queens: How Metaphor Shapes

Poverty Law," *Boston College Journal of Law and Social Justice* 34, no. 2 (2014): 233–66; at 235.

89. Noel A. Cazenave, *Killing African Americans: Police and Vigilante Violence as a Racial Control Mechanism* (New York: Routledge, 2018), 40.

90. Harvey, *The New Imperialism,* 63.

91. Cowie and Boehm, "Dead Man's Town," 357.

92. Harvey, *A Brief History,* 49–50.

93. Harvey, *A Brief History,* 50.

94. Cowie, "Nixon's Class Struggle," 283.

95. Alexander, *The New Jim Crow,* 47.

96. Roger Foster, "Social Character: Erich Fromm and the Ideological Glue of Neoliberalism," *Critical Horizons* 18, no. 1 (2017): 1–18.

97. Foster, "Social Character," 8.

98. Alexander, *The New Jim Crow,* 47.

99. Goldfield, *The Color of Politics,* 314.

100. Roberts and Mahtani, "Neoliberalizing Race," 253.

101. Cowie and Boehm, "Dead Man's Town," 357.

102. Cowie and Boehm, "Dead Man's Town," 358.

103. Shawn A. Cassiman, "Resisting the Neo-Liberal Poverty Discourse: On Constructing Deadbeat Dads and Welfare Queens," *Sociology Compass,* 2 no. 5 (2008): 1690–700.

104. Quoted in Cammett, "Deadbeat Dads & Welfare Queens," 255.

105. Nikita McMillian, "From Loving Mother to Welfare Queen to Drug Addict: Lebron v. Secretary of Florida Department of Children and Families and the Evolving Public View of the Poor as a Class of Sub-Humans with Sub-Rights," *Mississippi College Law Review* 35, no. 1 (2016): 197–239; at 211.

106. Cammett, "Deadbeat Dads & Welfare Queens," 245.

107. Cowie and Boehm, "Dead Man's Town," 358.

108. Lester K. Spence, "The Neoliberal Turn in Black Politics," *Souls* 14, nos. 3–4 (2012): 139–59; at 144.

109. Cammett, "Deadbeat Dads & Welfare Queens," 236.

110. Claudine M. Pied, "The Problem People and the Hard Workers: Whiteness and Small Town Response to Economic Decline," *Identities* 26, no. 1 (2019): 33–50; at 41.

111. Pied, "The Problem People," 46.

112. Alexander, *The New Jim Crow,* 49.

113. Alexander, "The New Jim Crow," 16.

114. Alexander, *The New Jim Crow,* 54.

115. Reiman and Leighton, *The Rich Get Richer.*

116. James Q. Wilson and George L. Kelling, "Broken Windows," *Atlantic Monthly* March (1982): 29–38, http://www.theatlantic.com/doc/print.198203/

broken-windows. See also Steve Herbert, "Policing the Contemporary City: Fixing Broken Windows or Shoring Up Neo-Liberalism?" *Theoretical Criminology* 5, no. 4 (2001): 445–66; Steve Herbert and Elizabeth Brown, "Conceptions of Space and Crime in the Punitive Neoliberal City," *Antipode* 38, no. 4 (2006): 755–77.

117. Herbert, "Policing the Contemporary City," 446; Herbert and Brown, "Conceptions of Space," 759.

118. Herbert and Brown, "Conceptions of Space," 759.

119. Marilyn A. Papayanis, "Sex and the Revanchist City: Zoning Out Pornography in New York," *Environment and Planning D: Society and Space* 18 (2000): 341–53; at 342.

120. Herbert, "Policing the Contemporary City," 446.

121. Bench Ansfield, "The Broken Windows of the Bronx: Putting the Theory in its Place," *American Quarterly* 72, no. 1 (2020): 103–27; at 111.

122. Katharyne Mitchell, "Zero Tolerance, Imperialism, Dispossession," *ACME An International Journal for Critical Geographies* 10, no. 2 (2011): 293–312; at 295.

123. Katherine Beckett and Theodore Sasson, *The Politics of Injustice: Crime and Punishment in America*, 2nd ed. (Thousand Oaks, Calif.: Sage, 2004), 134; Neil Smith, "Global Social Cleansing: Postliberal Revanchism and the Export of Zero Tolerance," *Social Justice* 28, no. 3 (2001): 68–74; at 69.

124. Mitchell, "Zero Tolerance," 296.

125. John A. Powell and Eileen B. Hershenov, "Hostage to the Drug War: The National Purse, the Constitution and the Black Community," *U.C. Davis Law Review* 24, no. 3 (1991): 557–616; David Rudovsky, "Law Enforcement by Stereotypes and Serendipity: Racial Profiling and Stops and Searches without Cause," *University of Pennsylvania Journal of Constitutional Law* 3, no. 1 (2001): 296–366; Katherine Beckett, Kris Nyrop, and Lori Pfingst, "Race, Drugs, and Policing: Understanding Disparities in Drug Delivery Arrests," *Criminology* 44, no. 1 (2006): 105–37.

126. Victor J. St. John and Vanessa Lewis, "'Vilify Them Night after Night': Anti-Black Drug Policies, Mass Incarceration, and Pathways Forward," *Harvard Kennedy School Journal of African American Policy* 20 (2019): 18–29; at 22.

127. Alexander, *The New Jim Crow*, 237–38.

128. Kathleen R. Sandy, "The Discrimination Inherent in America's Drug War: Hidden Racism Revealed by Examining the Hysteria over Crack," *Alabama Law Review* 54, no. 2 (2003): 665–94; at 671.

129. Sandy, "The Discrimination Inherent," 672.

130. John Gramlich, "Black Imprisonment Rate in the U.S. Has Fallen by a Third since 2006," *Pew Research Center*, https://www.pewresearch.org/fact-tank/2020/05/06/share-of-black-white-hispanic-americans-in-prison-2018-vs-2006/.

131. Philomena Mariani, "Overview: Law, Order, and Neoliberalism," *Social Justice* 28, no. 3 (2001): 2–4; at 3.

132. Mariani, "Overview," 3.

133. Sandy, "The Discrimination Inherent," 684.

134. Angela Y. Davis, "Masked Racism: Reflections on the Prison Industrial Complex," *Lola Press* 12 (2000): 52.

135. Davis, "Masked Racism," 52.

136. Davis, "Masked Racism," 52.

137. Earl Smith and Angela J. Hattery, "Incarceration: A Tool for Racial Segregation and Labor Exploitation," *Race, Gender & Class* 15, nos. 1–2 (2008): 79–97; at 90.

138. Smith and Hattery, "Incarceration," 84.

139. Becky Pettit and Carmen Gutierrez, "Mass Incarceration and Racial Inequality," *American Journal of Economics and Sociology* 77, nos. 3–4 (2018): 1153–82; at 1155. See also Naomi Murakawa, "Mass Incarceration Is Dead, Long Live the Carceral State," *Tulsa Law Review* 55, no. 2 (2020): 251–62.

140. Pettit and Gutierrez, "Mass Incarceration," 1153.

141. Pettit and Gutierrez, "Mass Incarceration," 1153.

142. Pettit and Gutierrez, "Mass Incarceration," 1162.

143. Priscilla Bustamante, Gaurav Jashnani, and Brett G.Stoudt, "Cumulative Dehumanization in Everyday Policing: The Psychological, Affective, and Material Consequences of Discretionary Arrests," *Analyses of Social Issues and Public Policy* 19, no. 1 (2019): 305–48; at 329.

144. Roberts and Mahtani, "Neoliberalizing Race," 254.

145. Alexander, "The New Jim Crow," 17.

146. Roberts and Mahtani, "Neoliberalizing Race," 253.

147. Williams, "Racial Mythologies," 838.

148. Luigi Esposito and Laura L. Finley, "Barack Obama, Racial Progress, and the Future of Race Relations in the United States," *Western Journal of Black Studies* 33, no. 3 (2009): 164–75; at 165.

149. Esposito and Finley, "Barack Obama," 165–66.

150. Esposito and Finley, "Barack Obama," 166.

151. Smith, "White Backlash," 102–3.

152. Esposito and Finley, "Barack Obama," 169.

153. Juliet Hooker, "Black Protest/White Grievance: On the Problem of White Political Imaginations Not Shaped by Loss," *South Atlantic Quarterly* 116, no. 3 (2017): 483–504; at 488. Likewise, the presidential campaign of Hillary Clinton in 2016 threatened the bastions of male supremacy.

154. Hooker, "Black Protest," 491.

155. Smith, "White Backlash," 91–92.

156. Luigi Esposito and Laura L. Finley, "Barack Obama, Racial Progress, and the Future of Race Relations in the United States," *Western Journal of Black Studies* 33, no. 3 (2009): 164–75; Luigi Esposito, "White Fear and US Racism in the Era of Obama: The Relevance of Neoliberalism," *Theory in Action* 4, no. 3 (2011): 1–24;

Leonard Zeskind, "A Nation Dispossessed: The Tea Party Movement and Race," *Critical Sociology* 38, no. 4 (2011): 495–509; and Adolphus G. Belk, "Fire on the Right: The Tea Party vs. Barack Obama," *Souls: A Critical Journal of Black Politics, Culture, and Society* 14, nos. 1–2 (2012): 77–87.

157. Hooker, "Black Protest," 489; Belk, "Fire on the Right," 79; Zeskind, "A Nation Dispossessed," 500.

158. Smith, "White Backlash," 90.

159. Banu Gökariksel and Sara Smith, "'Making America Great Again?': The Fascist Body Politics of Donald Trump," *Political Geography* 54 (2016): 79–81; Lindsay Pérez Huber, "'Make America Great Again!': Donald Trump, Racist Nativism and the Virulent Adherence to White Supremacy amid U.S. Demographic Change," *Charleston Law Review* 10, no. 2 (2016): 215–50; Henry A. Giroux, "White Nationalism, Armed Culture and State Violence in the Age of Donald Trump," *Philosophy and Social Criticism* 43, no. 9 (2017): 887–910; Banu Gökariksel and Sara Smith, "Intersectional Feminism beyond U.S. Flag Hijab and Pussy Hats in Trump's America," *Gender, Place & Culture* 24, no. 5 (2017): 628–44; George F. McHendry Jr., "White Supremacy in the Age of Trump: An Introduction to a Special Issue of the *Journal of Contemporary Rhetoric*," *Journal of Contemporary Rhetoric* 8, nos. 1–2 (2018): 1–5; Joshua Inwood, "White Supremacy, White Counter-Revolutionary Politics, and the Rise of Donald Trump," *EPC: Politics and Space* 37, no. 4 (2019): 579–96.

160. Inwood, "White Supremacy," 580.

161. Douglas Schrock, Benjamin Dowd-Arrow, Kristen Erichsen, Haley Gentile, and Pierce Dignam, "The Emotional Politics of Making America Great Again: Trump's Working Class Appeals," *Journal of Working-Class Studies* 2, no. 1 (2017): 5–22.

162. Schrock et al., "The Emotional Politics," 7.

163. Gusterson, "From Brexit to Trump," 210.

164. Schrock et al., "The Emotional Politics," 9.

165. Smith, "White Backlash," 108.

166. Terry Smith, *Whitelash: Unmasking White Grievance at the Ballot Box* (Cambridge: Cambridge University Press, 2020), 34.

167. Eduardo Bonilla-Silva, "Feeling Race: Theorizing the Racial Economy of Emotions," *American Sociological Review* 84, no. 1 (2019): 1–25; at 8.

168. Hooker, "Black Protest," 493.

169. Saharra Griffin and Malkie Wall, "President Trump's Anti-Worker Agenda," *Center for American Progress,* August 28, 2019, https://www.americanprogress.org/issues/ext/2019/08/28/478978/president-trumps-anti-worker-agenda/. See also Shanna Devine, "Workers Left Behind under Trump's OHSA," *Public Citizen,* 2018, https://www.citizen.org/wp-content/uploads/migration/trump-leaves-workers-behind-report.pdf.

170. Griffin and Wall, "President's Trump's Anti-Worker Agenda." The Trump administration also targeted for discrimination specific populations beyond the normative white working class. For example, the administration erected barriers to prevent people with disabilities from working and exposed LGBTQ Americans to employer discrimination.

171. Augustus C. Wood III, "The Crisis of the Black Worker, the U.S. Labor Movement, and Democracy for All," *Labor Studies Journal* 44, no. 4 (2019): 396–402; at 398.

172. Hooker, "Black Protest," 485.

173. Cheryl E. Matias and Peter M. Newlove, "Better the Devil You See, Than the One You Don't: Bearing Witness to Emboldened En-Whitening Epistemology in the Trump Era," *International Journal of Qualitative Studies in Education* 30, no. 10 (2017): 920–28; at 921.

174. "Trayvon Martin Shooting Fast Facts," *CNN,* June 5, 2013, https://www.cnn.com/2013/06/05/us/trayvon-martin-shooting-fast-facts/index.html.

175. Cazenave, *Killing African Americans,* 6.

176. Chase, "The Early History," 1096.

177. Jennings Brown, "One Year After Michael Brown: How a Hashtag Changed Social Protest," *Vocativ,* August 7, 2015, https://www.vocativ.com/news/218365/michael-brown-and-black-lives-matter/index.html; Jelani Cobb, "The Matter of Black Lives," *New Yorker,* March 7, 2016, https://www.newyorker.com/magazine/2016/03/14/where-is-black-lives-matter-headed.

178. Cobb, "The Matter of Black Lives."

179. Brown, "One Year After Michael Brown."

180. Brown, "One Year After Michael Brown."

181. Brown, "One Year After Michael Brown."

182. Alicia Garza, "A Herstory of #BlackLivesMatter Movement," *Feminist Wire,* October 7, 2014, https://thefeministwire.com/2014/10/blacklivesmatter-2/.

183. Chase, "The Early History," 1096.

184. Cazenave, *Killing African Americans,* 9.

185. Cazenave, *Killing African Americans,* 9–10; Jennifer Chernega, "Black Lives Matter: Racialized Policing in the United States," *Comparative American Studies* 14, nos. 3–4 (2016): 234–45; German Lopez, "Why Was Michael Brown Shot?" *Vox,* January 27, 2016, https://www.vox.com/2015/5/31/17937818/michael-brown-police-shooting-darren-wilson.

186. Cazenave, *Killing African Americans,* 9.

187. United States Department of Justice, "Justice Department Announces Findings of Two Civil Rights Investigations in Ferguson, Missouri," March 4, 2015, https://www.justice.gov/opa/pr/justice-department-announces-findings-two-civil-rights-investigations-ferguson-missouri. The complete "Investigation of the Ferguson Police Department" is found at https://www.justice.gov/sites/

default/files/opa/press-releases/attachments/2015/03/04/ferguson_police_department_report_1.pdf.

188. German Lopez, "What Were the 2014 Ferguson Protests About?" *Vox,* January 27, 2016, https://www.vox.com/2015/5/31/17937764/ferguson-missouri-protests-2014-michael-brown-police-shooting.

189. Chernega, "Black Lives Matter," 235.

190. Ransby, *Making All Black Lives Matter,* 6.

191. Denver Nicks, "How Ferguson Went From Middle Class to Poor in a Generation," *Time,* August 18, 2014, https://time.com/3138176/ferguson-demographic-change/.

192. Ransby, *Making All Black Lives Matter,* 6.

193. Taylor, *From #BlackLivesMatter,* 155.

194. Bryan Adamson, "Thugs, Crooks, and Rebellious Negroes: Racist and Racialized Media Coverage of Michael Brown and the Ferguson Demonstrations," *Harvard Journal on Racial & Ethic Justice* 32 (2016): 189–278; at 191.

195. Taylor, "From #BlackLivesMatter," 24.

196. Garza, "A Herstory."

197. Rickford, "Black Lives Matter," 36.

198. Taylor, *From #BlackLivesMatter,* 156; Cazenave, *Killing African Americans,* 8 passim.

199. Cazenave, *Killing African Americans,* 11.

200. Taylor, *From #BlackLivesMatter,* 164.

201. Cobb, "The Matter of Black Lives."

202. Ileana Jiménez, "#SayHerName Loudly: How Black Girls Are Leading #BlackLivesMatter," *Radical Teacher* 106 (2016): 87–96; at 87; Armond R. Towns, "Geographies of Pain: #SayHerName and the Fear of Black Women's Mobility," *Women's Studies in Communication* 39, no. 2 (2016): 122–26; at 122.

203. Melissa Brown, Rashawn Ray, Ed Summers, and Neil Fraistat, "#SayHerName: A Case Study of Intersectional Social Media Activism," *Ethnic and Racial Studies* 40, no. 11 (2017): 1831–46; at 1833.

204. Brown et al., "#SayHerName," 1833.

205. Hooker, "Black Protest," 483.

206. Hooker, "Black Protest," 483–84.

207. Rickford, "Black Lives Matter," 37.

208. Rickford, "Black Lives Matter," 37.

209. Brown, "One Year After."

210. Garza, "A Herstory."

211. Opal Tometi and Gerald Lenoir, "Black Lives Matter Is Not a Civil Rights Movement," *Time,* December 10, 2015, https://time.com/4144655/international-human-rights-day-black-lives-matter/.

212. Tometi and Lenoir, "Black Lives Matter."

213. Rod Bush, *We Are Not What We Seem: Black Nationalism and Class Struggle in the American Century* (New York: New York University Press, 1999); Dean E. Robinson, *Black Nationalism in American Politics and Thought* (Cambridge: Cambridge University Press, 2001); Darryl C. Thomas, "Black Studies and the Scholarship of Cedric Robinson," *Race & Class* 47, no. 2 (2005): 1–22; Katherine McKittrick, *Demonic Grounds: Black Women and the Cartographies of Struggle* (Minneapolis: University of Minnesota Press, 2006); Laura Pulido, *Black, Brown, Yellow, and Left: Radical Activism in Los Angeles* (Berkeley: University of California Press, 2006); Ahmed Shawki, *Black Liberation and Socialism* (Chicago: Haymarket Books, 2006); David Scott, "On the Very Idea of a Black Radical Tradition," *small axe* 40 (2013): 1–6; Laura Pulido and Juan De Lara, "Reimagining 'Justice' in Environmental Justice: Radical Ecologies, Decolonial Thought, and the Black Radical Tradition," *Environment and Planning E: Nature and Space* 1, nos. 1–2 (2018): 76–98.

214. Robinson, *Black Marxism,* 73.

215. Robin D.G. Kelley, *Freedom Dreams: The Black Radical Imagination* (Boston: Beacon, 2002), 54.

216. Kelley, *Freedom Dreams,* 54.

217. Tometi and Lenoir, "Black Lives Matter."

218. Tometi and Lenoir, "Black Lives Matter."

219. Katherine McKittrick, *Demonic Grounds: Black Women and the Cartographies of Struggle* (Minneapolis: University of Minnesota Press, 2006), x. See also Adam Bledsoe, LaToya E. Eaves, and Brian Williams, "Black Geographies in and of the United States South," *Southeastern Geographer* 57, no. 1 (2017): 6–11; Camilla Hawthorne and Kaily Heitz, "A Seat at the Table? Reflections on Black Geographies and the Limits of Dialogue," *Dialogues in Human Geography* 8, no. 2 (2018): 148–51; Douglas Allen, Mary Lawhon, and Joseph Pierce, "Placing Race: On the Resonance of Place with Black Geographies," *Progress in Human Geography* 43, no. 6 (2019): 1001–19; Adam Bledsoe and Willie Jamaal Wright, "The Pluralities of Black Geographies," *Antipode* 51, no. 2 (2019): 419–37; and Camilla Hawthorne, "Black Matters Are Spatial Matters: Black Geographies for the Twenty-First Century," *Geography Compass* 13 (2019): e12468.

220. Hawthorne, "Black Matters."

221. Tometi and Lenoir, "Black Lives Matter."

222. Cobb, "The Matter of Black Lives."

223. Garza, "A Herstory."

224. Garza, "A Herstory."

225. Garza, "A Herstory."

226. Taylor, *From #BlackLivesMatter,* 185.

227. Taylor, *From #BlackLivesMatter,* 185.

228. Rickford, "Black Lives Matter," 38.

229. Mike Elk, "How Black & Brown Workers Are Redefining Strikes in the Digital COVID Age," *Payday Report,* July 8, 2020, https://paydayreport.com/how-black-brown-workers-are-redefining-strikes-in-a-digital-covid-age/.

230. Bryce Covert, "Across the Country, Essential Workers are on Strike for Black Lives," *Vox,* July 20, 2020, https://www.vox.com/the-goods-2020/7/20/21327424/strike-for-black-lives-essential-workers-covid-19-racism.

231. Quoted in Covert, "Across the Country."

232. Quoted in Covert, "Across the Country."

233. Elk, "How Black & Brown Workers."

234. Elk, "How Black & Brown Workers."

235. Alexia Fernández Campbell, "As Protests Grow, Big Labor Sides with Police Unions," *Public Integrity,* June 5, 2020, https://publicintegrity.org/inequality-poverty-opportunity/as-protests-grow-big-labor-sides-with-police-unions/.

236. Yates, "COVID-19, Economic Depression."

237. Rickford, "Black Lives Matter," 38.

238. Quoted in Julia Wong, "As Ferguson 'Weekend of Resistance' Begins, Organizers Weigh How to Turn a Moment into a Movement," *In These Times,* October 10, 2014, http://inthesetimes.com/article/from-a-moment-to-a-movement.

239. Wood, "The Crisis of the Black Worker," 398.

240. "KJK: The Murder of George Floyd Is Not an Isolated Incident."

241. Tony N. Brown, Asia Bento, Quintin Gorman Jr., Lydia Koku, and Julian Culver, "'Who Cares?': Investigating Consistency in Expressions of Racial Apathy among Whites," *Socius* 5 (2019): 1–10; at 2.

242. Robin DiAngelo, "White Fragility," *International Journal of Critical Pedagogy* 3, no. 3 (2011): 54–70; at 54.

243. Uma M. Jayakumar and Annie S. Adamian, "The Fifth Frame of Colorblind Ideology: Maintaining the Comforts of Colorblindness in the Context of White Fragility," *Sociological Perspectives* 60, no. 5 (2017): 912–36; at 915.

244. Ashley Atkins, "Black Lives Matter or All Lives Matter? Color-Blindness and Epistemic Injustice," *Social Epistemology* 33, no. 1 (2019): 1–22; at 6.

245. Rickford, "Black Lives Matter," 39.

246. Amanda Seitz, "Facebook Groups Pivot to Attacks on Black Lives Matter," *Associated Press,* July 5, 2020, https://apnews.com/ca8c15794c65b1ae8e176deb9be5d718.

247. Teri A. McMurty-Chubb, "#SayHerName #BlackWomensLivesMatter: State Violence in Policing the Black Female Body," *Mercer Law Review* 67, no. 3 (2016): 651–706; at 702.

248. Geoff Ward, "Living Histories of White Supremacist Policing: Towards Transformative Justice," *Du Bois Review: Social Science Research on Race* 15, no. 1 (2018): 167–84; at 171.

249. Geoffrey Skelley, "How Americans Feel About George Floyd's Death and the Protests," *FiveThirtyEight,* June 5, 2020, https://fivethirtyeight.com/features/how-americans-feel-about-george-floyds-death-and-the-protests/.

250. Skelley, "How Americans Feel."

251. Civiqs, "Do You Support or Oppose the Black Lives Matter Movement," September 23, 2020, https://civiqs.com/results/black_lives_matter?uncertainty=true&annotations=true&zoomIn=true&net=true&race=White.

252. Barbara Applebaum, "Comforting Discomfort as Complicity: White Fragility and the Pursuit of Invulnerability," *Hypatia* 32, no. 4 (2017): 862–75; at 866.

253. ACLED, "Demonstrations & Political Violence in America"; Anti-Defamation League, "ADL Debunk: Disinformation and the BLM Protests," https://www.adl.org/resources/reports/adl-debunk-disinformation-and-the-blm-protests.

254. Anti-Defamation League, "ADL Debunk."

255. ACLED, "Demonstrations & Political Violence in America." For a specific example, see Josh Skluzacek, "Affidavit: Hell's Angels Member Believed to be 'Umbrella Man' Spotted Inciting Violence During George Floyd Protests," *KSTP,* July 28, 2020, https://kstp.com/news/affidavit-hells-angels-member-believed-to-be-umbrella-man-spotted-inciting-violence-during-floyd-protests-/5809447/.

256. Garza, "A Herstory."

257. Garza, "A Herstory."

258. Cowie and Boehm, "Dead Man's Town," 358.

259. Hooker, "Black Protest," 494.

260. Eric D. Knowles and Brian S. Lowery, "Meritocracy, Self-Concerns, and Whites' Denial of Racial Inequity," *Self and Identity* 11 (2012): 202–22.

261. Daniel Shore, "The Form of Black Lives," *PLMA* 135, no. 1 (2020): 175–79; at 178.

262. Shore, "The Form of Black Lives," 178.

263. Berg, "Geographies of Identity," 511.

264. That the media continually and, arguably, willfully misrepresents the aspirations of the Black Lives Matter movement contributes to the backlash of many whites. In an analysis of seven major newspapers, for example, Joy Leopold and Myrtle Bell documented that much of the coverage of the Ferguson protests failed to adequately explain the reasons for the protests and, in doing so, facilitated the construction of negative stereotypes about the larger Black Lives Matter movement. Notably, they conclude, "While many articles mentioned the deaths of unarmed Blacks at the hands of police, according to the publicized objectives and intentions of the BLM, these tragic incidents are just one aspect of a larger system of discrimination, racism, and injustice in the USA that the movement seeks to change." See Joy Leopold and Myrtle P. Bell, "News Media and the Racialization

of Protest: An Analysis of Black Lives Matter Articles," *Equality, Diversity and Inclusion: An International Journal* 36, no. 8 (2017): 720–35; at 730. The seven newspapers analyzed include the *New York Post,* the *New York Times, USA Today,* the *Wall Street Journal,* the *Los Angeles Times,* the *Chicago Tribune,* and the *St. Louis Post-Dispatch.*

265. Garza, "A Herstory."

266. Brown, "One Year After."

267. Garza, "A Herstory."

268. Alicia Garza, "Black Lives Matter 101," May 5, 2017, https://aliciagarza.com/black-lives-matter-101/.

269. Eddie S. Glaude Jr., *Democracy in Black: How Race Still Enslaves the American Soul* (New York: Broadway Books, 2016).

270. Glaude, *Democracy in Black,* 31.

271. David Gillborn, "The White Working Class, Racism and Respectability: Victims, Degenerates and Interest-Convergence," *British Journal of Educational Studies* 58, no. 1 (2010): 3–25; at 3.

272. Erik Olin Wright, "The Continuing Relevance of the Marxist Tradition for Transcending Capitalism," *tripleC* 16, no. 2 (2018): 490–500; at 493.

273. Cowie and Boehm, "Dead Man's Town," 369.

274. Cowie and Boehm, "Dead Man's Town," 369.

275. Baker, "Democracy, Class," 150.

276. Bush, *We Are Not What We Seem,* 224.

277. Bush, *We Are Not What We Seem,* 229.

278. Bush, *We Are Not What We Seem,* 230.

279. Taylor, *From #BlackLivesMatter to Black Liberation,* 161.

280. Taylor, *From #BlackLivesMatter to Black Liberation,* 162–63.

281. Taylor, *From #BlackLivesMatter to Black Liberation,* 163.

282. Cedric Johnson, "Who's Afraid of Left Populism," *New Politics* 17, no. 2 (2019), https://newpol.org/issue_post/whos-afraid-of-left-populism/. For thoughtful essays on the promise of solidarity among radical movements, see Chris Maisano, "No, the Racial Justice Protests Are Not at Odds with Class Politics," *Jacobin,* June 26, 2020, https://jacobinmag.com/2020/06/ross-douthat-nyt-racial-justice-protests-bernie-sanders/; and Curt Ries, "Our Path Forward After Bernie Must Include Rank-and-File Unionism and Class-Struggle Elections," *Jacobin,* August 9, 2020, https://jacobinmag.com/2020/08/bernie-sanders-campaign-unions-class-struggle.

283. Benjamin Balthaser and Bill V. Mullen, "Rethinking Socialism from Below in the Age of Covid-19 and Black Lives Matter," *New Politics,* June 30, 2020. https://newpol.org/rethinking-socialism-from-below-in-the-age-of-covid-and-black-lives-matter/.

5. The Emancipated Subject

1. Karl Marx, *A Contribution to the Critique of Political Economy* (New York: International, 1970), 20.

2. Erich Fromm, *Escape from Freedom* (New York: Henry Holt, 1969 [1941]), 16. See also Lawrence J. Friedman, *The Lives of Erich Fromm: Love's Prophet* (New York: Columbia University Press, 2013); and Mauricio Cortina, "The Greatness and Limitations of Eric Fromm's Humanism," *Contemporary Psychoanalysis* 51, no. 3 (2015): 388–422.

3. Fromm, *Escape from Freedom,* 16.

4. Fromm, *Escape from Freedom,* 276.

5. Roger Foster, "Social Character: Erich Fromm and the Ideological Glue of Neoliberalism," *Critical Horizons* 18, no. 1 (2017): 1–18; at 3.

6. Jason Read, *The Micro-Politics of Capital: Marx and the Prehistory of the Present* (Albany: State University of New York, 2003), 135.

7. Peter Lamb, *Socialism* (Medford, Mass.: Polity, 2019), 2.

8. Linda McDowell, "Work, Workfare, Work/Life Balance and an Ethic of Care," *Progress in Human Geography* 28, no. 2 (2004): 145–63; at 146.

9. Lynn Chancer, *Sadomasochism in Everyday Life: The Dynamics of Power and Powerlessness* (New Brunswick, N.J.: Rutgers University Press, 1992), 34.

10. Chancer, *Sadomasochism in Everyday Life,* 35.

11. Eric Fromm, *The Sane Society* (New York; Henry Holt, 1990 [1955]), 95.

12. Rainer Funk, *Erich Fromm: His Life and Ideas* (New York: Continuum International, 2000), 11.

13. Similar ideas are captured by David Riesman's *The Lonely Crowd,* Herbert Marcuse's *One-Dimensional Man,* and Jean-Paul Sartre's concept of the practico-inert in his *Critique of Dialectical Reason.* See David Riesman, *The Lonely Crowd* (New Haven, Conn.: Yale University Press, 1950); Herbert Marcuse, *One-Dimensional Man: Studies in the Ideology of Advanced Industrial Society* (Boston: Beacon, 1991 [1964]); Jean-Paul Sartre, *Critique of Dialectical Reason,* trans. Alan Sheridan-Smith (New York: Verso, 1991 [1960]).

14. Erich Fromm, *Man for Himself: Towards a Psychology of Ethics* (New York: Rinehart, 1947), 68.

15. Fromm, *Man for Himself,* 68.

16. Fromm, *Man for Himself,* 72.

17. Fromm, *Man for Himself,* 72.

18. Elie Wiesel, "The Perils of Indifference," http://www.historyplace.com/speeches/wiesel.htm.

19. Wiesel, "The Perils of Indifference."

20. Fromm, *The Sane Society*; Eric Fromm, *Beyond the Chains of Illusion: My*

Encounter with Marx and Freud (London: Abacus, 1983 [1962]); Erich Fromm, *The Anatomy of Human Destructiveness* (New York: Henry Holt, 1988 [1973); Erich Fromm, *The Art of Loving* (New York: Harper Perennial, 2006 [1956]).

21. Lynn S. Chancer, "Feminism, Humanism, and Erich Fromm," in *Erich Fromm's Critical Theory: Hope, Humanism, and the Future,* ed. Kieran Durkin and Joan Braune (London: Bloomsbury Academic, 2020), 101–14; at 105.

22. Fromm, *Escape from Freedom,* 4.

23. Neal Harris, "Reconstructing Erich Fromm's 'Pathology of Normalcy': Transcending the Recognition-Cognitive Paradigm in the Diagnosis of Social Pathologies," *Social Science Information* 58, no. 4 (2019): 714–33; at 719–20.

24. Fromm, *The Sane Society,* 30.

25. Chancer, *Sadomasochism in Everyday Life,* 35.

26. Chancer, *Sadomasochism in Everyday Life,* 36.

27. Fromm, *Escape from Freedom,* 140.

28. Fromm, *Escape from Freedom,* 162.

29. Fromm, *The Sane Society,* 30.

30. Cheryl E. Matias and Ricky Lee Allen, "Loving Whiteness to Death: Sadomasochism, Emotionality, and the Possibility of Humanizing Love," *Berkeley Review of Education* 4, no. 2 (2013): 285–309; at 291.

31. Fromm, *The Sane Society,* 123.

32. Fromm, *Escape from Freedom,* 144.

33. Fromm, *Escape from Freedom,* 154.

34. Matthew C. MacWilliams, "Trump Is an Authoritarian. So Are Millions of Americans," *Politico,* September 23, 2020, https://www.politico.com/news/magazine/2020/09/23/trump-america-authoritarianism-420681.

35. Amanda Taub, "The Rise of American Authoritarianism," *Vox,* March 1, 2016, https://www.vox.com/2016/3/1/11127424/trump-authoritarianism.

36. Matthew C. MacWilliams, "Who Decides When the Party Doesn't? Authoritarian Voters and the Rise of Donald Trump," *PS: Political Science & Politics* 49, no. 4 (2016): 716–21; at 717.

37. Fromm, *Escape from Freedom,* 255.

38. MacWilliams, "Who Decides," 720.

39. Daniel Burston, "'It Can't Happen Here': Trump, Authoritarianism and American Politics," *Psychotherapy and Politics International* 15, no. 1 (2017): e1399.

40. Matt Karamazov, "Erich Fromm on the Alienation of Modern Man," *Medium,* August 24, 2016, https://medium.com/@MattKaramazov/erich-fromm-on-the-alienation-of-modern-man-cdcb46d7e934.

41. Jennifer Mercieca, "Authoritarian Voters Pushed Trump to Victory. Can They Do It Again?" *The Guardian,* July 15, 2020, https://www.theguardian.com/us-news/2020/jul/15/authoritarian-voters-donald-trump-election.

42. MacWilliams, "Trump Is an Authoritarian."

43. Mercieca, "Authoritarian Voters."

44. Mercieca, "Authoritarian Voters."

45. Mike Lee (@SenMikeLee), Twitter, October 7, 2020, 11:24 pm, https://twitter.com/senmikelee/status/1314089207875371008?lang=en.

46. Paul Egan and Tresa Baldas, "Militia Group Plotted to Kidnap Michigan Gov. Gretchen Whitmer, Feds Say," *Detroit Free Press,* October 8, 2020, https://www.freep.com/story/news/local/michigan/2020/10/08/governor-gretchen-whitmer-kidnap-plot-militia/5921409002/; "6 People Charged in Plot to Kidnap Michigan Gov. Whitmer," *Associated Press*, October 8, 2020, https://apnews.com/article/michigan-checks-and-balances-archive-gretchen-whitmer-da09ca66cd8d5f36722021d3593425ff?.

47. Taub, "The Rise of American Authoritarianism."

48. Gajo Petrović, "Marx's Theory of Alienation," *Philosophy and Phenomenological Research* 23, no. 3 (1963): 419–26; Sean Sayers, "Creative Activity and Alienation in Hegel and Marx," *Historical Materialism* 11, no. 1 (2003): 107–28; Jan Kandiyali, "Freedom and Necessity in Marx's Account of Communism," *British Journal for the History of Philosophy* 22, no. 1 (2014): 104–23.

49. Kandiyali, "Freedom and Necessity," 107.

50. Martin Hägglund, *This Life: Why Mortality Makes Us Free* (London: Profile, 2019), 22.

51. Kandiyali, "Freedom and Necessity," 107.

52. Kandiyali, "Freedom and Necessity," 108.

53. Kandiyali, "Freedom and Necessity," 109.

54. Bertell Ollman, *Alienation: Marx's Conception of Man in Capitalist Society,* 2nd ed. (New York: Cambridge University Press, 1976), 81.

55. Kandiyali, "Freedom and Necessity," 109.

56. Contemporary scientists, from anthropologists to zoologists, may take issue with Marx's distinction between humans and animals; this is not the place to engage in a lengthy philosophical reflection on the veracity of Marx's claims, most notably his premise that humans are unique in their creative potential. The salience of Marx's assertion is how these ideas were—or were not—incorporated in the corpus of Marxist political philosophy and how these translated into the policies and programs of actually existing communist societies.

57. Kandiyali, "Freedom and Necessity," 109.

58. Ollman, *Alienation,* 114.

59. Hägglund, *This Life,* 23.

60. Ollman, *Alienation,* 116.

61. Kandiyali, "Freedom and Necessity," 110.

62. Fromm, *The Sane Society,* 204.

63. Fromm, *The Sane Society*, 31.

64. bell hooks, *Outlaw Culture: Resisting Representations* (New York: Routledge, 1994), 243.

65. hooks, *Outlaw Culture*, 243.

66. Hebah H. Farrag and Ann Gleig, "Far from Being Anti-Religious, Faith and Spirituality Run Deep in Black Lives Matter," *The Conversation*, September 14, 2020, https://theconversation.com/far-from-being-anti-religious-faith-and-spirituality-run-deep-in-black-lives-matter-145610.

67. hooks, *Outlaw Culture*, 246.

68. Fromm, *The Art of Loving*, 17.

69. Eduardo Bonilla-Silva, "Toward a New Political Praxis for Trumpamerica: New Directions in Critical Race Theory," *American Behavioral Scientist* 63, no. 13 (2019): 1776–88; at 1781.

70. Fromm, *The Art of Loving*, 19.

71. Ollman, *Alienation*, 155.

72. Ollman, *Alienation*, 155.

73. "Executive Order on Delegating Authority Under the DPA with Respect to Food Supply Chain Resources During the National Emergency Caused by the Outbreak of COVID-19," April 28, 2020, https://www.whitehouse.gov/presidential-actions/executive-order-delegating-authority-dpa-respect-food-supply-chain-resources-national-emergency-caused-outbreak-covid-19/.

74. Steven Greenhouse, "Trump Is Marching Meatpacking Workers Off to Their Deaths," *The Guardian*, April 30, 2020, https://www.theguardian.com/commentisfree/2020/apr/30/trump-executive-order-meat-processing-workers-coronavirus.

75. Fromm, *The Art of Loving*, 24.

76. Lydia Wood, Kate Swanson, and Donald E. Colley III, "Tenets for a Radical Care Ethics in Geography," *ACME: An International Journal for Critical Geographies* 19, no. 2 (2020): 424–47; at 428.

77. Fromm, *The Art of Loving*, 27.

78. Matias and Allen, "Loving Whiteness to Death," 286.

79. Fromm, *The Art of Loving*, 19.

80. Fromm, *The Art of Loving*, 21–22.

81. Andrew Power and Edward Hall, "Placing Care in Times of Austerity," *Social & Cultural Geography* 19, no. 3 (2018): 303–13; at 306. For helpful introductions, see Joan C. Tronto, *Moral Boundaries: A Political Argument for an Ethic of Care* (New York: Routledge, 1993); and Marian Barnes, *Care in Everyday Life: An Ethic of Care in Practice* (Bristol, UK: Policy, 2012).

82. Joan C. Tronto, "Care as a Basis for Radical Political Judgements," *Hypatia* 10, no. 2 (1995): 141–49; at 142.

83. Tronto, "Care as a Basis," 142.

84. Tronto, "Care as a Basis," 142.

85. Victoria Lawson, "Instead of Radical Geography, How About Caring Geography?" *Antipode* 41, no. 1 (2009): 210–13; at 210.

86. Matias and Allen, "Loving Whiteness to Death," 291.

87. Friedman, *The Lives of Erich Fromm,* 10–11; Cortina, "The Greatness and Limitations," 390.

88. Friedman, *The Lives of Erich Fromm,* 11.

89. Friedman, *The Lives of Erich Fromm,* 11; Cortina, "The Greatness and Limitations," 390.

90. Fromm, *The Art of Loving,* 1.

91. Matias and Allen, "Loving Whiteness to Death," 291.

92. Scottie Andrew, "The Psychology Behind Why Some People Won't Wear Masks," *CNN,* May 6, 2020, https://www.cnn.com/2020/05/06/health/why-people-dont-wear-masks-wellness-trnd/index.html.

93. Alec Snyder, Mirna Alsharif, and Theresa Waldrop, "Three Family Members Charged in Shooting Death of Security Guard Who Told a Customer to Put on a Face Mask," *CNN,* May 5, 2020, https://www.cnn.com/2020/05/04/us/michigan-security-guard-mask-killing-trnd/index.html.

94. Robert A. Kane, *A Contemporary Introduction to Free Will* (New York: Oxford University Press, 2005), 163.

95. Kane, *A Contemporary Introduction,* 163.

96. Hägglund, *This Life,* 24.

97. Kane, *A Contemporary Introduction,* 165.

98. Kane, *A Contemporary Introduction,* 168.

99. Susan Wolf, *Meaning in Life and Why It Matters* (Princeton, N.J.: Princeton University Press, 2010), 28–29.

100. Hägglund, *This Life,* 23.

101. Fromm, *The Sane Society,* 186.

102. Rebecca Shabad, "'It Is What It Is': Trump in Interview on COVID-19 Death Toll in U.S.," *NBC News,* August 4, 2020, https://www.nbcnews.com/politics/donald-trump/it-what-it-trump-interview-covid-19-death-toll-u-n1235734.

103. Hägglund, *This Life,* 25.

104. Ben Steverman and Alexandre Tanzi, "The 50 Richest Americans Are Worth as Much as the Poorest 165 Million," *Bloomberg,* October 8, 2020, https://www.bloomberg.com/news/articles/2020-10-08/top-50-richest-people-in-the-us-are-worth-as-much-as-poorest-165-million.

105. Steverman and Tanzi, "The 50 Richest Americans."

106. Matthew Yglesias, "What's Really Going On with the Economy," *Vox,* September 10, 2020, https://www.vox.com/21425031/economic-growth-unemployment; Aaron Ross Coleman, "Congress's Failure to Pass Stimulus

Has Had a Devastating—and Predictable—Effect on Minority Groups," *Vox,* September 14, 2020, https://www.vox.com/21433055/congresss-failure-second-stimulus-devastating-effect-on-minorities-unemployment-covid-bill.

107. Christopher Luu, "Black Lives Matter Protests Continue after Breonna Taylor Decision," *InStyle,* September 24, 2020, https://www.instyle.com/news/black-lives-matter-protests-continue.

108. Quoted in Luu, "Black Lives Matter Protests."

109. Peter Hudis, "The Seeds of Revolution Have Sprouted: What Is Now to be Done?" *New Politics,* August 6, 2020, https://newpol.org/the-seeds-of-revolution-have-sprouted-what-is-now-to-be-done/.

110. Benjamin Balthaser and Bill V. Mullen, "Rethinking Socialism from Below in the Age of Covid-19 and Black Lives Matter," *New Politics,* June 30, 2020, https://newpol.org/rethinking-socialism-from-below-in-the-age-of-covid-and-black-lives-matte/.

111. Paul D'Amato, *The Meaning of Marxism* (Chicago: Haymarket Books, 2006), 114.

112. D'Amato, *The Meaning of Marxism,* 114.

113. Lamb, *Socialism,* 15.

114. Curt Ries, "Our Path Forward After Bernie Must Include Rank-and-File Unionism and Class-Struggle Elections," *Jacobin,* August 9, 2020 at https://jacobinmag.com/2020/08/bernie-sanders-campaign-unions-class-struggle (accessed October 12, 2020).

115. Lamb, *Socialism,* 34.

116. Karen Brodkin Sacks, "Toward a Unified Theory of Class, Race, and Gender," *American Ethnologist* 16, no. 3 (1989): 534–50; at 542.

117. Brian Jones, "Continuing the Discussion on Black Politics," *New Politics* 17. no. 4 (2020), https://newpol.org/issue_post/continuing-the-discussion-on-black-politics/.

118. Fromm, *The Sane Society,* 33.

Index

JAMES A. TYNER is professor of geography at Kent State University and fellow of the American Association of Geographers. He is author of several books, including *War, Violence, and Population: Making the Body Count* and *Dead Labor: Toward a Political Economy of Premature Death* (Minnesota, 2019).